THE MISSING AMONG US

ERIN STEWART is a Canberra-based freelance writer who has written for a range of Australian and international publications including *Meanjin*, *Voiceworks*, *ABC Online*, *SBS Online*, *Daily Life*, *Overland Online*, *SELF*, *The Outline*, and many others. She has been an opinion columnist for *The Age* and made regular appearances on ABC Sydney Mornings to talk about books and the arts. Her writing has been anthologised in *Balancing Acts: Women in Sport*. An earlier version of this book was shortlisted for the Portobello Books Unpublished Manuscript Prize in the UK. She holds a PhD in non-fiction writing.

THE MISSING AMONG US

STORIES OF MISSING PERSONS AND THOSE LEFT BEHIND

ERIN STEWART

NEWSOUTH

A NewSouth book

Published by
NewSouth Publishing
University of New South Wales Press Ltd
University of New South Wales
Sydney NSW 2052
AUSTRALIA
newsouthpublishing.com

© Erin Stewart 2021
First published 2021

10 9 8 7 6 5 4 3 2 1

This book is copyright. Apart from any fair dealing for the purpose of private study, research, criticism or review, as permitted under the Copyright Act, no part of this book may be reproduced by any process without written permission. Inquiries should be addressed to the publisher.

 A catalogue record for this book is available from the National Library of Australia

ISBN   9781742236797 (paperback)
          9781742244907 (ebook)
          9781742249421 (ePDF)

Internal design Josephine Pajor-Markus
Cover design Alissa Dinallo
Cover image Nikita Buida/Shutterstock.com

Aboriginal words in this book use the preferred spelling of our First Nations contributors.

CONTENTS

Introduction		1
1	Grabbing headlines: Madeleine McCann, Azaria Chamberlain, JonBenét Ramsey	15
2	Lost in the bush: Cindy and Trevor's long weekend	29
3	An awful, awful thing: Sarah and the search for Q	48
4	When a parent abducts a child: Salma and Ayoub	74
5	Running for your life: Brandy's story	93
6	Searching: From divination to police procedures	125
7	More than one at a time: Wars and natural disasters	151
8	I don't have to limit my love: Looking for missing refugees in Europe	170
9	The bigger picture: Missing Children Europe	188
10	The Stolen Generations: Susan's story	200
11	Drinking the Kool-Aid: The attraction of cults	231
12	A point of connection: The Missing Persons Advocacy Network	263
13	Open ending: Living with ambiguity	280
Further reading		289
Acknowledgments		292

FOR LINDON.

INTRODUCTION

To be missing, you must be missed. You have to matter to others and they need to be worried by your absence. A person is missing when they aren't where we expect them to be. But location is only part of how we define someone as missing.

The Australian Institute of Criminology estimates that each year over 38 000 people are reported missing across the country. It's a prevalent national issue, and a global one. According to 2018/2019 data, in the UK 353 000 missing-persons incidents are recorded by police each year. In the US, the FBI states over 600 000 people are reported missing each year. Each agency stresses that missing persons are under-reported and the actual figures are therefore likely to be higher.

The concern of friends and family members fuels the figures. Every one of these cases is defined through the responses of those left behind: looking worriedly at the clock; making deals with themselves, like *I'll call them if they aren't back within the hour*; the anxious phone calls to friends asking if they've seen them. The difficult decision whether to involve the police. The oscillation between thinking they're overreacting and being terrified that something horrible has happened. Absence is both someone not being physically present, and that absence being felt by others. It is not just the space they used to occupy, it is the haunting gap of what they are to you.

By their absence, the missing person has violated their obligation to be *there* for others. They can no longer be a source of friendship, comfort, jokes; they aren't doing their job. They are missing not just because they're physically absent, but because they stop filling their usual roles.

'Missing person' is a designation applied by others, and can describe people who may not even see themselves as missing. After all, a person who's deliberately left home may know exactly where they are. As long as a person is not wanted by authorities, or involuntarily admitted to a psychiatric ward, any adult is legally allowed to leave their life and start afresh.

A woman whose brother disappeared told researchers: 'I always felt [he] would be horrified to know that he's been reported missing for a start, because he probably won't consider himself missing. He'll consider "Right, I've had enough of there, I'm off." Which, there's no law against that, he's free to do that.' Nonetheless, he was missing to his sister.

Because being declared a missing person is so contingent on the relationships left behind, not all who have disappeared are deemed missing. If nobody notices you are gone, are you really missing?

In 2005, a nine-year-old girl, Jessica Lunsford, went missing in the US. The case received intense media attention. As journalist Sarah Stillman reported, in the course of the investigation authorities dragged a lake and found a corpse. At the press conference, the Sheriff exclaimed, 'We have confirmed it is not our girl. I repeat, it is not our girl. And for that, we are very happy.' The corpse was not Jessica's, but it was somebody's. Yet there was little interest in the identity of the corpse, or how it had ended up in the lake. This human being may never have been missing because she may never have been missed.

❖

The nature of missing-persons cases is that they are frustratingly ambiguous. From the time someone is discovered to be missing, through the investigation – even if they are eventually located, and particularly if they are not – there are cavernous gaps between slivers of knowledge. We try to make the ambiguity more tolerable by putting up our own interpretations; we speculate, we hypothesise. Sometimes our efforts lead nowhere.

I was drawn to missing-persons cases for my own convoluted personal and intellectual reasons. I have always been intrigued by stories of those who fake their own deaths, who just pack up one day and leave their lives. As a child, I'd been frightened by stories of children being kidnapped, and I still remember the lessons of 'stranger danger' from school. But I came to write this book for a reason beyond voyeurism and fear. Counterintuitively, perhaps, my work on missing-persons stories began because I've been sick.

For years I have been enmeshed in the world of chronic illness. Though my symptoms are just about explained with diagnoses now, for most of my life they evaded definition. My daily life involved a disquieting array of symptoms I couldn't name, fatigue and pain I didn't know the source of, and challenges I didn't know how to explain. It was a frustrating experience. You go to the doctor with the expectation that if you list your symptoms and surrender to their expertise, they'll tell you what's wrong and give you a course of action. You take the pills, you have the surgery. Every problem is resolved within two to six weeks. The narrative you expect when you're sick is: something bad happened to me and then it stopped.

When you're diagnosed with a chronic illness, you're offered a story that explains what's wrong, but this story has its own frustrations. You might be able to manage your illness, or experience patterns of relapses and remissions; you can also learn to cope with it. But there's always ambiguity: you don't know when the symptoms will flare up next, or how long they'll last. You don't know what symptoms will get better, or what you'll need to accept as a new normal. You don't know what treatments will bring relief, so you're vulnerable to wasting your money, time, and energy in the search. You're also isolated by the nature of chronic illness. Those around you who've never experienced it themselves find it difficult to understand that sometimes health problems don't resolve. Sometimes there's no end to sickness – you neither get well, nor do you die.

From my place of ambiguity and isolation, I naturally became drawn to others who'd experienced wildly different versions of the same, essential problems. Nobody knows ambiguity better than those involved in missing-persons cases. These missing-persons stories became a distorted mirror of my own story – same themes, different details.

When I first learned how common missing-persons cases were, I was surprised, and when I mention the statistics to others, they are likewise surprised. We only tend to notice those rare cases that get weeks – or even years – of media attention, like missing British girl Madeleine McCann. But when I started properly considering missing-persons cases, I began to notice them everywhere. It was like learning a new word and then hearing it three times in the one day. I even discovered that missing-persons stories were threaded through my own life and family history. I had relatives who had been declared missing in action during World War I; I knew at least one person who was reported missing by their parents when, as a teenager, they unexpectedly stayed out all night and failed to call home because their phone battery died. Someone I'd worked with became – and remains – a missing person. I've had friends whose siblings have gone missing for disconcerting periods of time; a distant relative fell out of contact with the family for years until one day she was randomly seen on a TV news broadcast answering a journalist's vox-pop questions.

Most of us have been lost at some stage in our lives, if not officially 'missing'– perhaps as a child who wandered away at a supermarket, or on a bushwalk when the map stopped making sense. You may have fantasised about taking off from a stressful situation, travelling until you get to a place where nobody can bother you any more. Absences are far more common than a crime like murder – in Australia in 2018, 222 people were murdered, which means that there are hundreds of people who go missing for every person who is murdered – yet murder features more heavily in our awareness.

Why are missing-persons narratives so common yet subterranean? Why does their number surprise us, when it's likely that we have encountered disappearances in our own lives, however fleetingly? It's the ambiguity. As I learned myself, having ambiguity in your life is isolating. It's hard for others to understand the story, and you don't always want to tell it.

Ambiguity also goes against the way we're taught to tell stories. There is no simple beginning, middle and end.

Aristotle held that the aim of a well-composed drama was to bring about catharsis for the audience – a satisfying purge of emotions to relieve the tension built up over the course of the story. When Oedipus stabs his eyes out as punishment for killing his father and marrying his mother, we feel an outpouring of fear and pity. Although it's an intense scene, there is poetic justice; the natural order has been restored.

Others advise that stories must incorporate cause and

effect – we should know why a character did something, and how each action led to the next. Goldilocks is hungry and sleepy and so breaks into the three bears' house. She ends up being chased (and in some versions of the story, eaten) by the bears because she broke into their home. Everything happens for a reason; the story has a satisfying logic. Or the inverse, as in a murder mystery: we don't know who the killer is or why they did it, but we keep reading in the hope of finding clues that will enable the story to come to a clear conclusion.

The problem with writing about human experience – including things like chronic illness and missing persons – is that these structures don't apply. I don't know why I'm sick or when I'll get better. I don't know where this person is or why they left, whether they left voluntarily or were abducted, or even if they're alive. As a nonfiction writer, the fact that true stories – as well as interesting, important, and potentially instructive ones – might not get told because they don't fit a neat arc feels problematic. Ambiguous stories don't offer satisfying catharsis or even a small sigh of relief; we don't have the logic of cause and effect to draw from. The stories go something like a child's narration of events: 'And then ... And then ... And then ...'

Popular culture does, of course, have space for missing-persons stories. While there is discomfort with ambiguity, we are also pulled towards stories of disappearance. Some missing-persons cases – like those of Madeleine McCann and Melanie Hall in the UK, or Amelia Earhart and JonBenét Ramsey in the US, or the Beaumont children and prime minister Harold Holt in Australia – are continually revisited in the media and become cultural touchstones. However, famous missing-persons cases often don't allow ambiguity to linger respectfully. There can be violent speculation over these cases that can harm those left behind.

Absence is everywhere in popular culture, and always has been. One of the oldest surviving works of Western literature, Homer's *Odyssey*, is about a man missing at sea. It details his plight, as well as the complications his absence causes for his wife and child. The Bible describes Cain becoming a fugitive, forever lost, after killing his brother Abel. Missing people feature in Shakespeare, in plays such as *The Tempest*, in which stormy and indifferent seas are thought to have taken loved ones. More modern literary favourites also include characters who go missing. George Orwell's *Nineteen Eighty-Four* introduces readers to the concept of an 'unperson' – an enemy of the totalitarian regime who is swiftly and quietly taken away and will not be seen (or even spoken of or thought about) ever again. JD Salinger's *Catcher in the Rye* depicts the unfocused travels of a young man who can neither be at home nor at school and so runs away from both. Lolita goes missing in Vladimir Nabokov's novel to escape Humbert, her abuser, guardian and dead mother's husband.

Missing persons feature heavily in popular television shows like *Without a Trace*, *The Missing*, *Stranger Things*, *Mad Men*, and so on. As I've worked on this book, I've often sat down to read or watch something, only to realise halfway through that the story includes a missing person. While there's a continual pop-cultural loop of stories about missing persons, I never realised it was such a prominent theme until I began looking for it, and it started turning up everywhere. Absence is analogous to air in that its ubiquity doesn't call for contemplation.

But there's not a lot of space for the unresolved in real life. It can be difficult to make others understand. Friends may wonder why those left behind are still talking about a disappearance months later, and say things like, 'It's time to move on', or encourage them to assume the missing person is dead. The opposite can happen as well: sometimes friends will continually ask for updates, seeking any tiny clue that may promise closure. Either way, the story just hangs there, unresolved, which is intolerable. No one wants to hear the truth. Everyone wants the story to have the conclusion we've become accustomed to expect.

❖

We don't have a good vocabulary for talking about missing persons. Even the phrase 'missing persons' is stylistically strange. Technically it is the correct term, but feels inappropriately rigid and formal compared to 'missing people'. We say 'missing persons' because of an archaic grammatical rule. In the past, we would only use the word 'people' as a noun for an uncountable collective or population, as in 'modern people', while 'persons' was strictly the plural of 'person', as in one person, two persons, three persons, etc. – a role that the word 'people' now plays. 'Persons' is still widely used in a legal context, including policing. While 'missing people' is a term preferred by some (Missing People, for example, is the primary missing-persons charity in the UK), it isn't widely used. So, while 'missing persons' reads like an antiquated term, I've felt the need to use it anyway.

Other phrases present persistent challenges. 'A person has gone missing' sounds too casual, sharing a temporary, leisurely tone with phases like 'gone to lunch' or 'gone fishing'. 'A person has disappeared' is inaccurate, defying the laws of physics – a person must still be *somewhere*, even if we don't know where they are, or if they have died. Charities, police, and tracing agencies often refer to 'the family and friends of missing persons', a clunky phrase if used too often. But an alternative like 'those left behind' implies that the missing person chose to leave the people close to them, and we don't always know this to be the case. And yet, these terms are the best we have. I still use them.

This lack of good vocabulary may be evidence of a cultural taboo or anxiety around the topic: when we refer to concepts regularly, when they seem relevant to large groups of people, we find better, more various, and more precise ways of talking about them.

Linguist Anna Wierzbicka argues that all cultures have 'key words' that reflect their values – we have adequate vocabularies for the things most salient to us. A common interest – sport, for example – has a robust vocabulary attached to it. In cricket alone you can bowl or be bowled, bowl fast or bowl spin (and make distinctions between leg spin and off spin, wrist spin and finger spin). You can bowl a wide, or deliver, or concede byes, or drive, or hit fours and sixes, or take a wicket, or get out for a duck, or get dismissed, or shout 'howzat'. There's an exciting bouquet of words you can use to describe batting: hit, block, drive, pull, hook, slog, sweep, cut, flick, scoop, switch, glance. When we move away from something that brings pleasure, like a leisure activity, to something far more serious and challenging, something that brings no clear outcomes, we do not have such linguistic choice.

The wordlessness around the issue of missing persons has a grave ramification: if there is no vocabulary for your story, how are you supposed to tell it? Without words, there's no conversation about how the issues you face could be mitigated by your community, or through social or legislative change.

❖

Currently, very little research is conducted into who goes missing and why, how to prevent people from going missing, and how to protect missing persons from harm. We know very little about the consequences for those left behind, or about the long-term impacts of being abducted or having to run away. The silver lining is that a lot can be done – on personal, social, and political levels – to improve the lives of those affected by disappearances.

In this book I excavate the stories of the families of missing persons, those who have been missing, investigators of missing-persons cases, and other professionals in the business of searching for those missing and preventing future disappearances. These stories do not satisfyingly resolve, even where the person missing is found. They are subjective and showcase the points where knowledge collapses into interpretation, conjecture, and wishful thinking.

The ambiguities are uncomfortable but they are also important. Disappearance absolutely could happen to you, or someone you know, or anyone. And how to deal with the ambiguity of a disappearance is relevant for us all. As we learn more about the world through technological advances and scientific inquiry, we also see our own ambiguous futures. Climate change may displace an untold number of people and render parts of our land uninhabitable; our populations are getting older, with an increasing proportion too old to work and a decreasing proportion responsible for supporting them. How are we going to take care of each other? How will we take care of our planet? Paying attention to the problems of the world means facing uncertainty. The story of ambiguity is a story for all of us, whether or not the circumstances of our lives so far have attuned us to it. While many of us will mercifully never have to contemplate the terrible ambiguities of a loved one's disappearance for very long, we will have times of not knowing. These times will not be someone else's problem, or particular to the personalities and situations of other individuals. Ambiguity threads through life.

I have travelled to several countries in order to speak to people who've dealt with the issue of missing persons firsthand, and who offer reflections that don't get covered in the media around individual cases.

On my travels I came across the Magritte Museum in Brussels, dedicated to the work of Belgian surrealist René Magritte. Here was an artist who understood ambiguity. Painting after painting shows figures that are somehow both present and absent – ungraspable. One of Magritte's most famous paintings is *The Son of Man*, depicting a man in a bowler hat whose face is obscured by a large green apple. In another, *Not to Be Reproduced*, a man looks into a mirror only to see the back of his own head

'Every single thing which we see conceals something else,' Magritte said. 'We would dearly love to see that which we can see is hiding from us.' Absurdly, I find myself physically moving around – standing on tiptoe, moving my head from side to side – trying to see the face behind the apple.

These paintings seem to play with – and frustrate – our desire to solve mysteries. Not only is life mysterious, but we may not know what we think we know. We see a picture of a pipe and call it a pipe, but as Magritte warns in his painting *The Treachery of Images*, '*Ceci n'est pas une pipe.*' It is a representation of a pipe, not the thing itself. Perception and reality are two very different things. We may not always realise there's a gap between them, but when we do, we are left with another mystery.

Life – especially if it involves missing persons – is about dealing with unknowns. As Magritte suggests, we barely know ourselves. We look in the mirror and see the back of our own heads. How did I become the person I am? What am I capable of doing? What hardships can I survive? The answers only emerge over time, as we face life's challenges.

Absence crystallises what we don't know. Not having the answers suddenly matters a great deal. Who is this person who is inexplicably absent? Why did they leave? Are they alive or dead? When confronted by a mystery, we rehearse scenarios in our heads.

There are many alternative stories, for example, about the 1969 disappearance of prime minister Harold Holt. He was last seen swimming in the rough waves of Cheviot Beach on the Victorian coast. Over the years, people have answered the question of what happened to him with strange narratives involving mermaids, a convoluted Cold War plot, an extra-marital affair, and a Chinese submarine. He may also have simply drowned. I was captivated by the story – how could someone so high profile simply vanish? – and borrowed my brother's car one day to drive out to Cheviot Beach and see the tall waves striking the sharp rocks for myself.

For some, living with mystery leads to unusual responses. Early in 2017, a podcast launched titled *Missing Richard Simmons*. Simmons was an indefatigable exercise guru of the 1980s; the podcast's creator, American filmmaker Dan Taberski, had been one of Simmon's regular students. Alongside his prolific aerobic-centred media appearances, Simmons had run an in-person exercise class for 40 years. Taberski was surprised by Simmons's dedication – he regularly called students during the week just to catch up on how they were going; he'd invite them out to dinner and take them on tours of his house. When it all suddenly stopped and Simmons cancelled his classes and wasn't seen in public any more, Taberski had a similar question to mine about Harold Holt: how does someone so vivid, so exuberant, so famous, just vanish?

In a quest for answers, Taberski interviews Simmons's staff, his students, and his friends, and develops theories as to what might have happened. It turned out that Simmons wasn't really missing. He was still living in the same house, but had simply chosen to become reclusive. Which he has the right to do, if that's what he really wants. He is an adult. He has a right to retire from the public eye, and from aerobics teaching.

The real mystery then becomes why someone like Simmons would ditch the world. And the real wound for Taberski, it seems, is that Simmons renounced his social role. 'A lot of people who know him and whose lives have been changed by him,' says Taberski, 'they're worried. Or angry. Or full of grief. Some want to save him. Some just want to know he's okay.' Simmons is more than just a fitness instructor; he's played a key role in many people's lives. And those people want answers.

It's curious to me that the artwork associated with Taberski's podcast is based on Magritte's work. The logo is a version of *The Son of Man* but instead of a bowler hat, the man behind the apple has the afro hairstyle of Richard Simmons. Listeners are drawn into the mystery of the man behind the apple. Like me in the art gallery, they crane to see an unreachable dimension of the image.

Magritte's art is a guide for learning to live with mystery. It is filled with missing persons and artefacts, with things both there and not. They're just around the corner, under some fruit, off the edge of the canvas. The mystery itself, rather than its solution, becomes the object of fascination. Magritte says that mystery is poetry. It causes tension, yes, but 'The mind loves the unknown. It loves images whose meaning is unknown, since the meaning of the mind itself is unknown.'

My aim here is not to solve the superficial mystery of where a missing person is, it's to explore those other mysteries that are embedded in subjective life: our limits, the way our knowledge and perception are obstructed. It is the unknowns themselves that capture my attention. That individual stories are subjective and ambiguous is central to understanding them.

The point isn't to meticulously detail every single conjecture or piece of evidence available about a case so that others might hope to solve it. That's not really what these cases are like, and it's definitely not what life is like. There's no twist that comes and makes everything fall perfectly into place.

Overall, this book is about finding a space for those conversations about ambiguous circumstances in order to understand the complex issue of missing persons – what happens when someone goes missing, why they go missing, and how we can stop so many people from going missing every year.

Cultural attitudes towards missing persons reflect a deep ambivalence – a simultaneous attraction and repulsion. We are both curious and ignorant: intrigued by the cases yet lacking the vocabulary to talk about them; excitedly speculating on causes, yet not exploring the reality of living alongside absence. We are immersed in a world where disappearance is both common and subterranean. Etymologically, the word 'ambivalence' comes from Latin components – 'ambi' means 'both ways', and 'valence' derives from 'valentia', which means 'strength' – the equal and forceful pull of two opposing ideas. Embracing ambiguity entails a decision to sacrifice these competing, contradictory tendencies in order to focus on the murky realities beyond them. It may be unsatisfying and even uncomfortable. The nature of things can be understood in multiple ways, and we might never find out which understanding is best.

Ambiguity is part of normal life, but through the stories I've been told, and the research and reflection I've undertaken, I find a sense of what it's like to really contemplate it, and to carry it as a heavy parcel. It is disconcerting to commit yourself to not being sure, but by acknowledging our limits, we might learn how to deal with them. How do we talk about not knowing? How do we live with it? And what can we do in this place of doubt?

1

GRABBING HEADLINES

MADELEINE McCANN, AZARIA CHAMBERLAIN, JONBENÉT RAMSEY

They reported on little Maddie McCann's absence as if it were a natural disaster. The initial newscasts came live from the Algarve, Portugal, where she had gone missing during a family holiday, as though it were imperative we see what it was like on the ground. But unlike footage of a cyclone or an earthquake, there were no destroyed buildings or flattened trees, no drowned streets. There was less than nothing to be seen – an intact landscape, minus one girl.

The three-year-old British girl disappeared from her family's holiday apartment on the evening of 3 May 2007, some time between 8 pm and 10 pm. Her parents, Kate and Gerry McCann, had been having dinner only metres away and had been intermittently checking on her and the other children she was with that night. At some point they checked and she was not there and a heavy, dreadful stone fell into their stomachs.

This is not the whole story, but it's what we know.

Madeleine McCann is still missing. I was in my last year of school at the time the news broke. In Australia I was geographically far away from the story and had other things on my mind. But I still remember her going missing, the nightly news footage of parents who found an empty space instead of their beloved child. It has been a collective experience. The fate of Madeleine Beth McCann is a constant reminder of the possibility that malevolent hands can stretch out and snatch precious things in the night, a cautionary tale for parents that warns they should always, always watch their children.

People grasped for answers on a grand scale. As with a natural disaster, you could donate money to aid the victims. The reward fund to encourage anyone with information about the case to speak to authorities accumulated over £2.6 million. This sum was bolstered by donations from the likes of the Murdoch press, Richard Branson, Simon Cowell, and JK Rowling. It was also an individual tragedy. I have images in my memory of the parents – complete strangers to me, yet also familiar faces – clutching Maddie's favourite toy (a plush cat named Cuddle Cat) on the set of the *Oprah* show. I can close my eyes and see the silhouettes of grief under their eyes. I didn't know them but they left a mark. They make me sad and anxious, and their story makes me wonder.

I know I'm not alone because in the years since the disappearance there have been volumes of speculation on *what really happened* to Maddie (commentators often refer to her by her nickname). From late 2015 until 2019, I was living in the UK and it was a rare week that went by without her name being in news headlines: 'A paedophile took Madeleine McCann, not her parents', 'Madeleine McCann IS alive but hidden in plain sight', and 'Madeleine McCann will never come home'.

At first, the McCanns and the media had a symbiotic relationship. The McCanns wanted information on the whereabouts of their daughter and so raised awareness of her case. In turn, every time Madeleine appeared on the front page of a newspaper it sold, on average, 30 000 more copies than usual.

But then Kate and Gerry McCann – and the people they were dining with on the night of the disappearance (who became known as the 'Tapas Seven') – became implicated, and the media started portraying them as negligent parents, if not suspects, if not demons.

The way that the McCanns encouraged the media to follow the case so closely, engaged public relations consultants, and were so savvy in publicising their cause (for example, a month after Madeleine's disappearance, they orchestrated the release of balloons in 300 cities worldwide to raise awareness of her case and the issue of child abduction generally) was seen as suspicious by the Portuguese authorities as well as journalists. Were they trying to manipulate the public? Were they playing the role of grieving victims to hide *what really happened*?

All kinds of allegations were made against them in the media: that they and the Tapas Seven were swingers more interested in hedonistic affairs than their own children, that they had sedated their children with drugs, that they were not sad enough (this criticism was levelled against Madeleine's mother, Kate, in particular), and that they were guilty themselves (it was suggested that they had accidentally killed Madeleine with sleeping pills and hidden the body). The theories lacked any meaningful evidence and, accordingly, the McCanns were awarded damages from several newspapers for libel. They were also awarded damages from Gonçalo Amaral, a Portuguese police inspector heavily involved in the case, who decided to quit his job in 2008 specifically to write a book alleging that the McCanns had covered up Madeleine's death.

❖

In Australia, almost 30 years before Madeleine McCann's disappearance, a similarly fevered trial-by-media put the parent of another lost child in jail. Infant Azaria Chamberlain went missing in the outback, near Uluru, on the night of 17 August 1980. She was most likely taken by a dingo, as her parents suggested at the time. As with the McCanns, the media closely followed the story, capturing the Chamberlains' grief, until the tide turned and reporters became convinced that the story was absurd, that dingoes don't take babies, and that Azaria's mother, Lindy, knew more than she was letting on. Media speculation adversely affected the ensuing court case in 1982, which led to Lindy's wrongful homicide conviction and imprisonment. Azaria's father, Michael, was also convicted of being an accessory to the alleged crime. Though both were released from prison in 1986 when new evidence came to light, and both were pardoned in 1987, it wasn't until 2012 that a coronial inquest ruled that Azaria was killed by a dingo and denounced the particularly cruel and unjust treatment the Chamberlains had faced from the media.

The parallels between the public responses to the two cases are striking. There's a public hunger for more detail, and a persistent need to talk about the cases even when little in the way of new information emerges. In both cases, the grief of the respective families was only relatable for so long. At a certain point, it becomes difficult for others to comprehend the reality of having a child mysteriously taken from you. Instead of sympathising with that intolerable ambiguity, we wildly speculate, and we hold deep suspicions.

❖

Homicide cases frequently make their sad start as missing-persons cases, and this is true for another high-profile case, that of JonBenét Ramsey in Boulder, Colorado. JonBenét was six years old when she disappeared on Christmas night 1996. Her mother, Patsy, woke on the morning of 26 December to discover an unusually lengthy ransom note demanding the sum of $118 000 'if you want her to see 1997', but assuring the child's safety. The writer said they would call later that morning, but when the call didn't come, the police instructed JonBenét's father, John, to search the family's cavernous house. Eight hours after JonBenét was first reported missing, John found her in the basement. Her skull had been broken and a garotte had been tied around her neck; duct tape was stuck across her mouth and throat. There was evidence that she may also have been sexually assaulted. It was clear that she had been dead for some time.

Both investigators and the public were suspicious of the Ramsey family. There was no obvious sign of a break-in. Because the Ramseys' house was very large, it would have been difficult for a complete stranger to navigate their way to JonBenét's room and take her to the basement without waking anybody up. The ransom note was written on stationery the Ramseys had in the house, and the amount of money the ransom note demanded happened to be the same amount John had recently received as a bonus. Some speculated that the timing was beneficial for the Ramseys – because the police were understaffed over the Christmas holidays, their investigation was severely hindered and they'd even failed to secure the crime scene.

Two main theories about *what really happened* to JonBenét circulated. The first was that JonBenét had been accidentally killed (either by her parents, or even, some suggested, by her nine-year-old brother) and her parents had staged a kidnapping to cover up the family's involvement. The second theory was that JonBenét's kidnappers had botched the job. Something had gone wrong and they killed her – probably accidentally – before they were able to collect their ransom money.

Either way, from the moment the story first broke, there wasn't much sympathy for the Ramsey family, even among those who thought they were innocent. Much was made of JonBenét's involvement in beauty pageants. The media released dozens of photographs – without the family's consent – of JonBenét posed suggestively in grand, glossy outfits, her lips brightly painted. These were taken as evidence that JonBenét's parents had exploited and sexualised their daughter (writing for the *New York Post*, Andrea Peyser accused JonBenét of looking like a 'hooker'). Commentators speculated that her involvement in pageants could have attracted the attention of paedophiles. The Ramsey family were courting danger through this hobby.

Police were initially suspicious of the Ramsey family, believing that Patsy had written the ransom note herself. However, in 1998 authorities ruled that, as a result of new DNA analysis, the Ramsey family was no longer under suspicion. In 1999, after jurors had spent 13 months reviewing over 30 000 pieces of evidence and hearing statements from dozens of witnesses, no findings or indictments were made for the murder of JonBenét. Some members of the public were so displeased with the result that they protested. They continued to believe the Ramseys guilty, and held signs with messages like 'The ransom note is a confession' at a 'rally for justice for JonBenét'. In 2008, the Ramseys were cleared entirely – the district attorney even sent them an apology – although this was too late to reassure Patsy, who had died of ovarian cancer in 2006. Nobody in the family was ever charged with any crime.

The media obsession with the case was relentless for years. One journalist, Jeff Shapiro, attempted to befriend the Ramseys. He converted from Judaism to Christianity so that he could join their Episcopalian church and sit behind them as they prayed for solace. At the same time, Shapiro became a confidante of investigators. His close proximity to the case compromised investigations. He was present during conversations when the chief prosecutor discussed vital evidence. His involvement also lent credence to his speculation over Patsy's guilt. He's quoted in Lawrence Schiller's book about the case, *Perfect Murder, Perfect Town*, saying, 'I had never seen anyone pray for his own soul the way Patsy was praying for hers ... At that moment, I decided she was the killer.' Shapiro wasn't the only one prepared to make serious allegations about the family's guilt. Over the years members of the Ramsey family, as well as some of their friends, have filed defamation claims against media outlets covering the case; many of them have been settled out of court.

We still don't know what happened to JonBenét Ramsey. As with the other cases, new information doesn't need to emerge for media coverage to continue for years. There are innumerable documentaries about what happened, and constant claims of further twists in the case. A particularly strange documentary, *Casting JonBenét*, was released on Netflix in 2017. It's essentially a documentary about the making of a documentary about the case. Amateur actors who live in the Boulder area audition to play the roles of JonBenét and her family. Throughout, the actors are encouraged to speculate on the case and who they think was responsible. They rehearse finding the body, crying in the hallway. The small, made-up pageant girls, all of whom bear an eerie resemblance to JonBenét and wear spangled leotards, sit together in a line. At other times, you see rows of mothers in red knitted t-shirts; playful brothers one after another trying to smash a watermelon with a torch to see who'd have the strength to smash a skull (only a few are successful); sad fathers in button-down shirts. Each person is replicated, multiplied, honed for a perfect portrayal. The documentary, and the actors within it, are trying to create a rehearsed, understandable story from an ephemeral and confusing reality.

It all seems to suggest that these stories belong to us, and if we drill down far enough into the details, we'll get somewhere.

❖

I've looked at the cases of Madeleine McCann, Azaria Chamberlain, and JonBenét Ramsey because there are a few important elements that unite them. The first is that they received so much media coverage over so many years that even those who didn't give the cases their full attention would still recognise the names and know the basic facts of the disappearance. Many of us have been affected by the cases as well, perhaps because some of us were a similar age to the victims at the time, or because each of the girls reminded us of someone we knew. Perhaps these cases are distressing in the same way that watching footage from wars or natural disasters is distressing. They remind us that we live in a world where innocent children can be taken or killed arbitrarily.

I grew up with these stories constantly churning away in the background. They were reasons to view the world with trepidation, to make sure the doors were locked at night. The Azaria Chamberlain case – which I studied in my Year 9 history class – ultimately had less to do with the danger of other people than the other cases, but still spoke to the perils of the world, particularly the Australian outback.

The fear these cases induce in the public may explain the vitriol that has come with them. Perhaps it's easier to imagine the McCanns as bad parents who went too far in drugging their child, and to imagine that the Chamberlains and the

Ramseys murdered their children despite having no reason to do so, than to acknowledge that something so devastating could happen to you or someone you know. We'd like to believe that only specific people in specific circumstances could experience such a loss, people who have done something wrong or who are themselves malevolent. After a while, the constant coverage and discussion of these cases begins to look less like the frenzy of worry that follows a natural disaster and more like a desperate attempt at reassurance: *This could not happen to me.*

A case doesn't have to be a huge media event to make onlookers feel unable to tolerate ambiguity and to start pinning the disappearance on those left behind, or to try to complete the story. In doing so, they isolate those close to the missing person. People are very interested in missing-persons cases, but the strange contradiction is that they don't really want to go into the realities of the cases. They want to know the gory premise, but not the details of what it's like to actually live with ongoing loss and ambiguity.

A child going missing is a different experience to the death of a child. While a loved one's death is devastating too, people who have long-term missing family members are in an unresolved, ambiguous situation that others don't know how to respond to. It's not a unique situation – people go missing every day – but neither is it one with standard rituals like a funeral, or appropriate Hallmark cards. The mystery just continues and the realities of ongoing uncertainty are mostly left unspoken.

If someone's disappearance is not the topic of mass obsession and suspicion, it is a conversational dead-end. Lots of people, it seems, want to hear about the McCanns, the Chamberlains, and the Ramseys. But they don't want to hear about not knowing. With the exception of the McCann case, people may not generally regard these stories as missing-persons cases at all (the Chamberlain case is an accident of the natural world, the Ramsey case is a murder), but they each started out as one. And, as with all missing-persons cases, ambiguity lingers. Madeleine McCann's whereabouts remain unknown; Azaria Chamberlain's body was never found; JonBenét Ramsey's killer is still unidentified. All three cases highlight the uncontrollable, the unimaginable threats that none of us could ever completely pre-empt.

Of the millions of cases that are opened each year, these are three that captured the public imagination. But for every Madeleine McCann, Azaria Chamberlain, and JonBenét Ramsey, there are many, many more people who go missing who we've never heard of. Part of the reason for this disparity is to do with the identities of these missing children – young, white, female, from respectable backgrounds – which allows them to be easily seen as perfect victims, children who did no wrong, their disappearances easily read as tragic and unpredictable.

A number of studies have shown that there are inequalities in the media coverage of missing persons. In 2016, a Northwestern University study found that in four major US online news sources, missing white girls were granted disproportionately high coverage compared to the rate they actually went missing. Of course, missing boys also gain coverage – the cases of William Tyrrell and Jaidyn Leskie have both been well documented by the media, for example – but nonetheless, a general gender bias has been found. Earlier research from the years between 2000 to 2005 found that the child-abduction cases covered by US broadcaster CNN featured white children 76 per cent of the time, when only 53 per cent of actual child abductees in the US were white. Journalist Sarah Stillman writes that the disproportionate coverage worldwide of missing white girls is because they are seen in newsrooms 'as valuable "front-page victims"'. Others are treated as though they are 'disposable'. In addition, people from middle and upper socio-economic classes get more attention than those less privileged.

In his book *Chavs*, Owen Jones compares the frenzied coverage Madeleine McCann's case attracted with the case of Shannon Matthews, a nine-year-old white working-class girl who lived in a public-housing estate and disappeared from Dewsbury, in the West Yorkshire region of England's north. She had been on the way to her swimming lesson. Both disappearances were sudden and upsetting. Madeleine went missing in 2007, Shannon in 2008. Yet, while Madeleine's case amassed a reward for information of £2.6 million, Shannon's accumulated a relatively measly sum of £50 000. This difference alone seemed insulting to Jones – how can the safety of one girl be valued so much higher than another? But the class differences became even more marked when it was eventually revealed that Shannon's mother Karen had kidnapped her own daughter in a bizarre plan to pocket the reward money. Karen had tied up Shannon and drugged her so she wouldn't be seen or heard. Jones argues that the resulting media coverage demonised the working class in general – not the twisted actions of Shannon's mother as an individual. Shannon's neighbours searched tirelessly from the time she went missing until she was found. And yet, one commentator wrote:

> … [Shannon's] background, a scenario that encompasses the awful, dispiriting and undisciplined face of Britain, should be read as a lesson in failure… [Karen] is the product of a society that rewards fecklessness.

This tendency for the media to cover privileged young white victims over others is known as 'missing white girl syndrome'. Once you start paying attention to it, you see it all the time.

There are a range of potential explanations behind the inequality in reporting, such as the dominance of middle-class white people in newsrooms, which may lead to bias towards caring more about middle-class white children. It may also tie in with how people see victims. Norwegian sociologist Nils Christie looked at the sorts of people who receive validation for their victimhood in the media. It's important that the victim be understood as relatively weak and lacking in power, that they are respectable and involved only in innocent activities, and that they have not taken any risks such as being in a dodgy area late at night. It's important that the offender, if known, is big, strong, and unambiguously bad. It helps if they are a complete stranger. These cases get more sympathy, and more attention. Race, argues Stillman, is a factor that plays into the way a case is formulated as legitimate, and whether the victim's story fits the public narrative of the 'damsel in distress'.

Even if a child of colour and/or from a disadvantaged community is missing through no fault of their own, they aren't necessarily an object of concern. 'There's an assumption made,' argued Dori Maynard, president of the US Robert C. Maynard Institute for Journalism Education, 'that if a young white woman from a middle-class family is missing, something has gone terribly awry.' By comparison, a child with a less privileged background may be seen as a victim of their community itself. Unconsciously or otherwise, newsmakers and audiences may associate disadvantaged communities with cruelty, neglectful parenting, and crime. The disappearance of a child in such a context might not be easily read as something gone wrong, but rather an inevitability. Their disappearance seems somehow more reasonable, less ambiguous, less shocking. The case doesn't pique audiences' curiosity so clearly. They aren't driven to talk about it in the same way as the case of a missing privileged child.

Alternatively, as Chimene Suleyman argues for the UK newspaper *The Independent*, few stories about people from diverse backgrounds feature in mainstream white-dominated popular culture. And so it may be harder for white journalists and audiences to imagine that a missing child of colour could so easily be their child, or grandchild, or niece or nephew. This may limit their empathy towards the case. She writes:

> The multi-year coverage of Madeleine McCann's disappearance was often cinematic in its reporting, told to us in every step as though an enthralling and gripping thriller. Such fascination and importance has never been given to the Trang Nguyens or Hafsa Tarambis of this world. How can the public empathise with children like this when they have been faceless all their lives?

Suleyman's question is important. The demographics of missing persons show that young people from some minority backgrounds are more likely to go missing, but their stories are less likely to be covered. Trang Nguyen was born in Vietnam and in 2015 went missing from her local area in Nottingham at age 15. Concerningly, it's believed she didn't have shoes when she disappeared. Hafsa Tarambi – who wears a headscarf – also went missing in 2015 from her home in Luton, in England's south-east, at age 15. Bedfordshire police suspect that she might be in London, although concerns for her grow with each passing day. Where is the multi-million-pound reward that Madeleine inspired? The disaster coverage? The balloons? The vigils? Who do these missing children have to be for us to learn their names and repeat their stories over the water cooler?

If your child went missing you would hope the public would respond with the same level of obsession as for a Madeleine McCann, Azaria Chamberlain, or JonBenét Ramsey. This is the best-case scenario – if people are concerned, people are looking. And yet, under these conditions your character could be questioned, unthinkable accusations could be made against you. You could end up in prison. Even under these conditions, there's no space in the public arena for your story of what life is like after the disappearance. These cases demonstrate the apex of what public attention has achieved so far. I think we can do better.

2

LOST IN THE BUSH

CINDY AND TREVOR'S LONG WEEKEND

Settlers who've arrived in Australia recently – 240 years or so ago – often tell stories about getting lost. Films about white Australians and British backpackers getting lost in the bush or in the outback – from *Picnic at Hanging Rock* (1975) to *Wolf Creek* (2005), among others – function as warnings about the dangers of the landscape.

Based on Joan Lindsay's novel, Peter Weir's lush *Picnic at Hanging Rock* is set in 1900 and tells the story of students from a posh girls' school who disappear during their excursion to Hanging Rock, just north-west of Melbourne. They're apparently lured away by some supernatural force. At the rock, everyone's timepieces stop; a freshly baked heart-shaped cake is covered with poison ants.

Aboriginal people had lived in the area for at least 26 000 years before colonisation. However, by the time the girls arrive in their high-collared white dresses, the site has been untended for decades, the original inhabitants sent to a reserve more than 100 kilometres away in Healesville.

One girl is later found, collapsed in the wilderness, but she has no memory of what happened, or where the others are. There's no trace of them, and the case remains unsolved. That's the warning: Hanging Rock is mystical and dangerous.

Greg McLean's *Wolf Creek*, based on the true-life horror story of serial killer Ivan Milat, gives the same warning about the danger of the outback. In a painful echo of these killings, *Wolf Creek* depicts two young British women and their male Australian friend who take a road trip to Wolf Creek on the edge of the Great Sandy Desert in north-west Western Australia. The landscape is ancient, isolated from main roads and major cities. It's rare to see anyone.

When the travellers arrive, again, the clocks stop. The camera emphasises the vastness of the ground and the sky. They've entered a timeless, spaceless zone. When their car breaks down, a man named Mick passes by and offers to fix it at his place. In this environment, it might be the travellers' only chance of rescue. The gore and horror start soon after with long, convoluted scenes of torture, attempted escape, and murder. In the final scene, as Mick walks along an endless road under the endless sky, his figure vanishes supernaturally. The message is: it's not an evil individual that causes danger, but the outback and the ghosts within it.

These films feature lost adults and adolescents, but anxious stories on the dangers of the bush historically focus on lost children. In his book *The Country of Lost Children*, Peter Pierce traces stories that traverse art forms, including visual art, poetry, folk and fairy tales, newspaper articles, and pantomime, to show that from the 1850s onwards, settler stories were obsessed with children who went missing in the bush. The lost child 'is the symbol of essential if never fully resolved anxieties within the white settler communities of this country'. The anxiety has to do with the mysterious nature of the landscape – it's not what the new arrivals are used to. But there's also a moral ambiguity, the vague awareness that their tenure on the land results from the dispossession of First Nations people.

Henry Lawson's 1899 poem 'The Babies in the Bush' is emblematic of these stories. It describes children, drawn to the wonders of nature, who simply 'trotted away'. The poem asks:

> But what is the spirit that always leads
> The toddler's feet from home?

Their mother prays to the supernatural world, 'a spirit the bellbirds know', for their safety:

> To guide the feet of the lost aright
> And lead them on to a land of light
> Where the bush-lost babies go.

Similarly, the true story of the three Duff children who went missing for nine days in 1864 near Horsham in country Victoria became a fairytale told to generations of settler children. The Duffs survived on the food they'd brought for a picnic – damper and treacle – as well the quandong berries they found and the morning dew they sucked from leaves. The eldest child, seven-year-old Jane, protected the others from the cold by giving them her dress. They were found by a First Nations tracker – trackers were skilful navigators, enlisted for explorers' expeditions, and criminal investigations, and to search for missing persons. A verse version of the story published in Britain in 1866, *The Australian Babes in the Wood*, suggests the dangerous force in their story was nature itself: it describes the moon and stars of the night sky, and how 'Jeanie thought they smiled disdain'.

As Pierce points out, the stories of lost children told by Australian settlers are different to European ones. In Grimm's fairytales, for example, children go missing or deal with the threat of disappearance all the time. In *Hansel and Gretel*, siblings are abducted by a witch who lives in the forest in a house made out of gingerbread and wants to eat the children; in *Snow White*, the queen orders the murder of her stepdaughter, a fate the stepdaughter avoids by running away into the forest. It's never the forest that is the danger, it's people.

Similarly, the true story of stolen First Nations children told by Doris Pilkington in *Follow the Rabbit-Proof Fence* (adapted into the 2002 film, *Rabbit-Proof Fence*) affirms that it is harmful individuals and institutions that cause trouble, not nature. Under the government's policy of separating First Nations children from their families, three young girls are taken from Jigalong, a First Nations community in the Pilbara, and sent over 1600 kilometres away to the Moore River Native Settlement, north of Perth. The girls escape the settlement and manage to walk home across the desert. By comparison, says Pierce, the lost settler child 'stands in part for the apprehensions of adults about having sought to settle in a place where they might never be at peace'.

❖

I'm interested in getting beyond anxious stories of the dangerous bush to learn about the reality of survival and symbiosis. People *do* get lost in Australia, but these aren't always disaster narratives: it's also possible to work with nature.

Cindy Bohan and Trevor Salvado went missing in March 2019, a few months before we meet. They had gone bushwalking on Mount Buffalo, near Bright, a riverside town in north-eastern Victoria, and had become lost. Bright is a gateway to alpine regions that gather winter snow, and to the area's vineyards. I've visited Bright on school holidays once or twice and remember it as peaceful, the soft sunlight covering the landscape like a thin woven blanket. In autumn, the trees turn crisp, deep orange, yellow, and red. The mountain has large granite rocks and sheer granite cliffs, waterfalls, and views of the Ovens Valley below.

I meet Cindy and Trevor on very different terrain, in a café overlooking Flinders Lane in Melbourne's CBD. It's a cold morning that's promising to become a warm day as the sun peeks in through the windows.

They got lost on a Friday. They were meeting friends in Bright for the Labour Day long weekend but were there early and decided to take what Cindy describes as 'a short walk' of 'only' around four hours. They brought a Parks Victoria map with them, a camera, a Swiss Army knife, and picnic food – bread rolls, fruit, and some muesli bars.

'I don't even eat muesli bars usually,' says Cindy. 'But we had so many of them because we'd seen some in Bright and thought we'd try all the different ones.'

Cindy and Trevor had always loved the bush. Trevor was a Scout as a kid, and Cindy's father was a shooter and would take her out with him. Cindy doesn't like hunting herself, but remembers sitting in the bush thinking 'This is beautiful.' As a couple they'd regularly go camping and bushwalking, even after they moved to an inner suburb of Melbourne. For them, the bush is a place they can relax. 'It resets you,' says Trevor. 'You can go at your own pace.'

As they were walking, Cindy and Trevor's plans to head to a lookout were disrupted when they came across some snakes sunning themselves; they wanted to avoid disturbing them and getting bitten. They looked at their map and decided to take a smaller track to join up with a different track and walk back to their car. There were markers on the trees – little stones or streamers – but, as Trevor explains, 'It's remote up there. On some of the exposed rock areas you can lose the track because there's nothing to define it. All of a sudden, we're just in the bush and we aren't sure where we are.' I note Trevor's shift into the present tense, as though he's reliving these moments as we talk.

He doesn't know what happened. 'If we knew how we got lost, we wouldn't have got lost. It just happened so easily.'

This is a common story: you think you're following the path until, suddenly, you aren't, and you don't know how long you've been off track. It didn't help that their Parks Victoria map wasn't very detailed, a problem the organisation later acknowledged to the couple, and has since reviewed.

'At what point did you think, "We're lost"?' I ask.

'There was an expletive in there,' jokes Cindy.

'It wasn't far in,' says Trevor. 'Maybe five or six minutes after we left the track to join the other track. Maybe ten minutes at most.'

Cindy doesn't expect this answer. She turns to Trevor. 'When you say you knew we were lost,' she asks, 'how lost did you think we were?' And then she turns to me. 'Sorry Erin, I know you're the interviewer.'

I say it's okay; this difference of perspective underlines how uncertain this state of being missing is. I have two people, right in front of me, who got lost at the same time, and each had a different moment of realisation that they were lost.

'We were lost to the point where we couldn't backtrack,' says Trevor.

'I knew we were lost,' agrees Cindy, 'but I thought that we'd find a track. It wasn't until that evening that I thought, "This might be a little bit serious."'

They tried to navigate themselves back to the car, but the

bush was so dense it was hard sometimes for Cindy even to see Trevor walking ahead of her. 'It was interesting how thick it was,' says Cindy. This is the type of language they both use to talk about their experience – it was 'interesting'. They were curious about their surroundings, constantly making observations about it. Obviously, getting lost was not a desirable situation and they were keen to get home as soon as possible, but they talk about it as though it were a learning opportunity.

'We were calm the whole time,' Cindy says. 'We like the bush, so we knew we were safe.'

Nonetheless, adrenaline kicked in as they descended the mountain. It was steep going, but it was still possible to walk down, at times with the assistance of branches, or by making some short vertical drops, or by sliding over rocks. Although they were disoriented, when they saw boats on the lake below, they had some geographical clues, and they knew there were people close by. It helped that it was the long weekend, as the area had more visitors than usual.

'We were thinking we'd be down and out of the bush that night,' remembers Cindy.

Trevor agrees, 'Down and out by eight o'clock. In the Bright Brewery by ten.' He laughs. 'Little did we know.'

As the sun was setting, they found an opening in the bush. They approached a big rock, which they estimate would've plunged about 100 metres downwards. They couldn't get back up the mountain without climbing equipment, and when Trevor threw a stone off the drop and heard it bounce several times as it fell, they had no intention of following it. They were apparently trapped, and exhausted. But there was a water supply – a trickling creek nearby – so it was a good place to stop for the night. They ate some of their picnic food, which was now designated as provisions. They constructed the same kind of hut that Trevor had earned a Scout badge for as a child.

'It really came in handy for once,' Trevor laughs. 'It's like anything with memory: once you're put in the right situation, it all comes back.'

I ask them if they had brought a phone along and Cindy and Trevor exchange glances. They had not. 'That's a bone of contention with our family,' Cindy says. But reception on the mountain is limited anyway.

When it got dark, they could make out lights, and they could hear voices. They didn't know how far away the other campsite was, just that there was the murmuring presence of other humans. They tried to get their attention by taking a photo with the flash on. It didn't work. They went to their makeshift bed.

The nights were cold but not yet freezing – had they become lost a few weeks later, the overnight temperatures would've added an extra challenge. Insects were biting them, but they slept, in their words, 'okay'.

The sun hadn't touched their side of the mountain by morning, so they awoke to an icy cold. It was time to strategise. Trevor is a retired pilot and had been involved in rescue operations; drawing on that experience, they thought the fact there weren't too many trees around them would help searchers identify them from the sky. They decided to stay where they were to make search efforts easier. They ate some food, retrieved water, and improved on their hut by insulating the floor with leaves, raising it from the cold ground. They paced short distances to keep themselves warm and to have something to do. They watched birds and absorbed the breathtaking surrounds.

They could hear cows from somewhere below them and Cindy made up a story about a little farm down the mountain, and imagined a weekender cottage down there. The owners wouldn't be home, she decided. They could break in and sleep overnight and pay the owners back for the broken windows and the cans of food they took.

The sun set on another day. 'It was beautiful,' Trevor says. 'It really was.'

'We kept telling ourselves to think about where we are,' says Cindy. 'To appreciate it. We're in the bush, let's enjoy it. Let's soak it in.' And as they watched the darkening horizon, a helicopter flew over them. And with the sound of the mechanical whir, they knew they'd be found.

The next day – Sunday – went similarly to the day before. Confident they'd be rescued at any moment, Trevor taught Cindy how to put on a harness thrown down from a helicopter and get picked up from the sky. Through the day, they could hear the helicopter and see its bright floodlight. This noise was accompanied by the sounds of motorcycles – people searching via land. They tried to attract the helicopter's attention with their camera flash and by waving at it. It didn't work but they still felt reassured. As Trevor says, 'We could hear people looking for us.'

Something shifted for Trevor and Cindy by Monday morning, though. They had rested enough to no longer be exhausted, they wanted to see their kids, and they were down to their last muesli bar. They wanted to light a fire to stave off the cold, but they couldn't without a flint. Trevor sat quietly on their rock.

'I was just taking the beautiful morning in, and I saw a car,' he says. 'A white car, and it drove out of the bush – it just appeared. And then it turned, it turned left. So I knew there was a track down there.' From this information, they could get a better idea of where they were on their map. It had become clear by this stage that there was a way off the rock without falling or sliding. It looked rough, but possible. They had to decide whether they'd wait any longer to be rescued, or try to journey further by themselves.

'We sat around thinking about it,' says Cindy. 'We wanted it to be a sensible decision.' They knew that it's best to stay where you are if you're lost so that you don't wind up somewhere searchers have already scoured. They also knew they had access to water, even if their food supply was diminishing. They could hear a rescue helicopter above them. At the same time, they knew they could get off the rock, they knew there was a track, and they thought there might be a cottage lower down. The story Cindy told about the cows and the house wasn't factually correct, it later turned out, but working with what they knew, and entertaining what they didn't, they decided they'd descend the mountain further.

They'd have a full day to rest before walking on. They'd take their time, get off the rock, follow a little creek to a river, find a track (which was only about a kilometre away from where they were, they estimated), and walk another 5 kilometres or so to the lake they'd seen with the boats. They had contingency plans: they decided what to do if one of them got injured (the uninjured one would carry on, and make sure search and rescue teams would return to the site as quickly as possible), though it was important that they take their journey carefully to prevent any complications.

That night, they ate half their last muesli bar – a quarter of a bar each – and slept. They waited for the sun to rise again before finishing off the muesli bar and descending the mountain.

'It was the right time to make that decision,' reflects Cindy. 'Had we left on the day we got lost, or the next morning, we wouldn't have known what we were walking into.' Their time on the rock had allowed them to observe the terrain, assess some of the factors they didn't know, think through alternative plans, and imagine the weekender by the lake. They were still dealing with ambiguities, but they had enough experience and information to feel confident in the bush, and in their decision.

I wonder aloud if they were hungry. But even this was under control. 'I never felt hungry at all,' says Trevor. Cindy explains that when the body is just trying to survive, sensations like hunger are quelled. The survival-oriented sympathetic nervous system allows the body to thrive in stressful situations like this. You're alert, energetic; extra blood is sent to the muscles; non-urgent functions like digestion are slowed down until you're back to safety.

They gradually made their way around the rock. At the bottom of it, they came across dense brambles, even denser than what they'd encountered on the Friday. It looked impossible. 'But we were lucky,' says Trevor. 'We found wombat and wallaby tracks. They're like us – they're lazy and they don't like getting scratched by brambles. So we started following them, and they were essentially doing what we wanted to do: follow the creek and keep out of the brambles.'

Eventually, the brambles thinned out, the grass underfoot was brightened by the sun, there were fewer trees around and the ground was flat. And then they eventually got to a good-quality dirt road. Nobody was there, possibly because the long weekend was now over. But there were the cows they'd heard, and soon enough, the lake. This walk was far quicker than they'd expected it to be. They'd given themselves the whole day to travel around 6 kilometres, but it'd only taken a few hours. Once it was clear they'd get to see their kids again that day, the hunger set in.

As they walked, a busload of students who were out on a class trip pulled over. They had food. Apples and zucchini chips. And water.

The students were excited. 'They actually had canvassed the thought that "Wouldn't it be funny if we found those lost bushwalkers while we're on the lake?"' remembers Trevor. They called the police and reported them found.

Lost in the bush 39

In Victoria, the police are responsible for missing-persons cases, but the State Emergency Service (SES) supports them by conducting searches in the bush. The police are involved with searching as well, but not always – it depends on what resources they have, and how risky the case seems to be. In the year 2017–18, the Victorian SES supported police in 753 incidents. Not all these incidents would have been looking for missing persons (the SES also supports police with road rescue operations) but it does give you a rough idea of the frequency with which people become lost: it's a daily occurrence. The same is true in New South Wales, where the SES attended 450 search and rescue operations in the first six months of 2019 alone.

I call Hardy Clemens, an SES volunteer who's searched for people. Hardy is into hiking – he's travelled to various parts of the world, including Everest, to explore nature; he and his friends enjoy going on annual trips to Mount Kosciuszko on blizzardy days where everyone else has gone home.

'We do things a bit different to most people,' he explains, deadpan. 'It's about old blokes trying to prove we're still young.' He's joking, but these are the kinds of people you want searching for you if you ever get lost in the bush – people who love it, who've spent their lives in it, and who know the terrain they're searching.

At the start of a search, police have to establish that those missing are actually lost in the bush. For instance, police investigating Trevor and Cindy's case questioned the friends they'd planned to meet up with on the Friday night in order to rule out the possibility of murder, or murder-suicide. Some cases that look like someone's lost in the bush turn out to be cases of people intentionally going missing, or people who are missing as a result of a crime.

'We want to make sure that the people we're searching for are genuinely lost,' says Hardy.

Then you want some general information about the person. Their health, their experience in the bush, what equipment they have, and their age are all important factors that can impact their vulnerability. Someone's handedness can also be surprisingly important information. 'If they're strongly right-hand dominant, they tend to drift to the right when they get tired,' says Hardy. You also try to find out where they intended to go, which is why it's important for hikers to tell others their plans before setting out.

The personality of the missing person can also be important. 'Strong-willed people never believe they're lost.' Hardy remembers searching for a man for four days before he was located by air. When he asked the man if he was all right, his response was to ask why they were there. 'You're missing, mate,' said Hardy. 'No I'm not!' he replied. Some people, Hardy says, go out bush and 'have an epiphany', some kind of spiritual experience that makes them want to stay wandering. They change their plans, feel fine, and when they're eventually found they may not want to go back home. They don't understand that people are concerned for them. These are difficult cases because they keep walking. 'And they get further and further out of reach,' says Hardy.

Research gathered from the International Search & Rescue Incident Database shows that about half of hikers are found within 3 kilometres of the place they were last seen, although some are found much further away than that – Cindy and Trevor were about 6 kilometres from their car at their rock. Lost hikers tend to stay on tracks and seek shelter, and to seek higher ground for better phone reception – if, that is, they have a phone. They're usually found on a road, by a stream, or in a shelter of some kind. But you can't make assumptions – it's best to search thoroughly.

Searchers will divide up the landscape into one-kilometre squares and look through one square at a time. Anything could be a clue, so they look for little things like broken branches, or marks in the snow.

'You're looking for such minute details,' I say to Hardy. 'Do you ever worry that you're missing something?'

'Oh constantly, constantly,' he says. He remembers a case of two young Brownies who ironically went missing while learning compass navigation skills. When children go missing, it's automatically a high-risk situation, and the police need to establish if they're lost or abducted or if wild dogs have attacked them. In this case, the whole community was panicking. They searched all night, and even in the darkness they had to pay attention to every detail. In the end, the girls found their own way back at daybreak – they were good with their compasses after all, but had got distracted talking to each other and gone too far. They built a shelter – which they had learned to do in Brownies – and rested until it was light enough to walk back. Upon their return, 'there were 50 adults there who burst into tears'. It's a happy ending, but searchers are aware that not every case ends this way. And a searcher's capacity to notice things might be the difference between a happy ending and a sad one.

But some people have a knack for spotting this kind of detail. Hardy grew up spending a lot of time in the bush with his father: 'I've always been taught to look at my surrounds, 360 degrees, and to look for detail. It's just who I am and what I've been taught.'

And as well, says Hardy, 'I gotta say, it really lifts you up when you start seeing signs you're on their trail.' In one case he remembers, the searchers found a drag mark – the missing person had pulled himself along the ground with his arms – before seeing equipment the missing person discarded to reduce the load. Hardy interpreted these as signs that the lost person had injured his leg, and that he'd see him at any moment. Then he accidentally stood on him, 'because he'd covered himself up with leaves and branches to try and stay warm'.

Knowing how to use natural resources like this can be vital. 'A lot of bushwalkers don't have that skill,' says Hardy. They rely on equipment like tents – 'creature comforts, I call them'. While bushwalking once, he happened upon a group of hikers who had run out of water in the pouring rain. 'I bent down on my hands and knees and drank water out of a puddle,' demonstrating that fresh rainwater is drinkable. 'They just didn't see it.' It was as though water that wasn't from a tap or a bottle was invisible.

The best thing to do when you're lost, says Hardy, is to stop. 'Stop, make camp, make a good shelter, and wait. And you will be found. But people aren't taught to do that. Or they don't know they're even lost.'

Hardy obviously enjoys the bush, but when he goes hiking himself, 'I always plan that I'm going to be stuck for five days.' You need to plan to get lost, whereas 'most people don't even think of it'. You take more supplies than you think you will need. On one case he worked on, two men went missing in the bush; one was found alive and the other had died. The difference between them, as far as he could make out, was that the one who survived finished his bowl of porridge one morning while the other didn't.

An EPIRB is handy – a battery-operated device which can send radio distress signals to help rescue teams identify where you are. It's easy to fit in a pack, and it's a bargain if it ends up saving your life. And for those of us who aren't as happy to be mindfully observing their surrounds for days as Cindy and Trevor did, Hardy recommends taking along a deck of cards. Hopefully there'll be a moment during your thousandth game of patience where someone from a search and rescue team comes up behind you and tells you where to put the king to win the game.

❖

When the police picked up Cindy and Trevor, an officer told them their case had been 'big'. The search had been one of the biggest conducted in the state for a long time, with over 200 people on the mountain trying to find them. It was so big that the police wouldn't be taking them to the nearest police station in Bright. The media already knew they'd been found and would be gathering there. They went to the nearby town of Myrtleford instead. Their kids were at the police station, and so were some paramedics, who took Cindy and Trevor to the hospital. They were dehydrated, and obviously hadn't eaten enough, but after some IV fluids they were ready to face the media. They were happy to talk, because they were grateful to everyone searching.

'I think the experience was easier for us than for other people,' Trevor says. 'Because we knew we were well. We knew there was nothing wrong. It was just that no one else knew that.' A lot had happened while they were perched on their rock.

It was particularly stressful for the friends they'd failed to meet up with. They felt guilty that they didn't know where Cindy and Trevor had planned to walk. And, says Cindy, 'They'd think things like, "Trevor wouldn't murder Cindy, but Cindy might murder Trevor."'

Trevor and I laugh; it seems funny now. But questioning whether your friends would be capable of murder would've been challenging. Trevor says he was surprised by the reactions of some of his friends. Some had immediately assumed they were dead, while others had been calmer.

The searchers assumed they were alive, but hypothesised that Trevor had been injured and Cindy had stayed with him. 'For whatever reason,' says Trevor, amused, 'they thought if Cindy were injured, I'd have carried her out.'

I smile. 'That's very chivalrous of you,' I say. 'Hypothetically.'

Their campsite was also about the only part of the mountain that hadn't been searched. 'They thought there was no way we'd be there because it's just hideously dense,' Cindy says.

Some family members were in the media spotlight and responsible for liaising with police. 'They were under stress,' Cindy says of her kids, all aged in their twenties, 'but they dealt with it in their own way. And they never thought we were dead. They knew we were okay. I think the police didn't let them contemplate us not being okay.'

A local Bright family had let the kids stay at their house, and the police visited and updated them regularly. They'd also given them food recommendations and suggested a nice walk. Cindy reflects, 'The police were alert to the idea that an idle mind –'

Trevor finishes: '– is the devil's playground.'

I ask if they'd go back to Mount Buffalo again. Trevor says he would. He's curious to know how they got lost. 'It hasn't changed my view of the bush. In fact, I just want to get into it more and walk.' The couple have gone bushwalking in different areas since they were lost. 'It just goes to show that when you need to, you've got the resources to survive. I think our greatest quality is that we're very comfortable in the bush. Had we not been comfortable – especially at night, because there's a lot of noises in the bush – we would have freaked out.'

Cindy has a different answer. 'I don't know how comfortable I'd be back on Buffalo. I love the bush, I still love it. I'm not scared. But something's changed.'

'Is it a greater respect for it, in a way?' asks Trevor.

'No, because I've got a strong connection with the bush anyway. It's just an alertness that you can get lost. But that doesn't mean I don't want to be in the bush. Really, what happened to us is a really positive story.'

Trevor agrees. 'It restores your faith in human nature. All these people who didn't know us from a bar of soap were prepared to give up their time to come out and help. All the stuff we hear in the news is quite horrible, but this reinforces the fact that deep down, we just want to help.'

'The good news story is of Trevor and I being alive,' says Cindy. 'But it's also all those stories of people being kind to one another. The people who volunteered to search, or the family that offered their house, or our neighbours – we've got dogs and chooks, they stepped in to look after them. People were asking our kids, "Is there anything we can do?"… You just hear of that, the tentacles of people's kindness, and that's the best part of the story, for me.'

Despite its happy ending, Cindy and Trevor's story doesn't quite challenge all of the colonial fairytales about the bush. The reality is that it's easy to get lost, there are venomous creatures, and the landscape is complex to navigate. Sometimes people are ignorant of where they are and how to get where they want to go. And sometimes being lost is deadly. But to leave the story simply as a warning about the dangers of nature isn't right either. There's also a way of working with this ignorance to learn from the environment around you – to look for paths off a huge rock, for animal tracks to guide you through the brambles – and stay safe. The mysterious bush is a place that can inspire awe and respect. And within the unknown there's also room for human kindness. With the murmurs of surrounding campsites, carparks full of searchers' vehicles, a bus of students on alert for missing persons, and the helicopter flying above them, Cindy and Trevor were never alone in the bush. And so, despite being lost, despite having to deal with ambiguous circumstances, they enjoyed it.

3

AN AWFUL, AWFUL THING

SARAH AND THE SEARCH FOR Q

Quentin, who often went by the name Q, grew up in West Auckland, New Zealand. As a teen in the late 1980s and early 1990s he was part of a bustling household. He lived with his three sisters and two step-siblings, his mother Sarah Godwin, and his stepfather. He liked gardening and beekeeping and canoeing. The family could go just down the road and reach Manukau Harbour, on the west coast of Auckland, an airy blue beach that opens up to the Tasman Sea. Being close to these rough edges of the world suited Q. He liked to be outside.

When I meet her, Sarah says that she could imagine him happy in an outdoorsy career like forestry or agriculture. She also describes Q as a 'family person', caring and sensitive and good friends with his similar-aged stepbrother. One day, he went missing.

At the home she shares with her husband in a green village in Surrey, in England's south-east, not far from my own adopted home of Oxford, Sarah and I sit in a conservatory with cups of tea. It's not until Sarah switches on the ceiling light that I realise how little sun comes through the large window. It's grey outside.

Despite the fresh sea spray and the lively family life in New Zealand, Sarah tells me, 'West Auckland has got this tough, macho sort of culture': the boys with their ubiquitous black jeans and thick chains and tattoos, and a rising crime rate. 'It was quite heavy. And, you know, at a high school there's a lot of that around... Problem people, problem children.' Her nature-loving, sensitive son 'was also a teenager growing up in an environment where he had a lot of peer-group pressure,' she says. 'He dabbled in drugs, probably without us realising quite what his level of involvement was.' Q stepped through his urban landscape late at night with guys who carried cigarettes, drugs, and alcohol in their pockets.

'Was it hard,' I ask Sarah, 'for Q to be the kind of person who likes beekeeping around friends like that?'

'Absolutely,' she says, her long fingers cradling her tea. 'He was still trying to work out where to fit in, how to fit in, who he was.' Sarah's tone is thoughtful. Despite the age difference, some of the same things would have been as true for her growing up as they were for Q, and for me. Being yourself is not yet a habit when you're a teenager.

I become conscious that to retrace Q, who he was at that time, and what he went through, is an impossible act. Sarah doesn't completely trust her memory – it was 1992 when Q went missing – and from the beginning she has had to rely on others' accounts to flesh out the story. Moreover, we can't know what goes on in somebody else's head unless they want to tell us. Knowing someone is always a slippery thing, and never truly knowing is the risk we take when we give our love. Sarah's insights are gleaned from decades of introspection, but she still isn't sure what happened.

When Q went missing Sarah had been visiting friends and relatives in her native England, not far from where we're talking now. Q was 18 and one day after school he and his younger sister chatted briefly in the family kitchen before he changed out of his school uniform and into his work clothes – he was heading to his part-time job at the supermarket, just down the hill from their house. He cheerfully bade his sister goodbye and she thought nothing of it. But hers was the last confirmed sighting of him. As the family found out later, he never went to the supermarket.

That he didn't come home straightaway at the end of his shift wasn't worrying. He hadn't mentioned plans to go out, but he often did spend time with friends in the evening. His uneaten dinner meant nothing. Because he didn't live in the main house – he lived in a room above the family's garage – no one noticed his empty bed. Q's habits had their own rhythm.

His absence was first registered at breakfast the next morning. The family went outside and up the stairs to his room. It looked normal, except there was a note from Q on the bed. It said that he planned to go to Piha, a village on the coast west of Auckland.

'There's a big rock,' explains Sarah, her breathing growing faster. 'It's a place people jump [from] to commit suicide and all this sort of stuff.' She exhales slowly. The choice of location caused immediate concern, although how the family was meant to interpret the note is still unclear. It could have been a suicide note. 'Because it was, obviously, a fairly desperate note, they informed the police and the police took it seriously and started a search of the area,' says Sarah. At the same time, the note did not explicitly mention suicide. Sarah still isn't sure if it was a suicide note or an expression of sadness.

While Sarah was catching up with relatives on what had been a long-anticipated and otherwise enjoyable trip, the family was waiting to break the news to her. They'd hoped the police would be able to find Q quickly, and they didn't want to raise what could soon turn out to be a false alarm when there were long, expensive flights involved. But 24 hours after Q was discovered missing, they decided that Sarah needed to come home.

The New Zealand and UK time zones were 11 hours apart. As the sky above Sarah was fading into night, the phone call plunged her into the harsh brightness of a New Zealand day.

'It was the most horrendous phone call you could have,' she remembers.

The police put out calls to the public with Q's description and a number for them to call. Family and friends went door-knocking throughout Piha, an area framed by the rough, dark sea, black sand, and sharp rock faces. While Sarah was still in the sky, Q's informal search team asked the locals if they had seen him. After that, there are conflicting accounts as to what happened with the investigation.

'I remember being told about three days after he'd gone missing that some school friends had seen him out there and they told somebody this,' says Sarah. 'The police say they've got no record of that, so I don't know. We've got different versions of what happened.'

Sarah and I clasp our mugs of tea to gather the radiant warmth. How many times has Sarah gone over this story? And yet, the facts are not certain. 'A few people said they'd thought they'd seen somebody of that description sitting by the side of the road, or somebody walking along. But as in all these things, you can't verify if it is the person you want it to be. None of the reports were actually verified.

'There's a horrible sinking feeling when you realise something serious like this is happening. You know, and what do you do about it? Initially, you think that if you look hard enough, you'll find a person, or he'll come home. But then the days turn into weeks and the weeks turn into months and the months turn into years, and …' Sarah inhales deeply. 'You know?'

The search for Q continued. Family friends helped make posters. Sarah's then-husband used his job as a knitting-yarn supplier to extend the search – a poster and a letter was sent to every wool shop in the country with information about Q. Alongside shelves of colourful merino yarns were photos of Q's face. Their creativity was rewarded with leads, but the results were frustrating. While some people thought they had seen Q, it was impossible to tell whether or not they really had. And some promising reports were not adequately followed up.

'Six months after he'd gone missing someone said they'd seen him at Auckland railway station,' says Sarah. 'They were school friends of his and they had spoken to him. But we didn't get to speak to them because they told the manager of a shop and he forgot to take their names.' I cringe at this failure. The scope of the search was so big, with so many parts to manage. There were many stories about what might have happened.

And then there was nothing. 'Everybody does whatever physical thing they can think of,' says Sarah. 'But if it doesn't produce any results, you've got nothing to go on to do more searching. And although New Zealand's got a small population, it's a big country. And it's got a lot of really wild areas; even around Auckland. The bushland in between where we lived and the west coast is immense.' The coast west of Auckland is home to subtropical rainforests, roaring beaches and big waterfalls, and it's dotted with volcanic cones. It's adventure country: travellers come to hike and bungee jump and surf and hire four-wheel drives to explore the off-road terrain. It's a devastatingly big world.

'Somebody could live there for years without being found if they wanted to.'

When I ask Sarah why Q would go missing, she tells me that I have to understand the environment he was in. It was rough, and being sensitive wasn't easy. And at 17, Q was diagnosed with bipolar disorder, a mental illness that is characterised by extreme mood swings. She thinks his illness played a big role in his disappearance. Individuals with bipolar can spend weeks and even months in depressive turmoil or experiencing manic highs.

Although most people who live with mental illness don't go missing, as many as 80 per cent of the people who do go missing have some history of mental illness, from mild forms of depression to florid psychosis. Some missing persons with symptoms of mental illness will have received a diagnosis; some may never have sought support. Some abscond from mental health institutions – that is, they go missing in order to escape inpatient treatment. Some people go missing as part of a suicide plan. In the midst of anguish, running away can feel like an appealing option. It's a way to find distance. Sarah also thinks that just as being sensitive made it difficult for Q to fit in, so did his mental illness. It was another vulnerability.

In the lead-up to his diagnosis, Sarah had got a call from one of Q's teachers. At lunchtime one day, in the playground, a group of students circled around him as he showed off his karate skills. He kicked wildly and punched the air. He had told his teacher he was a karate expert but, says Sarah, 'He just wanted to think he was one.' He had no knowledge of karate at all. The teacher had noticed how Q's words ran into one another, merging into enthusiastic sequences that were difficult to follow. Although Q didn't do anything destructive, his staccato, aggressive display was frightening. As Sarah surmises, 'He was spooking the other kids a bit.'

Sarah had noticed a change in Q as well, but it didn't concern her at first. 'To us, it just seemed like he was just being rather super energetic. It was quite good because he wanted to do all sorts of things and was being incredibly busy.' But Q was barely sleeping, and his teacher's concern made the family seek the advice of a psychiatrist. After talking to Q, the psychiatrist decided he would visit him at home every day. He was not to go back to school.

'There's that tipping point,' says Sarah, 'where, if you're moderately manic, shall we say, it can be very productive and very creative. If you go too far, you become potentially a liability to yourself – if not a liability to other people – and you start to wreak havoc in everybody's life.' For example, it would have been easy for Q's boasting about his black-belt karate skills to go too far and turn destructive – particularly after a couple of drinks, particularly if others were looking for a fight. 'Or you just wear yourself out physically,' says Sarah. 'People who are manic will apparently just walk and walk until their shoes fall off and their feet are blistered and they'll keep walking, and walk their feet raw, and they don't know they're doing it.'

To prevent potential harm, Sarah remembers, 'For five weeks, I was his, sort of, warden.' Although 24-hour monitoring was impossible, Sarah says, 'Between us, as a family, I think we kept an eye on him pretty well.' They watched Q pace the house, expending his boundless energy in this safe place, stopping him from going out alone. 'He only went AWOL a few times. Like once or twice he got on a bus at five in the morning and went out to the coast, or something. Went missing. But, you know, he came back.'

By the summertime, Q's energies were more moderate. On the other side of mania, he looked back at his actions with embarrassment. When the next school year started, he changed to a new school to avoid the people who'd remember his karate displays.

'When he had the manic episode it really shook his confidence socially – because the kids had seen him as being weird,' Sarah says. It was a quieter time for him. 'If anything he was, in some ways, more homebound afterwards because it was where he felt, perhaps, a bit safer. But at the same time, he was reaching out and trying to carry on.'

The manic version of oneself can be an incredible thing to experience – there is nothing to worry about, you feel capable of anything, you are full of energy and new insights and ideas. These are very high highs to fall from. Especially when people with bipolar are also in danger of falling into depression.

'Was there a point where you began to trust that things were getting a bit better?' I ask.

'Yes,' says Sarah. She did begin to trust regular life again. Q's experience had shaken him but he was recognisable now. Together, they began to imagine his future – tertiary studies, a career. 'I was too trusting, looking back, in that, I don't think anybody really warned us what the signs were to watch out for in terms of depression. Tipping the other way.'

'You couldn't have known,' I say.

Sarah agrees, but there's caveats too: 'He was quite open to talking about things but, looking back, I think we should've had … more guidance as to what the illness meant long-term. Because my picture of it was, okay, he got over the manic episode. Yes, he might have to take lithium or some other medication for the rest of his life but, you know, that's it, we've done it … I was a bit naïve, or a bit ignorant.'

❖

It's natural to wonder about a missing person. Why would they leave? Would they still be here if I'd done something different? Elizabeth Davies, a social worker who has studied the effects of a family member's absence, has found that people try to pick out possible warning signs and berate themselves for not heeding them. But, she writes, 'almost invariably, there's no warning, no clear indicator to suggest that a loved one will become a missing person'. Despite their intense scrutiny of the case, many families, even months and years on, still have no idea if the person left of their own volition.

There were no warning signs that Q would go missing. And so, ten days before his disappearance, Sarah left for her visit to England without a worry. Q was, after all, not being left alone – the rest of his family was around. It wasn't evident that he was going through anything more than the usual difficulties of a young man embarking on adulthood.

'I think, looking back, I shouldn't have done that,' Sarah says heavily. 'But then, how can you tell these things? And if I had stayed there, would it have made any difference? I don't know. It's one of the things that haunts you though.'

After her family's phone call to her in England, Sarah wanted to get home as quickly as possible. But between her and home stood half a planet. She'd have to travel from London Heathrow to Los Angeles, then from Los Angeles to Auckland.

Sarah's journey was even tougher than an average long-haul flight. For the first 11 hours of the flight from Los Angeles to Auckland (following the 11-hour flight from London), Sarah sat tense and sleepless in the dry, pressurised air of the cabin, watching the small screen showing the incremental progression of the plane across a map of the world. She clung to the hope that soon she'd be able to *do* something to help find Q. But then the tiny plane on the screen made a sudden U-turn.

The weather conditions in Auckland were too bad to land,

so the plane diverted to Fiji. If conditions didn't clear in a few hours, they would have to disembark because the crew would've been working for too long to safely continue the journey. The conditions did not clear. Passengers disembarked onto a tropical island.

'We had to spend a whole day in Fiji and I just couldn't believe it, you know. It's never happened to me before in all of my life, going backwards and forwards from New Zealand and the UK. It had to happen then.'

Sarah called her family from a featureless airport hotel room. There was no news. By the time she got to Auckland, she had been in transit for 50 hours.

'I think I was in another dimension mentally.' She laughs and I smile too; it releases some of the tension. But then she adds, in an understated manner I come to find characteristic of her, 'It was, yeah. It was a nightmare.'

This feeling of being suspended over the planet, of waiting for the opportunity to search and to see her son again, didn't end when Sarah's plane finally landed in Auckland. According to sociologist Susan Hogben, when a loved one goes missing, life can go 'on hold'. Hogben spoke to a family who wanted to move to mainland Britain from their home on the Isle of Wight, but felt unable to. They were afraid that if they moved, their missing son wouldn't be able to find them. Their response to ambiguity, says Hogben, is 'literal immobility'. Family members sometimes feel they need to wait until the case is resolved before they can begin to imagine – let alone embark upon – the future.

Missing someone is a lot like waiting for them. The time that passes without the person isn't full of possibility like normal life. It's a hurdle between the present without them and the possibility of a future with them. Time becomes something all too expansive, something to be *killed*. Eventually, the challenge for family members waiting for missing persons is to start moving again.

When I meet Sarah, it's clear that she is not stuck in the place she was when Q first went missing. Literally, she's living in a different country. Her house in this little village has an air of solace. It's so quiet there. One of the reasons Sarah wanted to move back to England was to avoid those nosy onlookers who constantly demanded updates on Q's case. The move – about three years after Q's disappearance – allowed her some much-needed distance from the questions, from the noise.

In time, Sarah begins to speak of Q more often, but did so on her own terms. One day, she says, 'I suddenly thought that by not talking about him, I'm denying him. So I made myself talk about it more, but it wasn't easy.' The ordinary conversations she has when she meets new people are always fraught. She'll be at a convivial event, holding a glass of sparkling wine. She'll start talking to someone new. They'll ask each other about their lives. Do you have kids? How many? What are they doing? In those moments, it would be easier for Sarah to pretend that Q never existed. But that's not true. So, she says that he's missing. She says she isn't sure what happened to him. She talks about her other children too. She chooses to recognise Q, to show that he is valuable, and while he is not literally present he is nonetheless on Sarah's mind. She carefully imparts a small sense of what having a missing son is like. But the conversation always moves on. I see in Sarah a protective reluctance to set out the rawness of her experiences in the crystal air of the conservatory in which our interview takes place.

'You can't pour the story out,' she says. 'You can't depress people by telling them how awful it is. So you shut up about it.'

From where we sit, we can see Sarah's garden. It has been drizzling with rain on and off all day. But the sun is now beginning to softly light up the flowers and the pale walls around us. In this contained space, nature blooms behind the glass. It seems to me that Sarah looks at her loss the way we look at her garden now. It's still very real, it's there in vivid colour. But we are not in it. Even though it's big, it is possible to turn away.

This isn't an easy thing to do. The open questions of a missing-persons case trap friends and family members in an all-encompassing state of crisis. In the wake of someone going missing, there flows a tremendous, harsh kind of grief. Psychologist Pauline Boss calls this grief 'ambiguous loss'. It occurs when individuals aren't sure whether or not their loved one has died, as in cases of missing persons, or where a person is physically present but not themselves, or deteriorating for an unknown length of time into the future, as in cases of dementia or terminal illness. Boss says that 'ambiguous loss is the most stressful loss people can face'. The intensity changes over time, but these feelings don't go away entirely because the situation doesn't go away. Sarah tells me, 'Certainly for a few years – and everybody's different – you're a mess.'

For every person who goes missing, it's estimated that 12 further people – family, friends, colleagues left behind – will be affected. In the case of someone like Q, who grew up as part of a large and boisterous blended family, the ripples would have spread even further. The burdens of worry and stress are enormous, potentially affecting every aspect of a person's life. It's overwhelming. When someone dies, there's nothing left you can do to change things, but when someone is missing there's always a chance that the person could come back or their fate could be discovered. It's a huge responsibility, to keep searching.

Sarah describes driving around after Q's disappearance and scanning the surrounding areas for any sign of him. One eye is always dedicated to the missing person. Even ordinary things like going out with friends to watch a film become complicated by the cost of putting the search aside for a few hours.

The stress of having a missing loved one can be physically draining, too. Extreme stress is associated with elevated stress hormones and blood pressure and, in turn, chronic muscle tension and pain, heart and endocrine problems, fatigue, disrupted sleep, and digestion problems. It can exacerbate pre-existing conditions such as asthma. Psychologist Geoffrey Glassock found that some family members attributed the stress of a person's disappearance to ailments such as low immunity, broken bones, and pneumonia.

Stress is compounded by the difficult logistics of the search itself. It's most common for families to conduct their own searches alongside police efforts. They may phone everyone and everywhere they can think of, including favourite cafés or bars or shops, and get in touch with banks, hospitals, embassies, and airlines for any information. Many families and friends set up social-media pages to share photos and information that could help locate the missing person. They may look to the mainstream media to publicise the case, or engage the services of a private investigator, or even go to a psychic for clues. If families suspect that their loved one is lost in the wilderness, they can obtain technical surveys of the geographical area as well as information about tides and weather conditions. They may search those difficult terrains themselves, or recruit volunteers to help them. Some of these possibilities are expensive, particularly where international travel or professional services are involved. Even printing signs and posters can be surprisingly costly. Often people take time off work to do these things, which can also deplete their finances.

'How do you cope with that?' I ask Sarah. She gazes at the point where the wall meets the ceiling. There's no easy answer.

'I think I'm just lucky I didn't ever fall into the trap of taking heavily to drink or using drugs or anything. Perhaps I haven't got the sort of personality that needs that. But it's just been a matter of finding ways to deal with your own mind, really.' Life plunges us all into difficult realities and we suffer because of that. But a frantic mind – one that constantly asks, 'What if?', that replays the same awful moments over and over again, that builds and retells narratives of guilt and shame – is really what brings suffering into technicolour.

Sarah tried counselling as a means of coping but found it was of limited help. Sarah Wayland, a social worker and health researcher, explains that ambiguous loss isn't well understood by professionals. Pauline Boss suggests that counselling for ambiguous loss should not focus on moving on from the situation – it is inherently ongoing. Accordingly, support needs to focus on developing 'tolerance for the unknown'. Yet not all counsellors have specific training in ambiguous loss, as Sarah found out.

'They can deal with grief, they deal with divorce, they can deal with relationship troubles, whatever. But I remember the last guy I went to see – I spent two or three sessions trying to explain to him what it was like. Well, I was paying him. You know, he should've been paying me.'

Perhaps because ambiguous loss can be so all-encompassing, Sarah has come to think that coping can involve a range of different strategies. She has found a strong social network she can rely on and talk to. She practises tai chi. She reads. She writes for herself. Over time, she's become more involved in advocating and fundraising for missing-persons organisations. She's a family representative and trustee of the charity Missing People in the UK. Part of the satisfaction of this charity work is helping others in a similar situation feel supported.

'It's trying to find a way of helping people get just a little bit of emotional rest.'

As difficult as ambiguous loss can be to live with, to remain unsure or even hopeful is realistic. It's not that families necessarily experience false hope. Indeed, Sarah Wayland's interviews reveal that family members may not have optimistic expectations for a case, particularly over time. Hope is complex, diverse, and changing. People 'weave' between hoping for a happy outcome, hoping for answers (happy or otherwise), and hoping for themselves – hoping that they can learn to live in the aftermath of a person's disappearance while simultaneously accepting the possibility that the missing person has come to harm. Wayland writes:

> All of the participants spoke of the awareness that they had to be flexible with ideas about the return of the missing person. For them, to live in one space perpetually, where they either believed a return would not occur or were hopeful that one would eventuate, did not correspond with the unresolved nature of loss that accompanies a missing person's investigation.

They came to understand that although you'd prefer to know, sometimes you just can't.

Not everyone feels compelled to accept the unresolved nature of a missing-persons case. In some situations the facts may lead those left behind to conclude that hope for the missing person's return may not be appropriate. When Rachel Funari disappeared from Bruny Island off the coast of Tasmania in 2011, her family never entertained much hope of finding her. The slippery path Rachel took on a lone hike was dangerously close to the edge of cliffs 300 metres high. Her sister Nicole told the ABC that her first impressions of the area were, 'I thought it was so beautiful. And I thought, "They're never going to find her … This is a lost cause".'

Within 18 months of the disappearance, Nicole accepted that Rachel was dead. She felt strongly that if Rachel were alive, she would have made contact. She gave away Rachel's possessions, only vaguely wondering if Rachel might one day become upset with her for doing so. In lieu of a gravesite, she sees the rough, picturesque island as her sister's final resting place. Rachel's mother, Phyllis, expresses an even stronger certainty of Rachel's death.

'The minute they called us I knew Rachel was dead. I immediately accepted it … It was easier than hoping.'

❖

The threads of Q's mental illness, the social stigma and lack of education around mental illness, the tough peer group he was part of, and his tentative quest to understand where he fitted in can all be considered factors that might have led to his disappearance. That there are so many factors and that each – alone and in combination – is so complex and slippery adds to the ambiguity of his case. There was a lot going on that Sarah has been left to disentangle.

Sometimes in a missing-persons investigation the family discover confronting realities about their missing loved one, for instance that they were involved in crime or drug use. Those secrets may offer important leads to their social circle, the places they frequented, and the dangers they were exposed to. But in soliciting new information, it may be hard to distinguish between shocking-but-true facts and a cruel hoax.

As the physical search for Q continued, and he remained missing, Sarah and her family had to try new methods. They went to the media to ask the public for more information. It's a good idea. As one missing-persons investigator said as part of a study into missing persons and policing, 'For me the single most important part of a missing person enquiry is the media appeal, because there is no point in four sets of eyes looking for somebody if you can have 400 sets of eyes looking for [them].'

In the process you can end up getting information you'd never envisaged. Around a year after his disappearance, Q's case was covered in a documentary, a magazine and, notably, the New Zealand television series *Crime Watch*, which re-enacted unsolved police cases and provided a phone number for viewers who thought they could help.

'They were very, very good,' says Sarah. 'I mean, they were an amazing crew of people and very careful and caring in how they enacted it.' All the same, it was a 'bizarre' experience to watch the show. They deliberately cast an actor who looked like Q to play him. He wore Q's hat on camera. They filmed him in Q's bedroom, which had remained untouched since Q first went missing. They filmed the actor from the back, the angle from which his resemblance to Q was most striking. He pottered around in the garden, tending to plants, just as Q used to do.

'It was pretty powerful stuff,' says Sarah. 'You look at it and take a step back and say, "Hopefully Q might see it, or somebody who knows what's going on with him might see it."' But 'nothing came of it'. At least, 'nothing concrete'. The contact they did get was troubling.

'We had these phone calls from a woman who said she was his wife and they had a baby and ... said that they were living on the South Island of New Zealand.' When police traced the first call – which, given the technology available at the time, was far from instant – they found it had been made from Auckland Central Library, on the North Island. 'So, you know, we couldn't go any further with that.'

About three years after Q's initial disappearance, a second

call was made to Sarah's house and she answered it. 'I spoke to the woman and again, she said, "We've got this baby daughter and I'd love you to meet her and I'm trying to get Q to, you know, be in touch with you again, and blah, blah, blah." And, of course, I was absolutely shattered by the call and the thought of it all, but the police officer who had been talking to us all this time came straight round and we traced the call straightaway to a house in south Auckland.'

The call had come from a share house. When the police officer asked the collection of young people who lived there if anyone knew who'd made the call, each of them shook their heads. 'They absolutely, categorically said they hadn't made the call,' recalls Sarah in disbelief. Someone had to know something.

The police officer gave Sarah a choice: she could seek to identify and prosecute the likely caller, or she could leave the matter. It was a hard choice. Perhaps the caller really knew something important. And, if not, then they should receive some penalty for harassing a family that had suffered such a tremendous loss. Yet by this point Sarah had decided that she would move back to England. She was scheduled to depart within days.

'I literally couldn't stand trying to work out what was going on,' she says. All these frustrations, these false leads, had come to feel ridiculous and enraging.

'Why would someone do that? Call and pretend they were his wife?' I ask. I don't understand the motivation at all.

Sarah shrugs and shakes her head. These are questions she's asked herself many times. She answers me with more questions.

'Why do people make hoax calls? If it was a hoax, why did they do it? And if it wasn't a hoax, what was going on? I don't know to this day what was going on there.' She still wonders about the significance of the call, whether it was genuine or not. There's no explanation that makes sense. There's no benefit to lying. Even if it's someone's idea of fun ('But who'd find that fun?' I ask), they're opening themselves up to prosecution. And if it's not a lie, why hasn't Sarah been able to find her son after all these years? What is keeping Q away? How did he manage to hide so well? The sky outside clouds over, grey again. Threats of rain come and go. The call is most likely nothing more than a hoax, but the painful fact is that Sarah can't be sure.

Hoaxes are not uncommon in the search for missing persons. One of the most disturbing examples was in the case of Amy Billig, as recounted in the book *Without a Trace* written by her mother Susan and journalist Greg Aunapu. Amy was 17 when she went missing in 1974 near her home in the US state of Florida. She was last seen hitchhiking. Throughout the following 21 years – until 1995 – Susan was harassed with explicit phone calls about her daughter. At first the caller would simply hang up after Susan answered, leaving Susan to fear that the caller was Amy looking for help but having trouble getting her message through. Then the calls grew even more agonising. She was told by an anonymous male that he had Amy, that she had been abducted by a biker gang, that Amy was his sex slave, that Amy had been taken to various international locations and sold as part of a sex ring. He would describe, in graphic detail, her sexual activities. He told Susan that he had cut Amy's tongue out of her mouth. It was unrelenting. Even though the police and Susan felt that these calls were hoaxes, they still compelled Susan to put herself in some very dangerous situations in order to follow up the leads – just in case. She visited biker-gang headquarters and went to various locations – alone – in attempts to meet the caller. Eventually the caller was tracked down and identified as Henry Johnson Blair, a law enforcement officer. He'd never seen Amy in his life. He was convicted of stalking. Although

Susan was relieved by the ruling – the calls had stopped – on another level she was also saddened that there was no longer anyone telling her that Amy was alive.

The lies themselves are a nuisance and a danger, but the real wound that's opened by a hoax is that it makes a cruel game of the ambiguous situation family members find themselves in. When you don't know the person's whereabouts or what compelled them to go missing, it's impossible to separate what's absurd from what could be a meaningful lead. Those left behind are more aware than most of the slipperiness of knowing someone else. When the feeling of familiarity shatters, any story becomes possible. Even if a call sounds suspicious, loved ones are so desperate for information that they're likely to err on the side of taking it seriously. Just in case.

❖

After talking to Sarah for an hour, we get to what I feel like is a natural place to end the interview. In the three years after her son disappeared, Sarah's life changed dramatically. She got divorced, and moved back to her original home of England. These upheavals were devastating, but she coped.

'I sometimes do think of what would I be doing now and what would I be like now if I hadn't had this experience in my life,' Sarah says. 'I guess I have become stronger, I've become better able to deal with other situations because I think when you've been through something as traumatic as this – and you hear people freaking out or you see yourself freaking out about relatively minor things – you think, that's not really important, that doesn't really matter. So, you get a different sense of what is important in life. And what isn't.' When Sarah's youngest daughter moved to Italy, for instance, and then back to New Zealand, Sarah would be asked if she worried about her being so far away. Her answer was always no. She missed her daughter very much, but she knew where she was, she could speak to her. For these things she was grateful. 'So, I think it's made me better able to deal with other emotional situations, and keep things in a different perspective.'

Sarah talks quickly as she lists these silver linings. This isn't how she wants this conversation to end. She will not let the story wrap up so nicely, because it doesn't wrap up so nicely. She points this out in the subtlest of ways, after a pause. 'There is one other point really, if you want me to carry on for a bit?'

I tell her yes, of course.

'Even after all these years it still is a changing and unfolding scenario. There's not many years that have gone by when something hasn't come along as a rumour, or a possibility that we have to check up.'

Several years ago, Sarah set up a Facebook page for Q. It helps her keep in touch with his old friends. It was also through a message to the page that Sarah received some new and potentially vital information. A friend of a friend of a friend in New Zealand sent Sarah a message saying that Q was killed shortly after he went missing. The woman saw a gang of four boys 'playing hooligans', recklessly driving their cars around a local carpark. According to her, they ran Q over. The woman said she hadn't given this information earlier because the boys threatened to kill her if she did.

One of the men is now dead. The other three have histories of getting into trouble with authorities. The police were informed but although they interviewed the woman and the men she named, nothing came of it.

'Funnily enough,' Sarah says sarcastically, 'they have all denied any knowledge of the situation, or the story.' The police closed the books.

Sarah is left to imagine the possibility that her son's last moments took place in a carpark, his life cut short as a heavy car controlled by a reckless, laughing driver knocked him over and took the breath out of him. It's possible.

'It's an awful, awful thing of not knowing,' says Sarah. 'And you know, since I first heard this information – obviously, it's pretty sad and pretty upsetting to hear it – I've at least thought to myself well, if he was killed, you know, that's what happened and that's what we have to learn to live with.' She looks me in the eye. Even though Q's case is cold, it's not frozen. Sarah may still one day get a conclusion, a different thing she will have to learn to live with.

As new information emerges, cases change, and the experience of missing someone may also change. Eventually, search efforts become more passive. It is no longer a matter of trying to find further options to exhaust. Instead, it's 'just looking' – letting your eyes roam around the missing person's favourite places. Your wandering eyes acknowledge this old, continuing loss. On the podcast *This American Life*, reporter Miki Meek describes a phone booth in Japan that some people use to leave messages for their loved ones who went missing in the 2011 tsunami and earthquake. The phone isn't even connected to any line, but many users nonetheless dial the old telephone numbers of their missing loved ones. Some are silent on the phone, others give updates on their lives, or express their sense of loss. They recognise that the missing person is still present in their lives, still there.

In the longer term, families can also opt to bring the case to a coroner to find a presumption of death. A family may do this to seek closure, or for pragmatic reasons like settling a person's estate. This was the case with British aristocrat Lord Lucan, who went missing in 1974 on the night that his child's nanny, Sandra Rivett, was murdered. Lord Lucan came to be a main suspect. His wife, Lady Lucan, alleged that he had attacked her on the same night. After the attack, the bloodstained car Lord Lucan had borrowed from a friend was found abandoned. Nothing more remained of him.

In the years following there were, according to the BBC, 'dozens of unverified sightings' in places as far afield as France and even Australia. Some family members thought he had fled to Africa. Nonetheless, his family were legally allowed to access his assets as a result of a 1999 court ruling that posited his return as unlikely. Then, in 2016, some 42 years after his disappearance, Lord Lucan's death certificate was issued. The certificate allowed his son, George Bingham, to inherit his title and take a seat in the House of Lords. Bingham told the BBC: 'I am very happy with the judgment of the court in this matter … It has been a very long time coming.' He explained that since his father went missing – when he was eight years old – he had always believed him dead.

The likelihood that a coroner will officially presume the death of a missing person depends on the specifics of the case, including how long the person has been missing, and if there were suspicious circumstances. In the absence of a body, other evidence is needed to officially presume death, such as witness statements, information about the person's state of mind at the time of their disappearance, or bank statements showing that an account has fallen into disuse. In New Zealand, as Sarah would discover, being unable to find a person is itself considered evidence that they are dead.

Sarah has never sought a presumption of death. Q had no assets and she's always maintained the possibility that he is still alive. But the police nonetheless referred Q's case to the coroner without telling her. Sarah heard about this procedure second-hand, in a Christmas card from a relative in New Zealand. She did not want an inquest, and tried to stop it.

'It's a bit like assuming somebody's guilty unless you can

prove they're innocent, to me,' she says. She feels there is no clear evidence that Q did, in fact, die. 'But the inquest went ahead and the coroner's findings were that probably he committed suicide, which I know is a possibility and I've always accepted that, but I felt that it was not necessary to declare him dead if we didn't want it declared and we had no financial or legal reason for it to be necessary.' Sarah is annoyed. This procedure goes against her sense of justice, and her acceptance of ambiguity. The conclusion of death is a contrivance, based on only limited information.

In presuming Q's death, the New Zealand authorities have asserted that there is no hope for his case. Further investigations will be frustratingly difficult to open should new evidence be found, and the way Sarah tempers her hope in her changing understanding of the case – how she lives with the ambiguity of it all – has been undermined. The possibility of return persists in many cases, and so a narrative that a missing person has died could one day be contradicted by the person themselves. Even though it may sometimes be appropriate for those left behind to assume a death, the possibility of return should be respected too. What we onlookers – whether police officers, judges, bureaucrats, well-meaning friends, or voyeurs – reckon happened doesn't reflect the real uncertainties involved in being left behind. Wayland argues that the shifts in hope dictated by the outside world can be traumatic for those left behind if they don't occur with deference to their ongoing, daily experience of the case. A conclusion would be ideal, but it's better to be on this ambiguous voyage forever than to impose a fictive one. 'It never closes,' Sarah says.

Even when cases grow cold, there's no stable ending, no specific meaning. When you think you understand it, that surety is prone to slip away with contradictory facts, or new interpretations. French philosopher Jacques Derrida uses the term 'deconstructionism' to describe the fluctuating, fragmentary nature of life. 'What is really going on in things, what is really happening, is always to come,' he says. Our conclusions dissolve and evolve, and force new and unexpected paths.

These days, Sarah is interested in sharing what it's like to wonder about where a loved one is for so long. Once, she related her insights on stage in front of a large crowd at the O2 arena in London as part of her advocacy work with Missing People.

'They'd shown a five-minute video of me talking in the garden about my son,' Sarah points outside to the garden beyond the window. 'And that was a really weird experience. It was sort of like, there's me on the big screen behind and here's me on the stage.' She stretches her arms to illustrate how impossibly large the screen and the arena were. She would never have dreamed of speaking at such an enormous venue before she started her advocacy work. But things change.

There are limits to sharing stories of absence: you're asked to talk about the shocking reality of a fresh case and the emergence of new clues that could be used to track down the person. You focus on the known facts, the pet theories. The full realities of cases, and the lives of those left behind, are flattened by gaps in our collective vocabulary and our aversion to ambiguity. The deeper stories are made two-dimensional in the same way that video footage flattens people and movement. But Sarah is also still there, on stage, in person, and in three dimensions. Her story is bigger and speaks to something more complicated, something ambiguous, something true.

When Sarah received the coroner's report in the mail it was filled with basic errors about Q. Both his name and date of birth were incorrect, and although Sarah didn't want the report to be filed in the first place, it was up to her to request corrections. After the ruling of suicide was made, someone from the court asked her if she wanted his death certificate. She'd have to pay a fee.

'I said, "Well, no I don't, thank you."' Sarah laughs. Although her humour is dry, her smile is also genuine. The idea that she'd want such a meaningless thing is comical. 'What do I need it for?'

4

WHEN A PARENT ABDUCTS A CHILD

SALMA AND AYOUB

I take a fast train from the UK to meet Griet Ivens, a case worker for Child Focus, an organisation based in Brussels that aims to prevent Belgian children from going missing, whether they're at risk of running away, being abducted, or otherwise vulnerable to exploitation. The first-floor office is standard-issue beige and blue-grey. Griet has arranged for me to meet a woman I will call Salma (all the names of this family have been changed), whose eight-year-old son Ayoub had been taken from his small town outside Brussels by his father a few years ago. He was taken all the way to Portugal. Griet was assigned the case. It was her job to establish communication between Ayoub's parents and to help bring him back home.

Griet briefs me about what we're going to do, where we're going to go, and what kind of story I'm going to hear. Working with Salma has been one of Griet's more memorable cases, she says. Although everything she did – organising legal help, providing ongoing support, attempting to mediate with both parents of a missing child – was all part of her job, it was far more involved than usual. Plus, she says, 'It was a good outcome.' Not all of them are so positive. She tells me of parents who never get to know where their child is, of a 12-year-old girl found dead in the woods after being missing for two weeks. 'She was murdered by someone in the village.'

Griet and I leave her office in one of the organisation's cars. We're near one of Belgium's most famous landmarks, the Atomium. It's a towering steel statue, an inflated model of an atom which stands in recognition of the importance of the atomic age. Once we are out of Brussels, we quickly approach Salma's town. It's June and it takes on a summer vibrancy, enhanced by its pastel-coloured houses and scattered green squares with their bright playgrounds. It looks like a nice place to grow up. It's quiet enough to feel safe but there are things around for kids to do and it's close to central Brussels. It occurs to me that the panic of losing your son – *where is he?* – would have been strangely juxtaposed with this calm environment of quiet, colourful blocks, half an hour from the giant atom. The threatening things are invisible here.

Griet and I knock on the door of Salma's townhouse. She smiles, invites us in, and she and Griet exchange pleasantries in Flemish. The three of us sit on two couches, Griet in the middle – she will translate my questions into Flemish, and Salma's answers into English. At points, Griet joins in, contributing her own impressions and memories of the case. The tiles on the floor beneath us are cool. The windows face away from direct sunlight.

In this comfortable room, I hear the terrible story of Salma having her son taken from her and not knowing if or when he'll be back. I learn about the hidden dangers of seemingly safe places, and safe relationships. Then, I learn about the challenges a parent faces once that son is back. How do you get along with the father of your child when he was the one who took that child away? Once again, the story starts before the actual disappearance. Once again, it still hasn't ended.

❖

Child abduction as a crime has a short history. Not because people haven't taken children in days long past, but because it wasn't seen as a crime against the rights of children until relatively recently. In medieval England, the closest thing to child abduction was a type of property crime called 'ravishment'. The law protected human members of a household as the patriarch's possessions and punished people who took those possessions. Wealthy young daughters would not be allowed to elope and therefore risk the family fortune without the permission of their father; unhappy wives were not allowed to be taken from the home by a new suitor (consensually or otherwise); and potential heirs were likewise protected by law to ensure the continuity of the family.

Concerns about the specific vulnerability of children didn't emerge in England until Georgian times in the late-18th century. At this stage, abduction was labelled 'child stealing', which was understood to be more serious than property theft. In Georgian England, a society of burgeoning wealth and commerce, children were more visible than ever before. Lavishing attention and gifts upon children was a way to spend one's increasing leisure time and disposable income. 'Children,' writes historian Elizabeth Foyster, 'were cherished as companions to their parents and shared with them the new pleasures and pastimes of urban life.' Some children were dressed in tailored clothing and appeared in public spaces as stylish, animate toys.

With this trend grew the appreciation of mothers and

motherhood. For women, to be a mother was the highest achievement possible. This was a problem for women who were unable to conceive, and some addressed it by stealing children. Often acting alone, and targeting children under the age of six from across the socio-economic spectrum, women in their twenties and thirties tried to attain the status afforded to motherhood through criminal activity. These women tended to treat the abducted child well, caring for them as their own. Nonetheless, being stolen was traumatic.

In other cases, children wore vestments of such monetary value that people would take a child so they could remove their clothes and shoes to sell them. They would then discard the child, leaving them naked on the street.

Today, opportunistically nabbing children for their expensive clothes or to achieve motherhood seems absurd. And children's rights have been codified into international law under the UN Convention on the Rights of the Child. Legally parents and schools are responsible for protecting children, and most kids are taught the principles of 'stranger danger'. I remember at the age of five, or even younger, being told that it's important, no matter what, not to go with someone I didn't know, or to let them into the house. I was warned not to take sweets or other treats from strangers, and not to trust them even if they made it sound like they knew my parents. If the stranger said they were a police officer, I should ask to see their badge. Real police officers wouldn't get mad at you for asking that. Nobody ever articulated the motivations of dangerous strangers. They're harder to understand than an attempt to gain status, or wealth. They're paedophiles and murderers, perhaps even child traffickers.

Stranger abduction accounts for a small proportion of all child abductions. Even so, 'stranger danger' programs implicitly assert the agency and autonomy of children – a striking contrast to their legal treatment as chattels in medieval times. The programs not only cast abduction as a serious crime worthy of preventative effort and education, but also cast children as individuals who could potentially prevent their own abduction in certain circumstances, if given the right tools. A national UK study shows that in 75 per cent of cases, an attempted abduction is abandoned – often the child is able to avoid abduction entirely.

Salma's son, Ayoub, knew that he would be abducted. He told Salma an ominous story of how his father had bought a house in Portugal, and that if he ever went on holiday with his father, they'd go to Portugal. Over time, the story got darker. 'We're going to move in February,' Salma reports him saying in December that year. 'We're leaving; we're going to live in Portugal.'

Salma took the words of her then eight-year-old son seriously. She contacted her ex-husband, Adam, and asked him about it. 'Adam said, "No that is not true. I don't know where Ayoub gets this from, it's not true." But I know what my son tells me is true. He is not somebody that makes up a story like that. I know that what my son says is true.'

A work colleague told Salma that abduction was a possibility. They told her it was important that Adam not take Ayoub out of the country. It was at this stage that Salma contacted Child Focus and Griet helped her apply for a judgment stating that neither parent would be allowed to take Ayoub abroad without the other's consent. Although Salma's application was successful, it didn't stop Adam from enacting his plan.

Despite the emphasis on 'stranger danger', most cases of child abduction usually don't involve strangers at all. According to 2018 data collected from 26 European countries by Missing Children Europe, 38 children were abducted by somebody who wasn't their parent. In almost half of these cases, the child was abducted by someone they already knew, such as another family member or an acquaintance. That same year, over a thousand children were reported as abducted by one of their parents and brought across international borders. Another 786 cases of parental abduction were still open from previous years and under the attention of missing children's organisations across Europe. According to 2015 figures, the average age of children abducted by their parents is five (although ages ranged from 0 to 16). Of the cases opened in 2015, only 24.8 per cent were resolved within the year. Successful resolutions were usually attributed to effective mediation between the child's parents. Within a family situation, according to the Illinois State University's research, a perpetrator of child abduction is likely to be male, usually the biological father of the child. The place most likely for a child to be taken from is their home. Usually only one child is abducted by a single person, with nobody else directly involved in the case. It is uncommon for weapons to be used in cases of parental abduction or for the child to come to any physical harm.

It was Adam's job to pick Ayoub up on the last day of school before the Carnival vacation (held over February–March), and he had custody of Ayoub for the two weeks. Ayoub's teacher told Salma that Ayoub had mentioned at school that day that he was going to be leaving Belgium. Salma was so concerned at the possibility that Adam might take Ayoub out of the country that she went to his house. No one was there. The car wasn't in the driveway. Inside, there was rubbish strewn around but no furniture. 'Then I knew,' Salma says.

She called the police. There technically wasn't much they could do for those two weeks while Adam had custody of Ayoub. Salma wrung her hands and waited. She did not feel hopeful. When Ayoub didn't show up at school on the first Monday back, the police commenced the investigation. They found that Adam had cancelled his address in Belgium and had given his mother's address in the Netherlands to his neighbours. The police visited her house; Adam and Ayoub weren't there. It was becoming clear that Adam had probably gone to Portugal, although because he also had contacts in Morocco, Salma was afraid he might have taken Ayoub there. If he went outside the European Union, the case would become even more complicated.

As Salma tells the story, Griet's brow furrows. She's compelled to recount her own experience of Adam's brazenness.

'The way I see him,' Griet tells me, 'he's very manipulative, he wants things to go like he wants, he has his idea and he won't change it, he wants to have the control over the situation.' She thinks that Adam's motivation in taking Ayoub had nothing to do with the welfare of his son but was to gain a sense of power over Salma.

According to the US Department of Justice, there are a number of reasons why a parent may abduct their own child. The abductor may 'confuse' their hostile feelings about their marriage (or former marriage) with a negative judgment on the other's parenting skills; they may want to seek revenge by 'taking' something the other parent 'wants' (that is, their child); or they may want to remove their child from a real or perceived threat. In the cases detailed by the Department's report into parental abduction, abduction was about power. For example, Liss, who as a child was abducted by her mother, shared her thoughts: 'My mother was not really acting under a misguided notion of what was best for me as she claimed, but instead operating out of a desire to inflict a mortal wound upon my father.'

The report details the dehumanising hardships some abducted children go through. Some are forced to take on a new name, a new appearance, or a new identity in order to evade authorities. Some are falsely told that the parent left behind is dead, or hates them and doesn't want to see them any more. Who the child actually is and the love the parent left behind could offer them doesn't matter. This is a grievous component of the crime of child abduction: it exploits what the child represents – in Ayoub's case, Adam's ability to disrupt Salma's life. At the same time, it objectifies the child and denies them their right to a voice.

To help me understand Adam's motivations, Salma tells me about her relationship with him. It started out as loving. Salma was raised in Morocco and met Adam – originally from the Netherlands – while he was visiting one of her neighbours there. Griet translates for me: 'They met each other and they *fell in love*.' Salma understands her English and laughs at the translation, and then Griet laughs too. It's a sarcastic laugh, acknowledging that Salma's previous feelings for him have faded. When Adam's holiday ended, he went back to the Netherlands for six months before returning to Morocco once more. He returned for Salma. They married there in 2003. He was 30 years her senior.

'Wow,' I say, as Griet tells me this. Salma laughs again.

They stayed in Morocco for a little while, but then moved to the Netherlands. Salma doesn't remember many problems at the start. Adam seemed kind, even egalitarian. He was raised as a Catholic but there was a dramatic indication that he could see other points of view: he converted to Islam while he was in Morocco. And so, the two seemingly shared a belief system. A year and a half later, Ayoub was born. This is where Salma thinks the problems started. By the time Ayoub was six, they had separated.

Parenthood can emphasise cultural differences and bring existing tensions to the fore. The average couple experiences a drop in marital satisfaction in the first three years after their first child is born as they adjust to having a new family member. This ordinary drop in satisfaction is stronger, on average, within intercultural marriages. It seems to be a particularly tense time because different cultural views on the basic elements of child-rearing – such the levels of discipline, independence, autonomy, and obligation a child should experience – may emerge. The differences can be a challenge, or they can be an opportunity – a way to discuss and clarify a unified vision for family life.

In this case, the opportunity was never taken. Salma recounts the message she was given by Adam after the birth of their son.

'There was actually no discussion about Ayoub,' Salma says. 'He decided everything. I wasn't allowed my opinion, there was never a discussion. "You must do this, you must do that, the end."' He was empowered by his home-ground advantage in the Netherlands, and her inexperience in Europe.

Psychoanalytic researcher Annie Stopford says that spouses who move to a new country for their marriage report feelings of 'alienation, estrangement, and loss provoked by cultural differences and misunderstandings in their relationships'. It's common for individuals who have moved away for love to feel disturbed by the things their partners do or say that unexpectedly reveal a chasm between them. Understanding another person is always ambiguous – you never know if your impressions of the other are completely accurate. Sometimes, telling moments reveal ignorance, completely displacing a sense of understanding and communion. Where they once thought there was an intense understanding that transcended their differences, suddenly they were 'lost' to each other. Their shared language becomes *just words*. It was shocking to Salma how controlling Adam was about Ayoub's upbringing. Not only was it frustrating to feel she was not listened to or understood, it was lonely. How well had she really known Adam? Who was the man she had uprooted her life to be with? The loneliness set in for Salma when she realised that Adam wasn't who she had thought he was. 'I don't know what happened to him,' she says.

Although the problem is worse now than it was during their marriage, anti-Muslim sentiment in Belgium has been growing in the years since the 9/11 attacks in the United States. Salma came to Belgium at a time when far-right parties, which condemned multiculturalism and Islam in particular, were coming to prominence. Adam played a curious role in bringing those nervous feelings about Islam into the family home despite being a Muslim himself, says Salma.

'He was afraid that his son would grow up to be a *real* Muslim.'

'What does that mean?' I ask. 'A real Muslim?'

'He didn't wish for a Muslim education for his son.'

Islam places an emphasis on holistic education. It intertwines academic learning with spiritual and social studies. It involves learning Arabic. It's a bit different from what secular public schools offer. This is not to say that Salma demanded such an education for Ayoub; what she wanted was a dialogue so that she and Adam could explore and decide together. And that didn't happen.

Salma goes on to wonder why Adam even became a Muslim. She doesn't know. And her not knowing things is key to this story. I ask several times why Adam did something or thought in a certain way and Salma never knows. 'I don't know why he did any of these things,' she tells me. She can guess, but they didn't really talk about themselves in that kind of way. They barely knew each other at all. That's particularly hard for Salma, because when she first met Adam, she thought they understood and loved each other.

Salma did not accept Adam's attempts to dictate what life

was going to be like for Ayoub. 'I shared my thoughts,' she says. 'But it didn't matter to him.' She felt exhausted, that she was in an impossible position where there was no negotiation, no meeting point between them.

Stopford writes that a lack of understanding – while devastating – is a normal part of a relationship. It's painful to realise that what the two of you think doesn't always correlate, but it's a normal pain. It's likely, Stopford argues, that if you feel complete unity and understanding within your relationship, you're delusional.

I think of all the times when I've dropped a subject with a friend or with my husband, not wanting to pursue it any longer. I think of the times I've felt forced to agree to disagree, without feeling that my thoughts have been understood. I think of times I've given up trying to explain my decisions, beliefs, or feelings, because sometimes it's easier to let those subjects go. It's hard to translate your interior life into words. So, I tell myself to try again later. These limitations are in play in relationships where we share the same native tongue and we have no desire to hide the truth. But realising the chasm is there might be an important step to getting closer. You realise that all this time you weren't really completely unified, so now you can aim for something a bit better than before, move a little closer to mutual understanding.

Perhaps completely closing the chasm is impossible. Perhaps it's made much harder when your cultural backgrounds or linguistic differences keep pushing open the gap. But even if it is impossible, you have to keep trying. You have to realise the importance of the other person's thoughts and feelings and you have to want to understand them and want to be understood. If you give up as Adam did – arms in the air, saying that the chasm is too big to overcome, that you don't want to try any more – it's already over.

Adam and Salma's relationship had already disintegrated by the time they separated. They had slept and eaten separately for years. 'I decided to leave,' Salma says. 'That is no way to live any more. There was nothing. No love.' For a while – even before the separation – they lived in different cities. Ayoub lived with Adam in a Belgian village while Salma worked in Antwerp. Salma then moved to be closer to her son and his school. After the separation, the two parents shared custody of Ayoub. Salma also moved on. She remarried. She became pregnant. Then Adam abducted Ayoub.

It didn't take long for Griet to make contact with Adam after Ayoub was recorded missing – only about a week. She procured his email address and simply sent him an email. Thinking it was unlikely to work but worth a try, she asked him where he and Ayoub were.

'He answered right away,' Griet says.

My head moves backwards with surprise. 'What? Really?'

'I know,' says Griet. 'It was weird.'

When Griet was able to tell Salma that Ayoub was in Portugal and they had an address, some of the terrible ambiguity Salma had felt was eased. The days and days of not knowing where Ayoub was had been filled with breathless anxiety. But once those days were over, the ceaseless worry remained – it had just been transformed.

Even when Salma found out that her son was safe and knew roughly where he was, she experienced that ambiguous loss of not knowing how long she and her son would be apart, as well as all the psychological, physical, financial, and other burdens ambiguous loss brings with it. The stress was compounded by the fact that she was pregnant and had to manage her health, and her concerns about her future mobility when it came to attempting to see Ayoub with a newborn in tow. Perhaps Ayoub was not technically 'missing' after those first few weeks because his whereabouts were known, but he certainly was missing to Salma in the sense that he was far away and out of reach.

Missing is not just a geographical state, it's a state where relationships shift. The absence of Ayoub meant that Salma couldn't fulfil her role as his mother. She couldn't be *there* for him. And he couldn't fulfil his quotidian role of being a son who gave her warmth and love. Although Salma was always optimistic that Ayoub would come back and their lives would be restored, in her darker moments she wondered if Ayoub would ever get to know his half-brother, due to be born within months of Ayoub's disappearance.

Salma was not alone. She had her husband, who supported her and felt the loss of Ayoub strongly himself. She had friends; she also had Griet. But nobody else could quite apprehend her devastation. She knew it. And so did they. 'The months that went past were like years,' Salma says.

There was another small moment of relief when Griet helped Salma negotiate contact with Ayoub through a mediation process. They agreed that Salma should be able to talk to Ayoub on the phone twice a week. They organised a regular schedule. But still Adam did not bring Ayoub back. And still Salma did not know when or even if he would.

Griet, along with legal experts, helped Salma file an international legal case on the basis of the rights she had as a parent under the Convention on the Civil Aspects of International Child Abduction. Under the Convention – which both Belgium and Portugal are signatories to – the parent left behind in an abduction case can file to have the child returned home. Because the case is international in nature, the process is convoluted. Essentially, they had to apply first to the Belgian authorities. If the application was successful at that stage, the Belgians would then liaise with Portuguese authorities to request Ayoub's return. It would then be the responsibility of the Portuguese authorities to rule on the matter.

Salma says she never felt worried that her case would be rejected. Her case was the kind that the Convention was set up to rectify – that is, a clear-cut example of an unlawful abduction where one parent has unilaterally decided to take their child out of their home country without the consent of the other. There were also no evident risks that Ayoub would come to harm if he returned home, another key condition of the Convention. Not every case that is brought under the Convention is as straightforward. Most people who are pursued under its terms are primary caregivers (usually mothers) who have fled with their child in order to find support among friends and family in their country of origin. There are no clear figures on how many of these parents are actually fleeing domestic violence, but in these situations, attempting to balance parental rights and child protection can become fraught. Here though, Adam's actions were clearly defined as wrongdoings.

But while Salma felt reassured that the legal system was on her side, she still worried about Adam. She was afraid that he might do something that would make it harder to get Ayoub back, such as going missing, or going abroad yet again. Another source of anxiety was the question of how long she would have to wait to see her son. Justice can be a slow process and she was never given even an approximate timeline for progress. The situation was terrifyingly ambiguous.

She also worried for Ayoub. When Salma talked to him over the phone he mentioned how at night he dreamed of returning to Belgium, seeing his friends and family again, going back to his old school.

'It was very difficult to hear my son talking like that,' Salma says. He seemed upset, but also afraid of Adam and, Salma suspects, afraid of telling her everything he felt about the situation. And the situation was very stressful – he had to suddenly learn Portuguese, live in a new house, go to a new school. Everything had changed for him.

'I know he did not feel good, but he could not say anything,' says Salma. She didn't know what else she could do.

In its report, the US Department of Justice explores some of the difficulties experienced both by abducted children and the parent left behind. For the child, grief can shade their time away from home. Liss, mentioned earlier, who was abducted as a child, explains: 'Think about what it is like to lose someone you love. Losing one, single, loved one is enough to send an adult into a tailspin. Overnight, I had lost not just ALL my loved ones, but every single person I had ever known in my entire life. Can you even begin to imagine what that would be like?'

The parent left behind may also experience grief, as well as 'fear, helplessness, and anxiety'. These feelings may be triggered in 'inopportune' places and times, when the parent sees a united family in ordinary settings like the shops, or at a restaurant. Yet, 'even as the searching parent worries about [their] missing child, [they] must also be the driving force that brings the child home'.

Salma decided that she could no longer wait. She had to resolve this by herself. She was heavily pregnant with Ayoub's half-brother and knew that once she got closer to her due date, and straight after the baby was born, she would not be able to travel. After months of legal procedures and confusion and waiting, she planned to fly to Portugal and visit Ayoub.

Just before she was due to take off, the Portuguese authorities made their ruling. Five months after his abduction, Ayoub was to finally return home. As per the judgment, Adam got to choose how he would take Ayoub back to Belgium. He could have flown or taken a series of fast trains. Instead, over two days, he slowly drove across several countries. 'It was nerve-racking,' Salma recalls. He could so easily have travelled somewhere far away. There are ferries that run between Spain and Morocco and the ports aren't far from Portugal – Adam could have got to Africa within a day.

'From the moment that the decision came, and the judge gave him that freedom, from that moment I was really scared. I expect anything from Adam.' Salma told the authorities about her fears but felt hopeless. 'What could I do? I was really scared.'

Griet kept in touch with Adam throughout his journey, checking in on his progress. She suspects he was deliberately taking his time as one last act of manipulating Salma. When he finally arrived in Belgium he was required to deliver Ayoub to a local police station where Salma could pick him up. Under the Hague Convention, parental abduction is dealt with as a civil matter, so it doesn't necessarily lead to a criminal conviction. Adam received two slaps on the wrist. When he arrived in Belgium, the police decided to keep him in a cell overnight. He also had his custody rights reduced – he could only see Ayoub one day a month between the hours of 9 a.m. and 5 p.m. It's an opportunity he has taken up just three times in the last year. He continues to live in Portugal.

❖

Parental abduction isn't always taken seriously. All victims of parental abduction – the child, the parent left behind, the child's concerned friends and family members – may have to face people who don't think of abduction as a crime. According to the US Department of Justice, often people think of child abduction as a custody issue and don't want to get involved in what they see as a family drama. It's very easy to hide an incident of parental abduction too. Because the abductor is a legal guardian of their child, they can make decisions and arrangements for them without suspicion. They can enrol them in a new school or take them to a doctor or travel with them, no questions asked. The abducted child may themselves not even realise they've been abducted, particularly if they love their abductor, and particularly if they've been told lies about the other parent being dead or not wanting them.

The parents left behind are sometimes told by well-meaning friends that it's no big deal, not that bad, because at least the child is with their other parent. But it is bad. It violates the humanity of the child and uses love as a form of artillery. It's too early to know what the long-term impacts of his abduction will be for Ayoub. According to the US Department of Justice's report, depending on their coping style, how old they were when they were abducted, how long they were away for, and the conditions they experienced while missing, many abducted children will face long-term consequences as adults. They may feel their life is unstable, or have a reduced ability to trust others. The trauma of being torn away from home remains. One adult quoted in the report who was abducted as a child said, '[I] live in constant fear that all I have manifested will disintegrate into thin air.' They may also experience lingering rage, desire for revenge, depression, anxiety, and self-destructive tendencies.

Despite the potential negative long-term effects, the majority of previously abducted children surveyed in 2000 by Geoffrey L Greif seemed to be progressing well in life. It seems that the seriousness of parental abduction doesn't preclude a happy outcome, given the right support. Even so, it's a huge risk to the child's lifelong wellbeing – another ambiguity for both Salma and Ayoub to live with.

Fortunately, Ayoub had maintained some contact with his mother and knew throughout the months he was away that she loved him. For some abducted children, being reunited with the parent left behind can be as traumatic as being taken in the first place. They may have thought that this parent abandoned them and wasn't searching for them. If they were lied to and told that the parent was uncaring – or dead – reunification could be very confronting. Abducted children may also deeply love their abductor, so reconciling their actions with that love can be challenging. Salma feels that there is reason to be optimistic for Ayoub's future, though.

'I see Ayoub as really happy. He has also changed a lot. He has become more open' – and, in the time since being back home, 'more restful'. She continues, 'If Ayoub is happy then I am happy.'

However, it has taken her a little longer to find calm after his abduction. 'In the beginning I was afraid he would be taken again by Adam, thinking, "Maybe one time he'll come." It's those little things I keep thinking … Sometimes, when Ayoub is playing in the park with his friends and he is away for too long, then I will go and look and see if he's okay. Since I know that Adam is in Portugal, I don't think about it too much … That real fear from the beginning is now reduced. Yes, maybe Adam would do it again. And I expect anything from him,' Salma says again. 'Since he did that, I expect anything.' The few occasions when Adam visits Ayoub for the day are particularly difficult. 'From the moment he's here it's stressful. I count the hours until 5 o'clock.'

Salma has to continually manage her anxiety about Adam. While she fears that he could abduct Ayoub again, she also believes that parenting should be cooperative. And so, the risk and the doubt and the turmoil never really go away as she needs to keep talking to Adam; she needs to keep that relationship alive.

'It's important that Ayoub has both his parents and that we are both there for his education, and to make decisions. When a boy is older, like 12, 14, they need a father. This has always been my view.'

But how do you sit with someone who refuses to sit with you?

'After the abduction was resolved, we had a few meetings with the mediator. We met one, two times. That was hard.' They decided to stop mediation because it wasn't working. 'So that's what I'm thinking about now, for the future: how do we make decisions about our son like normal parents? It's hard. For me, he's nothing. That man is nothing to me. After doing that, to me, he's not a man. He's not a father. He doesn't have emotions. He had no feeling, no perspective.'

Salma is beginning to feel better. Ayoub is close to his stepfather and his other family members, and her fear is dissipating.

'I'm truly happy … From where I was, I was more worried, always quick to fear, always. But we are really happy.'

The sun grows more vibrant in the previously shadowy room as we move closer to the afternoon. Our meeting ends on this note of fragile optimism. Things are better, yet also still in doubt, still ambiguous. Salma has decided to face that ambiguity so that her son may know his father, a scary proposition, but in keeping with her values. I thank Salma for enduring this disruption to her day, and I thank Griet for her translation efforts. A few more Flemish words are exchanged between Salma and Griet and soon Salma is taking long steps out of the room and up the stairs. When she returns she brings out Ayoub's younger brother, born just after his return home. He has just finished his nap. He wears little blue socks and his hands stretch out into the world, and he smiles and stares with wide brown eyes. I wish there were a way to preserve this openness, this happiness.

5

RUNNING FOR YOUR LIFE

BRANDY'S STORY

I shall wear a crown, I shall wear a crown, when it's all over.

When Brandy Bonner was just reaching adolescence, at age 12, maybe 13, she listened to the gospel choir in her church in Kansas City, USA. The space was shadowy, but sparks of light and life and music hummed under the high ceiling. The choir had learned a collection of new hymns. 'They called it candlelight music, so they would walk down the aisle with candlelight, and they would sing all these great songs,' Brandy says.

The hymn 'I Shall Wear a Crown' spoke to her. 'They were singing this song, and while they were singing it my hands went up and tears were streaming down my face. I *so* felt that song.' There was comfort in the candlelight: space to experience the feelings echoed in the voices of the singers.

I'm going to put on my robe, tell the story how I made it over.

'That so resonated with my soul. It was a soul anthem for me,' Brandy continues. 'And right before I got on the call with you, my daughter said, "Put on your robe, Mom, and tell your story of how you made it over."'

I'm startled by this reminder that talking to me is an act of courage. It feels strange that Brandy's school-aged daughter felt compelled to give her a pep talk to prepare her for my questions. Brandy takes her daughter's words literally. I am in the UK, at my Oxford flat, and Brandy is in the US; we are speaking over Skype and when she pops up on my screen, I see a person wearing a crown of her own design. It's not studded with rubies or diamonds, but it's nonetheless regal. It's a top hat, adorned with pink and white ribbons fashioned into a flower. 'I do it subconsciously when I pick these things out,' Brandy says. 'They represent me putting on my crown and putting on my robe and telling the story of how I made it over.'

Brandy ran away from an abusive home when she was 17. There is no typical missing person, but teenage girls are the most prevalent demographic of individuals who go missing. A report from the Voices of Youth Count in 2017 found that around one in 30 Americans between the ages of 13 and 17 experience homelessness as a result of running away or being thrown out of home each year. UK figures are not directly comparable, but nonetheless are also striking, with 2011 figures showing that around 9 per cent of those between the ages of 14 and 16 had run away at some point in their lives. Similarly, in Australia, young people account for half of all reported missing persons, with young women between the ages of 13 and 17 being most at risk. Most (but not all) of them are runaways.

The realities behind all this running away and the impact it has can be profound. Even from Brandy's vantage point of retrospection, *being* a missing person is mired in ambiguity, just like being left behind. It isn't clear where her story even starts or ends. And although running away is rife with uncertainties about where to live and how to survive, Brandy's circumstances before she went missing were just as uncertain.

I ask Brandy if there was a point when, after running away, she felt she could settle down and establish a sense of home.

'Erin, if I were fully honest with you – even in my full queen garb and all of that – I still am a very terrorised person. I do still have quite a few terrors. The other day I realised that I spent my whole life scared that somebody was gonna – my whole life from 17 on – scared that somebody was going to rape me,' she laughs, dryly. 'I carried that with me. That was always a fear whether I was at college, whether I was here, putting gas in my car, whether I was at a hotel with my husband, just wherever.'

The US Centers for Disease Control and Prevention says that childhood trauma – or adverse childhood experiences – is so closely linked to long-term health consequences that child abuse is a population health issue. As I mention this, Brandy nods in recognition.

'I have high blood pressure. I've come to realise that my blood pressure is probably just higher than normal people's because my body learned at an early age to be in a state of terror all the time ... And so even if things are good, it's still pumping at a higher level. Like literally, my heartbeat is always at a rapid rate,' she says.

For Brandy, 'normal' was her mother's face in her face; her eyes up close, wide and fierce; and hearing her mother's threats. It was being punched in the face – again, by her mother – and feeling the teeth fall out of her gums. Normal was goosebumps, the sense of being watched all the time by the man who'd been introduced to her household, the sense that those watching eyes were a precursor to violation. It makes sense that through this baseline 'normal', Brandy's heart would feel high in her chest, it would pulse rapidly and rarely slow down.

The story begins almost a decade before she ran away, when Brandy was eight, after her mother married her stepfather. It started as soon as the families merged and began to live together. This happened despite Brandy's mother having heard allegations that her new husband had sexually abused his own children from a previous marriage.

Brandy remembers that her stepfather began abusing her and taking nude pictures of her from the time he moved in. He and her mother fought constantly and violently. Meanwhile, Brandy's mother shrieked and hit her in response to minor, childhood indiscretions (Brandy doesn't remember what she did wrong exactly). Brandy also had a brother who was five years younger than her. She looked after him. They would sit together, bored, in the stagnant air of the family car, while their mother would go elsewhere for hours. They didn't know where she went, and Brandy was always in charge.

'I was in a state of terror all the time,' she says. 'I had enough sense to be afraid. The things that were happening – from the word go, from the time we moved into the house – really looking back on it, it's like watching a scary movie.'

Brandy began to wheeze one night, six months after her stepfather moved in. She tried to breathe deeply but her bronchial tubes spasmed and tightened in the darkness. She couldn't get any air into her lungs. She was rushed to the hospital where she was treated for her asthma attack. As she regained the ability to breathe, staff at the hospital became concerned. As she lay in the starchy bed, gazing out of the window, a doctor came into her room. He listened to her lungs with a stethoscope and in the antiseptic air asked her outright, 'Has anyone touched you inappropriately?'

'By then he had,' Brandy says to me now. But by the time she opened her mouth to take another precious breath to answer the question, her stepfather had suddenly materialised at her bedside. He was forever lingering nearby, listening in. 'He was a very – I want to say a cuss word if you don't mind?' I tell her to go ahead; I think the catharsis of a well-placed cuss word would be good right now. 'He was a very bold son of a bitch. Right off the gate he started bothering me.'

Brandy has the sense that somehow he knew her deepest vulnerabilities and fears, how her mind worked, and what was important to her. He knew these things not out of warmth or love, but just the opposite. He used this information to manipulate her.

'My fear that he would hurt my mom, he used that against me.' Brandy was willing to keep quiet about the abuse if it meant avoiding another scene of violence between her mother and stepfather. Brandy also feared her mother and the violence she was capable of. Her stepfather used that fear against her too. 'He knew that we had a violent relationship as well as a very strained relationship. I kept as many secrets from her as possible, so I was the perfect target.'

Brandy told no one. There was no place to get away from his watching eyes. Even if she could find somewhere, she couldn't give voice to what was happening to her.

'How do you say it? And who do you even tell?' Brandy reflects. 'He molested me, and I stayed in that house, keeping his secrets, and actually having a relationship with him in order to protect my mother and to keep things copacetic.' To keep things copacetic is to keep things running smoothly, to pretend that everything is fine, to do whatever you can to avoid conflict. Brandy became a peacekeeper. I begin to see why she might need a robe and a crown to bolster herself before talking to a stranger about all this. Staying silent and pantomiming happiness was her job. It was what she had to do to stay safe.

Later, when Brandy was around 15, she heard a clicking sound in the family basement. She searched the room for the source of the noise, moving around and noticing when it was getting louder or softer. Her search led her to a cupboard where the clicking filled her ears. She opened the door. There were wires everywhere. And then she saw the tape recorder – the source of the noise. Following the wires, Brandy discovered the secret trail that had hung through her house the whole time. Her stepfather had bugged the phones. Every call made to and from the house was being recorded.

'My stepfather was very sneaky … He was an engineer … His brain worked in a very crafty way all the time. None of us were savvy enough to imagine what he was doing,' Brandy says. Her words make me feel tense and I feel a shiver down my back.

There's no clear way for a child to improve their abusive living conditions. As Brandy surmises, 'You just know that your mom's been beat all your life, all the way up to this point. And you don't want to see her get killed, and you don't want to see her get hurt, and you just need to keep this stuff copacetic and get along. And that's what I did.'

It's much easier for a child to blame themselves for the things that go wrong in the home than to face the fact that their caregivers – the people they are utterly dependent on for everything – are dangerous. As psychologist Alice Miller observed in her book *Thou Shalt Not Be Aware*, 'I have never known a patient to portray his parents more negatively than he actually experienced them in childhood but always more positively – because idealisation of his parents was essential for his survival.' It was easy for Brandy to see peacekeeping as her responsibility. Its failure was her failure. The tapes kept rolling and clicking as part of the normal beat of life.

Puberty was a scary spectre for Brandy because she was afraid the sexual abuse would increase. In her bedroom, she barricaded the door at night, only sleeping peacefully when she could be sure she'd remain alone.

'I still slept under piles of clothes for fear that he was going to come to my room,' she remembers. Around the house, she dressed protectively. On top of her regular clothes, she would add a dressing gown. Around the gown she'd tightly fasten a leather belt. Brandy likens it to a chastity belt. These small measures, she hoped, would be an obstacle for her stepfather. These small measures were all she had available to keep herself safe. In fact, as Brandy developed into her teens, her stepfather stopped sexually abusing her. But the absence of the abuse created its own intense uncertainty.

'It stopped abruptly,' Brandy says, 'and I never knew when or if it was going to come back.' She suspected it could happen again at any point. He was just waiting for her vigilance to falter.

'How did you survive?' I wonder aloud. A smile grows on Brandy's face and in her voice. She speaks of her school and of her candlelit church. 'Both places represented where I went to get away,' she says. At school, she could feel like a normal person among friends and use her work as an outlet. At church, she could feel her robust spirituality and find support in her community.

'It's who I prayed to, it's who I begged for help, it's where I took hope. It's where God was. It's a place where they always had something for me to do and there was always somebody there who was responsible for me or cared about me.' She remembers churchgoers seeking her out and taking her aside to ask for advice. They told her what was going on in their lives and wanted her to help them come up with what to say in their prayers to God. Putting the right words together was Brandy's talent. 'I knew how to get a prayer through, I knew how to get right to the heart of the matter. I could see very clearly what somebody needed.' She relished understanding others' problems and reflecting them back in elegant phrases. She noticed how others would drop their shoulders and exhale with relief when their problem was rendered comprehendible and fluent.

For years Brandy was protected enough that she could survive these difficult times. And from the outside, it was nearly impossible for people to know what she was facing. Her mother had spoken at length to their pastor about the difficulties in her marriage, but she hadn't mentioned the children and how they might be suffering. Other members of the church saw the problems Brandy's mother and stepfather were having too. One night, when Brandy was being dropped off home after church in a minibus, she found a note on her front door instructing her to go to the hospital. She showed the note to the driver and they went to the hospital to find that her stepfather had hit her mother so hard in the eye that it had swollen to the size of a golf ball. The livid purple bruising did not prompt questions about Brandy's welfare. Brandy's heart duly responded, rapidly pumping blood. And so, such scenes remained part of normal life.

❖

Brandy remembers watching television one night with her brother and stepsister (the stepsister didn't live with them, but happened to be around at the time). They were all sitting around in Brandy's bedroom upstairs. She doesn't remember what they were watching, but it was the early 1990s, and TV sitcoms were populated by wholesome families who conquered Serious Issues in half-hour allotments while wearing cosy, colourful jumpers. Child sexual abuse was mentioned as the glow of the television light touched the three engrossed faces.

'He used to do that to me,' Brandy's brother said. His eyes didn't leave the screen. As the show continued, the changing movements and colours on the screen flickered over his face. But he did not move. It was almost as though Brandy had imagined his matter-of-fact statement. But, as her eyes snapped towards him, so did her stepsister's.

'Our heads just about spun off our shoulders,' she says. They'd both heard it. It was real. With that comment, Brandy realised that her stepfather had abused all three of them. But there was little time to dwell on that realisation. Brandy and her stepsister had questions. 'We kind of started quizzing him a little bit about it, but then the craziest thing happened … While we were trying to figure out what the heck he just told us, my parents came storming up the steps. They were screaming, "What are you up there talking about?" And we're like, "What? Where were you? How did you hear this conversation?"' Nothing was said inside the house that wasn't overheard. Had Brandy's stepfather been bugging their rooms as well as the phone? Or were his ears just alert to dangerous admissions?

'That began a very creepy time,' says Brandy. 'I found out that he had molested my brother. My baby brother, who I felt fully responsible for all his life. And I was just devastated.' In the years since the last time she had experienced abuse, it had never occurred to her that her brother would be in such danger. 'I couldn't – because I was a little kid, I didn't have a point of reference that a man would do something like that to a boy. So, I didn't know that he needed to be protected.' She continues, 'Once that came out, I just knew for sure that my mom was going to leave, Erin. I knew that, you know, the bags are packed, we're out of here. And she didn't leave. She stayed.'

Brandy seems to stare right at me as she says my name. She repeats it occasionally through our conversation and it always swings me back into the immediacy of the moment. Although our words are being transmitted via fibre optic cables deep in the Atlantic Ocean, she feels very close. It almost feels as though she's whispering in my ear even though she's enunciating her words clearly and they're emanating from my laptop speakers. The confusion in her voice, her anger, the fact that she remains so mystified by her mother's immobility, is palpable. *How could she not leave?*

Australian journalist Jess Hill spent years reporting on domestic-abuse issues and in her book *See What You Made Me Do* she characterises the question, 'Why didn't she leave?' as a distraction from the truly fundamental question: 'Why did he do it?' When we want to address domestic violence as a social issue, our focus should be on identifying what makes perpetrators continually enact violence.

On a personal level, though, Brandy felt betrayed and mystified by her mother's inaction. But as Hill notes, inaction is common for women in abusive situations. 'It doesn't make sense,' she wrote in *The Guardian* in September 2015, 'that even women who are smart and independent will stay with a man who treats them like dirt.' She says that the relationship between an abuser and a victim is analogous to that of a captor and a prisoner of war. Long-term abuse can instil a feeling of abject hopelessness, as if there's nothing the victim can do to change the situation. 'Survivors who have escaped this systematic abuse often emerge from it confused and utterly disoriented.'

Teenage Brandy paced her room in frustration, a feeling that echoes in the tone she uses to describe the events to me today. 'Nobody's making any friggin' moves,' she growls. I notice her use of the present tense. The memory is still so alive.

Where she expected to watch her mother leave, she instead saw her turn to drugs, having amassed a potent collection of pill bottles that she kept around the house. Plan A – for her mother to protectively take her children out of her house – had failed. Brandy's Plan B was to stop talking to her stepfather. She wanted to just get through her last year of school, to graduate, to go to college and get out of the house.

Plan B also did not work. 'They wanted to keep me in their insanity,' surmises Brandy. As she fitfully kept to her bedroom, she could hear her stepfather in the distance, yelling at her brother, 'Tell her it didn't happen!' If the story was retracted – banished to the realm of imagined, slanderous accounts – things would be fine again. But her brother would not say those words. So next, Brandy remembers, her stepfather formed an ultimatum.

'He started torturing my mother, telling her that I couldn't eat his food or use his utilities or anything in the house if I wasn't going to talk to him.' He knew that Brandy's mother would do the work of policing this ultimatum on his behalf. And she did. Brandy's mother attacked her. Again, this doesn't make sense but it isn't unheard of either. Partners of child abusers may be well aware of the allegations made against them – deep down, they may even believe them – but they can also be unwilling, or unable, to act in the interests of the child.

Christina Enevoldsen, who is based in the US and a co-founder of the online resource 'Overcoming Sexual Abuse', writes on the site in her essay 'Confessions of a child molester's wife' that she was sexually abused by multiple family members as a child and yet still married someone who had told her upfront that he had a history of sexually abusing children. She felt bonded to him by his confession; she wanted to uphold his trust in her.

'That kind of intimacy was what I craved and I was eager

to escape my lonely-making family,' she writes. The couple married and had a baby. One day, Enevoldsen was changing her infant daughter and found blood. She confronted her husband. He confirmed he had abused his tiny daughter. He seemed 'remorseful' and told Enevoldsen that it wouldn't happen again. But over their daughter's childhood, such incidents kept occurring anyway. Her pastor advised her to stay with her husband, reassuring her that it would stop.

'I tried to do everything I thought would help my relationship with my husband. I never said no to sex and I listened to everything he said.' When they finally divorced, her daughter had reached adulthood and finally told Enevoldsen that her efforts to please her husband to protect her daughter had been in vain. He'd just become better at hiding his actions.

Like Brandy, Enevoldsen's daughter had been pressured into silence. She wanted to keep the family happy. Besides, it's not hard to keep a secret from someone who doesn't want to know the truth. Enevoldsen says: 'I ... imagined that all he did was fondle her. That's bad enough, but how did I think a little fondling would leave blood in her diaper? I had minimised the abuse in my mind to protect myself from the truth – and the guilt that came with it.' While her husband manipulated her into thinking that he was contrite and committed to changing, she blames herself for wilful ignorance.

Brandy's situation was compounded by the fact that her mother was not merely complicit, but also abusive herself. The room that Brandy had tried to make a safe haven over the years was invaded. Her mother barged in, the door swinging open with the full force of her strength, the wooden frame shuddering with her energy.

'She had actually come into my room and she was so angry that she was screaming and crying, telling me she was going to kill me, and that I was to no longer eat any food in the house,

I was not to take a shower ... And I was scared and I believed her, with all my heart ... She had a habit of hitting me and throwing me around. And so, I didn't know. As angry as she was, I didn't know if she was actually going to attack me right then. So, I sat on my bed just hoping and praying that this session was going to come to an end and I was going to have my life still intact.' She sat still and heard her mother's words and watched her violent gestures (the flinging of arms, the pounding of fists). It seemed to last ages, but even the energy of her enraged mother faded eventually.

'And when it did finally come to an end I packed as much as I could pack in my backpack, and I said a prayer that if I ever left, that I would never ever come back.'

Brandy's home life had always been unpredictable. She would never know if she was about to get yelled at, or injured, or molested. She carried the fear and uncertainty with her always. It pounded at the centre of her body, in her heart. Now, she was seriously wondering if she was going to be killed. This ambiguity had finally become intolerable.

Somehow, Brandy slept that night. The next morning, she got into her mother's car. It felt dangerous. When she closed the car door she wondered if it was the last action she'd ever choose to make. But to be taken away, she'd have to get in. Brandy's mother dropped her off at her school bus stop, yelling at her throughout the entire journey.

'It was a very risky moment, it was a very risky time. It was very scary. Sometimes it's kind of hard to even go back and really put my finger on the emotions of it, because it was so heavy.' Brandy says she switched off, she could see her mother's lips moving, but didn't take in the words. She thought to herself, 'If I put up any fight I might not make it there, so I just need to be silent.'

Brandy spent the day at school; she tried to concentrate on

her classes, she made a few phone calls to try to find a place to stay. She never did go back to that house.

❖

Running away involves trading one set of ambiguities for another, surrendering to a different kind of uncertainty. And while surely, for Brandy, it was a case of better the devil you *don't* know, uncertainty is still hard to navigate. First, there are practical questions. Up until this point, Brandy had had a routine, a place to live. She remembers asking herself, 'What am I going to eat? Where am I gonna sleep?' Then, there were immediate uncertainties and fears: 'Is my mom gonna get killed? Is my brother gonna get killed? How do I save myself? Are they gonna show up at my bus stop and kill me, you know, take me back? Are the police gonna make me go back home? You know, what's gonna happen? What's gonna happen?' Brandy asked these questions through the day: as she walked to classes, as she gathered her books from her locker, as she looked out the window and saw the floating clouds, as she acted like a focused student.

Young people who run away face huge risks in finding a safe place to stay and avoiding harm. Although most can find refuge with a family member or friend, sleeping rough or accepting shelter from strangers are common measures people take when they run away. There's a certain amount of savviness involved in running away – at a minimum, you need reliable social contacts and the rhetorical skills to persuade these people to let you stay with them. These skills are especially needed when you factor in that most teenagers don't have a regular income and have little experience caring for themselves. It's often an invisible struggle too – according to the UK charity Railway Children's *Reaching Safe Places* report, only around one-third of runaways are reported missing. Some don't get reported because families don't want to attract the attention of authorities, or think that family problems should be sorted out within the home. Some don't get reported because others don't realise the runaway is missing; for instance, in homes where parents aren't often around, it's possible that nobody will notice their child's absence. If the young person is habitually away from home because they're always out with friends, their absence may seem unremarkable. Some don't get reported because the young person frequently runs away, and so the logic is that there's no need for concern or to bother police (although, in fact, someone who has run away multiple times is actually at greater risk of coming to harm).

It's common enough for young people to calm down after a fight with their parents by spending a few nights at a friend's place. But what underlies running away might not be as simple as an ordinary fight. A US National Longitudinal Study of Adolescent Health found that 38 per cent of runaways report having been physically abused at home, 66 per cent report verbal abuse, and 10 per cent report sexual abuse. These rates of abuse were substantially higher in young people who ran away compared to those who hadn't. The Railway Children study in the UK says that the 'recurring themes' in young people's stories of running away include 'family instability, violence, abuse, [and] neglect'. In other cases, where the families of runaways are supportive, the young person can still struggle with feelings of failure at school, loneliness, mental illness, substance abuse, or bereavement. As Brandy puts it, 'Nobody runs away for no reason. If a kid runs away, there's something going on there.'

❖

Brandy's testimony is at odds with one vivid picture we get of runaway young people in popular culture. In Mark Twain's classic story *The Adventures of Tom Sawyer*, Tom runs away to an island with some friends because he's bored at school. While they're having a free, fun time, their whole town is looking for them, fearing they've died. Tom can't help but wait to see his own funeral, and hides up in an unused church gallery to listen to the proceedings. He makes a grand reveal: he's alive! And people are happy he's well and he has no sense at all of the full gravity of the situation. He is selfish – letting his loved ones suffer for his own entertainment. He doesn't represent missing runaways. But this image of a kid running away for a lark affects the way runaways are perceived within their community.

A more accurate portrayal, perhaps, is found in Vladimir Nabokov's *Lolita*. Humbert Humbert falls in love with a young girl, Dolores (whom he calls 'Lolita'); he marries her mother and becomes Lolita's guardian, which gives him the opportunity to abuse her. When her mother starts to suspect Humbert, she suddenly dies in an accident. For a short while, the predator has Lolita all to himself. He tells her that she can never leave or tell anyone what is going on or else she'll be sent to an orphanage where she'll suffer terribly. He gives her gifts while he watches her movements closely. Eventually, she is able to leave. Humbert searches desperately for her but fails. Lolita lives with a different predator, another older man who wants her to star in pornographic films. Then she escapes him too. She works as a waitress and by the age of 17 she decides to reach out to Humbert, but only because she needs money. She is married and pregnant and struggling. Humbert reflects:

> … unless it can be proven to me … that, in the infinite run it does not matter a jot that a North American girl named

> Dolores had been deprived of her childhood by a maniac
> ... I see nothing for the treatment of my misery but the
> melancholy and very local palliation of articulate art.

In short, he's upset about what he did, although his penalty is that sadness alone, which can be alleviated. Not for her, though. Lolita escaped because she suffered, not because she was bad. When she escaped, she faced more danger. And these traumas followed her.

Sometimes missing young people are more aptly called 'throwaways' than 'runaways'. A UK Children's Society survey in 2004 found that 2 per cent of people between the ages of 14 and 16 had been forced out of home. About 23 per cent of these young people said that they were thrown out because they didn't get along with other people in their households, usually a parent. Most cases were directly preceded by an argument between the young person and other members of their household. The conflicts tended to arise from different views, different expectations and boundaries, issues between parents, and tension caused by changes in the family structure (for instance, a young person not getting along with a new step-parent).

Sometimes the line between 'runaway' and 'throwaway' is murky. How could Lolita not accept what appeared to be a passage to safety when the alternative was abuse? Brandy consciously chose to get out of her parents' house and go into the unknown, yet, as I listen to her story, I wonder what else could she have possibly done. She was in a hostile environment where her stepfather was seriously threatening to cut off her food and resources unless she interacted with him – a man who had abused both her and her beloved brother. She had genuine fears for her safety, even her life, as her mother literally threatened to kill her. Telling someone about what was going on didn't occur to Brandy at that stage; it didn't even seem possible to articulate what was happening. Even though running away was her choice, there were significant factors that pushed her in that direction, to the point where it didn't seem like other viable choices existed.

On the day Brandy left home, an older friend from church picked her up from school. Once Brandy was in the car, her friend started describing the relationship between her husband and Brandy's stepfather. They were good friends. Brandy could stay at their house for a bit, but they didn't want to get in the middle of whatever family drama was going on – it could compromise the friendship. Brandy remembers the pang of disappointment in her stomach. Still, at least for a short while, she was safe. The car stopped. Brandy walked up the driveway and into her friend's house. She asked to use their phone. Through a series of calls she arranged to stay at another friend's auntie's mother's house, using the full extent of her social networks to secure somewhere to live.

The house of this distant family member of a friend was small but – at least at first – Brandy paired it with freedom. She and the homeowner – a stranger, essentially – agreed that they had to ascertain Brandy's rights in the situation. It wouldn't be right to illegally harbour a minor, and the homeowner didn't want to engage in any custody dispute. So, Brandy sat at the kitchen table and called the local police. She was nervous. In some US states, running away from home as a minor is illegal and a runaway can be taken into police custody and ordered back home, into the care of Social Services or even into juvenile detention. Even where running away as a minor isn't a crime, runaways get nervous about letting authorities know about their situation from fear of being sent back home. They try to keep quiet about their situation. But Brandy was reassured when the police told her that, in her jurisdiction, at 17 she couldn't be forced to live with her parents. So she stayed in that small house for the next three months, until the homeowner told her it was time to find somewhere else to live.

Brandy was only technically missing in the few days between leaving home for the last time and calling police to ask them about her rights. As police define it, a person is missing when their whereabouts are unknown and where there's concern for their safety. It's inherently concerning when a minor (in most US states, a minor is a person who is under 18) has gone missing. It's a matter worth investigating, even if the minor has voluntarily chosen to leave, in order to make sure that the person has the competency to make that decision, and in order to ensure that their leaving will not cause them or others any harm. But once it was established that Brandy – who was on the cusp of legal adulthood anyway – had thought through her decision, the police were satisfied that she had a right to leave. I can see her retrospective relief through her webcam as she sits back in her chair after a long period of leaning forward. 'That was the music that I needed,' she says.

She was not 'missing' by police definitions at this stage. Yet, her story from this point forward still rings true to many of the themes of a longer term missing-persons case. She was still in an ambiguous space. Her legal guardians only roughly knew where she was living and where she was going. Brandy was both physically absent from their home as well as absent from the role she played there as a daughter, a stepdaughter, and a sister. She was no longer their peacekeeper. This absence was problematic for them. It wasn't as though Brandy had left home as part of a regular rite of passage, like going off to college or moving into her own house as an adult. She chose homelessness. Her refusal to play the roles she'd been given disrupted the façade that everything was fine. She hadn't told the secret yet, but that was now a live risk.

Brandy doesn't know what she did for Christmas that year, which was shortly after she ran away. She doesn't remember it at all. She spent that winter floating between places, staying with different friends and changing houses before anyone could get irritated by her presence. This movement, this floating, is often part of what it's like to be a missing person. UK research that collates the narratives of formerly missing persons reflects these themes – in many of the stories there is no big plan, just an oscillating desire to remain absent. There is little stillness. Those missing often feel free while in motion, but there are other feelings too: worry about being found, confusion as to what to do next, surges of adrenaline, or the opposite – a sense of quiet calm. Everything, for better or for worse, is in flux.

The researchers observe that being missing is less about finding a new space as much as it is a state of movement and experiencing new rhythms. It is an uncertain, ambiguous way to live. Brandy moved to several different places to find shelter. But even if she could stay in one spot for a few months, her thinking was oriented around movement. Eventually, she did find a steady arrangement. The mother of one of her friends agreed to let her stay with them until graduation. But even then, she had to pre-empt the possibility of overstaying her welcome and plan what places she could go to next. She regularly stayed with other friends for a night or two to reduce the likelihood of being asked to leave. So, each day was no longer the same routine sort of day divided between school, church, and home. There was no guaranteed shelter, and no familiar landscape to serve as a predictable backdrop for her experiences. The researchers say that this type of scenario is an exhausting, 'arrhythmic' state to be in.

It's tempting to see running away as a chance for a clean break to start a new life, but the bounds between old and new are always fluid. Some people who deliberately disappear change their name, disguise their appearance and even cultivate new identities, but still the break is never clean. You can't escape the fact that you carry the past with you. You are the same person. The connections with your old life linger in the same body, and in your memories.

When Brandy ran away, she still went to the same school and she kept her identity. She maintained her distance from her parents but, even while physically absent, they persisted as people she couldn't get away from. Her mother and stepfather had used the Tom Sawyer trope about young runaways to explain to churchgoers and friends why their daughter no longer lived with them. They told them that she couldn't follow the rules, she was a bad kid, she was breaking up the family and needlessly upsetting them. Her friends were also curious about why she wasn't living at home any more. The people around Brandy began to ask questions. She had to acknowledge her past in order to embark on her future away from her parents. If she didn't explain herself, their side of the story would be the official story, and she'd be pressured to move back in with them.

'It was like I had to release the story just to stay ran away,' she says angrily.

The first time Brandy told someone why she had left home, she could almost see the words in front of her. 'I felt like I wanted to take them back out of the air.' She had just told her boyfriend, whose immediate response was rage. His whole body tensed up, he began to yell.

'He wanted to find my stepfather, kill my stepfather, tell somebody.' Brandy tried to calm him down with even-toned, soothing words, noting the irony that she should be the one to comfort him. 'I realised how big it was, that normal people couldn't carry the weight of it.'

At church one day, Brandy's pastor approached her. He told her about how her mother had come to him, distressed and crying. Brandy was, reportedly, breaking her heart. It could only heal upon Brandy's return. Brandy frowned at his words and shook her head. That wasn't right. 'You guys got to be fucking kidding me!' she thought. She was compelled to tell the story. Again. She was dismayed that those around her just couldn't trust in the fact that she needed space, that she didn't want to talk about it. But as soon as she started talking, she couldn't stop. 'The lights started going on,' she says. And when her pastor argued that she should try to make amends with her family despite the harm they'd caused, her sense of injustice only heightened, becoming more real, and louder. I still hear it in her voice today.

As Brandy realised, there is a function to having a continuous, detailed narrative of your past. It stops people from bothering you. Not that simply talking always works. Stories of abuse aren't always believed. Psychologists from the University of Oregon identified that myths about child abuse persist, such as: 'it's normal for people to pretend they were sexually abused as a child', and 'child sexual abuse is not truly abuse'. The likelihood that someone will believe a story of abuse varies. The story is more likely to be believed if the narrator found the incidents particularly memorable. The problem is that in some households, abuse is so commonplace that it may be hard for survivors to remember specific incidents. In cases where the listener knows the abuser, the narrator being believed can be even more fraught because it introduces a contradiction. If the alleged abuser seems like a nice, 'normal' person, it can be harder to accept that damning stories about them are true. Brandy faced this problem because her stepfather was perceived as being a good man within his community.

'He was very outgoing, which made it very difficult when the story did start to unravel, because the people at church loved him,' she says. 'He was the Sunday school superintendent at the time, he was the coach for the ladies' softball team, so all the ladies were always hanging out, hanging off of him. He had the good job, and the pretty wife.'

Physician Roland C Summit wrote that there are two traumas involved in child abuse. The first is the abuse itself; the second is the rejection felt when others don't believe it. Children even learn to retract stories where it's clear they're not believed. Brandy found that her friends believed her, which was reassuring. Eventually, in her spate of talking, she also told the school counsellor what had happened, and the counsellor reported Brandy's story to authorities who, in turn, commenced an investigation into her stepfather.

Other people did not believe Brandy as readily. Aside from her own mother, who was in denial, Brandy was disappointed by members of her church who refused to take her story seriously.

'They were confused. They heard the story, many of them were just in disbelief and they never moved from the shock and awe and disbelief of it to realising that this really happened. A lot of them never really made the transition. They just left themselves at "This couldn't be."' She thinks the failure to believe the allegations was related to the fact it would mean that they, as a community, had failed Brandy and her brother. It also meant that they would have to face the disturbing thought that they had trusted Brandy's stepfather with their own children. 'While all this is happening, he had kids over at the house all the time.'

'Belief,' she continues, 'would mean that you had to go home and talk to your own kids and ask your own kids those same questions.' They would have to wonder if the smiling man involved in their children's Sunday school education had hurt their own children too. 'People don't want to face that.' At this time, Brandy's place for God, for sustenance through difficulty, for protection – her church – became a place where people turned away from her. Another expectation – that of acceptance within her refuge – was shattered.

'I can't imagine. It's baffling,' Brandy says of people who hide from the reality that there is a chance that their child has been harmed. I agree. I'm mystified too. I see my fingers clutching at the table in front of me. And yet, I tell Brandy about the scary research I've been unearthing. I mention Christina Enevoldsen's story and how the 'warning signs' were like neon lights in the darkness – direct confessions and bloodstains – and she still did nothing. I see Brandy shuddering slightly. But ultimately, she nods.

'Even my pastor – he eventually, in his older age, apologised to me fully. He said that he didn't know. That's what he kept saying. After I was fully, fully grown and we came back to interact together my pastor just kept saying, "I really didn't know", or "I knew but I couldn't believe it and I worked with the information that I had, with information that I could compute. And your mom wanted to keep your family together and so that's what I was trying to help her do."'

Sometimes people don't want to know the truth. They can't hear it. It's more convenient to believe that the teen who ran away was just a problem child, doing it for attention or out of selfishness. It's impossible for them to question what they think they know about a man who seems nice and might have spent a lot of time around their own children. The implications are too much. It means that horrible things have occurred within what they thought of as happy homes and happy families. It means that victimhood may be far more widespread than anyone wants to admit, or deal with. It means that danger could thrive in places that are uncomfortably close.

The denial of abuse points to another ambiguity involved with running away as a teenager. Not only is there a need to engage with the past when trying to forge ahead with a new future, and a lot of confusion about what that future will hold, there's also a moral ambiguity. Brandy had to contend with the fact that her reality conflicted with what others were prepared to accept as true. As a result, she had to deal with people questioning *her* character and motivations, because they could not question her stepfather's character and motivations. What she perceived with her five senses was dismissed.

Brandy and I turn off the Skype video function at some point during the interview to save bandwidth and speed up the connection, so I can't see the expression on her face. But her voice hums with outrage, that people would dismiss her experiences – and her – so readily and with such little reflection. Her speech quickens, twisting with disbelieving question marks; the condemnation of her community comes steadily and from her core.

❖

Running away can lend itself to different kinds of journeys. Railway Children identifies two types of narratives lived out by young people who run away. The first is circular. The person leaves home, has a number of experiences, then at some point goes back to where they started. Most people arrive back home very quickly. Sometimes people go back because after their short break from the normal rhythms of life they seek a more predictable experience again. Sometimes they are located by police or friends or family members and are compelled or feel obliged to come home.

Then there are missing persons who, like Brandy, take another sort of journey – Railway Children calls it a linear journey. People on linear journeys never go back after running away. Some new place emerges as home, and life takes on a new normal. Linear journeys can be risky, and the missing person is likely to be homeless for a greater length of time than those who experience a more circular pattern. But runaways on a linear journey are also more likely to move towards a sense of self-determination and responsibility. Even if initially running away was an impulsive reaction to a difficult situation, it eventually becomes an active life choice. 'There was unanimity that moving on meant taking a conscious decision to stay away from some people and situations,' says the Railway Children report. Things had to change, and so they did. Regardless of the particulars of the conflict at home, what caused the young people to leave, whether they made risky decisions, or who was to blame, a linear story of running away is a story of personal resolve. It's a story of trying to transform the conditions in your life when you lack the resources to do it in other ways.

After her high-school graduation, Brandy was homeless. While authorities said that too much time had lapsed to investigate any abuse she had suffered, they did investigate her stepfather's abuse of her brother. Brandy's stepfather wanted her mother and brother out of his house, and so did the authorities – after all, it was inappropriate for a boy to live with the person being investigated for abusing him. The only place her mother and brother could go was her grandmother's retirement home, which was where Brandy joined them for the summer.

Brandy was no longer missing, or a runaway, and she was even living with her mother temporarily, albeit in a claustrophobic space for four people to squeeze into in the sweaty heat. Still, that September, starting college was a relief for Brandy, even though it came with its own struggles. She moved a few hours away from home, in the same state of Missouri but far enough away that it would be difficult for her family to pay her a surprise visit and bother her. She drank a lot. She became depressed, unable to leave her dormitory for weeks. After her first semester, her college threatened to kick her out for under-achievement unless she could offer them a reason for it.

'I had to write the school a letter telling them how tumultuous my senior year had been and my life had been, and like literally telling my story, and they let me back in school on probation.' By letting her back in, they implicitly told her that her story mattered. She saw a counsellor to address her depression and disturbing nightmares. When her college dormitories closed each holiday, she became homeless again. She sometimes stayed with her mother for a few weeks or she'd go to a friend's house.

Eventually, during this time, Brandy's stepfather had to answer for his crimes against her brother. He agreed to a plea bargain where he could say he was guilty and forgo jail time as long as he never worked with children.

'The things that he was found guilty of were gruesome,' says Brandy. 'I can't even – I couldn't even fathom it. It was so hard to deal with emotionally and intellectually, all of it, that this had happened on my watch, you know? When my mom told me on the phone exactly what happened … because by then they were going to court, and he was having to tell the story, she had called me on the phone one day and told me what he had done and how long, like it went on for a good, strong five years, Erin. This gruesome, gruesome, gruesomeness that he was doing to my brother – I collapsed to the floor when she told me. I literally collapsed on the floor in my dorm room when she told me what had happened.'

Even today, over two decades later, Brandy still lives with the guilt of what happened to her brother. She recalls the times she had left him alone with his stepfather as she frantically tried to spend time with their mother.

'I was trying to figure out how I could get her to love me, you know, so I thought maybe we [could] spend time where she wasn't focused on [my brother].' While they were out of the house together, Brandy didn't get the bond she was looking for. And the cost was far greater than she could have anticipated. 'Those were the very times that he was bringing harm to my brother. The guilt is lighter now, but it's quite the baggage to try and carry with you.'

Brandy's story of what happened to her in the years subsequent to her leaving reminds me a lot of what Sarah said about Q's case, and how even though time passes, these events continue to have a fluctuating influence on day-to-day life, fading at times, returning with unnerving force at others. As with having a long-term missing loved one, going missing might not be a life event that ever really resolves.

While she was in college, Brandy was out of that house, and out of any immediate danger. But the story wrapped itself around her life. It was suffocating. She hadn't digested it; she couldn't. She destroyed all but one of the journals she'd made as a lifelong diarist. 'I had destroyed all the rest because I could not believe how horrible my story was,' she says. At the same time, in her college years, Brandy also came to relate to her story differently, to see its potential power. The facts stayed the same, and sadly always would, but what her story meant could still evolve.

An example was when she toured eastern Europe as part of a religious program to talk about trauma and faith. Faces stared up at her as she spoke on stage, and their responses showed that her message was speaking to something many in the audience had experienced themselves.

'When I told my story, like the whole church broke down,

crying. That's kind of where I learned my story had power. I wasn't just a victim; I was a victor. And that there were thousands of people who had my same story, and had never had the guts, or the gall, or the confidence, or the support to tell their story. I heard many first-time stories from grown-ups, who were 60-something years old, to teenage kids, who had never told anybody. And that became my thing.'

Over the last few years, Brandy has had to revisit these events in painful depth in order to have a good relationship with her daughter. Mother–daughter difficulties are a tradition in Brandy's family: not only was her mother abusive, but so too was her grandmother. She had to pay attention. The problem Brandy encountered was swinging too far in the opposite direction of this legacy. She describes herself as 'overprotective'. When her daughter was small, she would volunteer at her day-care centre to keep an eye on her. Every minor incident that could be perceived as a slight against her daughter – if a staff member accidentally forgot to hand her a piece of paper to draw on – enraged Brandy. She would begin yelling, and 'kicking butt, and walking out'. She assumed that 'everything that went on had to be on purpose'. Eventually, the day-care centre kicked out both mother and daughter. Then it happened again, on multiple occasions with multiple day-care centres. Brandy laughs as she tells the story, and I laugh too, even though I imagine it would be terrifying to be on the receiving end of her shouting. Her fierce love had become a problem, and its force was leonine.

To coincide with her fortieth birthday, Brandy mapped out the timeline of her abuse and her running away. Using the source material of her single surviving journal, she revisited every incident she had wanted to forget, and every painful feeling.

'I came face to face with myself, it was the Michael Jackson "Man in the Mirror" song ... Was I the kind of person – the kind of mom – that a kid could be with 24/7? And so, I came face to face again with my depression, face to face again with my anger, face to face again with my scepticism, face to face again with me being in a state of terror all the time. I just came face to face with myself again, and it became an emergency. I needed to transform immediately in order to be able to be the kind of teacher that I would have wanted for my daughter – and that my daughter would be happy to be home with ... I'm still a work in progress, but I'm getting there.'

Today, she has a loving family, and a career as a self-employed business coach who caters to women entrepreneurs, which she finds meaningful and freeing; she's received accolades within her field, such as her ambassadorship with the US National Black Chamber of Commerce. The worst of what happened to Brandy is over, while it lives on in ways she could never have imagined – in her lingering terror and racing heart. Life is painful and it's good and sometimes it's both simultaneously.

❖

Creating a life story that's painfully true is an act that Danish philosopher Søren Kierkegaard understood as ethical. Through forming their life-view, he wrote, a person:

> ... becomes conscious as this specific individual with these capacities, these inclinations, these drives, these passions, influenced by his specific social milieu, as a specific product of a specific environment. But as he becomes aware of this, he takes responsibility for it all.

The person is no longer a silent witness or an unaware puppet in the flux of life events. To tell the story shows that you see what has gone on, you have a view of it and you can voice that view. With awareness, you have choice. Becoming aware is courageous – as Brandy found, it requires paying careful attention to traumatising things that are more easily avoided. It means you can no longer justify your verbal tirades against day-care centre staff. It is ultimately constructive though: forming your story is a sign of being true to yourself rather than letting others dictate who you are and what you do. In the telling, you also recognise the power you have going forward rather than giving that power away to fate or the cruelty of others. The story is the crown, the robe.

Kierkegaard argues that it doesn't matter that the story you tell about yourself is subjective and at odds with others' accounts. Most people want to reinforce the status quo, reiterating accepted facts rather than digging into new possibilities. Others will call your story a lie if it makes them uncomfortable. Even if you know this, their contradictions can still be painful. I hear – again – the rage in Brandy's voice when she talks about how her stepfather came to her old pastor's funeral a couple of years ago. Brandy didn't go, but her brother did, and his stepfather spoke to him as though nothing had ever gone wrong.

'He sat three rows behind my mom and he went up to my brother and spoke to him… in the church, in the midst of all of these people who supposedly knew what happened. And he was able to walk in free and clear and walk out free and clear. That's how much people never transition from awe and disbelief to really believing it.'

Her sense of injustice remains – not just about what her stepfather did, but about what this community failed to do. They kept welcoming him through their doors, letting him sit, untroubled, in what was supposed to be a moral place, a house of God. This is to be expected, Kierkegaard said: 'the crowd is untruth'.

The objective facts of the world, by themselves, are cold, he said. The individual has to render the facts meaningful by interpreting them, figuring out what those facts mean and how they are important. Brandy tells me that she's consciously trying to see life through rose-coloured glasses.

'When people refer to rose-coloured glasses,' she says, 'they always say it negatively, like "She always sees things through rose-coloured glasses, she never can face reality." Well, it's a gift to be able to see positivity in negativity, to be able to see strength in perceived weakness. That's my gift, to be able to see treasure in trash; to be able to see all of these positivities in a world where everybody only sees the negative.'

She even has a literal pair of rose-coloured glasses that she can put on to remind herself to fashion the facts in this way. We turn on the video function again and she shows me the glasses. The round, John Lennon–style pink lenses are suspended in a thin silver frame. Yes, they remind her that she struggled. But also that she got herself out of danger. She's used what happened to her to help free others from their own difficult pasts. I borrow Brandy's outlook and think that 'runaway' is quite the wrong word for who she is. She didn't run away from her problems. She survived them.

6

SEARCHING

FROM DIVINATION TO POLICE PROCEDURES

At the North Melbourne branch of the National Archives of Australia, I find a method for locating missing persons, set out in yellowing 75-year-old papers. These documents are different from most of the archival material I have found about missing persons. Most are letters addressed to government authorities asking for information about a missing person. But the documents in front of me are unique in that they offer authorities a solution. It's the correspondence between a 21-year-old man, John, a farmer from the town of Mudgee, 260 kilometres north-west of Sydney, and the Australian Army Inventions Directorate, a now-defunct body that took submissions from the public about ideas that could hold some military value. I sit captivated in the Archive's reading room, which is flooded with pale natural light.

Since he was a teenager, John had been studying water divination – a procedure to find ground water by holding twigs and rods in elaborate ways. His method to divine the location of missing persons follows the same principles. The idea, he writes, is to find 'a beam of natural force' emitted when objects spatially align, the same way that the Earth and the sun and the moon align during a solar eclipse. The beam will then lead you to the person.

The first step is to get a few of the missing person's possessions. It's important that the objects are different in their nature and composition. Their pencil, John explains by way of example, will emit wooden 'vibrations', and so, if another object of theirs is wooden as well, there's going to be a force between them independent of anything else. Accordingly, the only unifying quality of the objects you choose must be that they belong to the missing person. So, John suggests, using their pencil with their leather bootlace will work more reliably.

The second step is to make a divining rod. This requires a 2-metre piece of number 10 black wire with the last segment folded so it can hold one of the possessions you've collected.

Then you mark a circle that's divided into eight segments. Each segment is demarcated by a piece of differently coloured paper and ascribed a different cardinal point. A piece of violet paper, for instance, is placed on the north sector, blue on the north-east, and so on. The missing person's second possession is placed at the centre. Then, if the missing person is dead, another possession is placed on the black sector. If they're alive, it is placed either on the white or grey sector (you may have to play around with which one – in general, says John, the possessions of missing men are better placed on white and those of women on grey, but in his experience, there's no sure rule). If you put the possession on the wrong colour, there will be no beam. If you don't know if they're dead or alive, you'll have to make a guess.

The next step is to pick up the rod and walk in a square formation around the circle. You'll feel the beam as you walk into the cardinal direction the missing person is in. The beam, explains John, is about 30 centimetres wide. It's similar to a radio wave but you can feel it, like magnetism. You can then slide a piece of tin along the rod to ascertain how far away the person is. The tin will pick up the beam at a place which roughly correlates with their distance from you.

The Army Inventions Directorate would have been interested in techniques to find missing persons, particularly in 1944 – the year these letters were written – as many soldiers and civilians alike became lost in the chaos of World War II, or died without anyone being able to recover their bodies to confirm their deaths. The Directorate's response to John's letter is included in the documents. The Secretary writes that 'the contents' of his letter 'have been noted with interest'. On further pages, the Army Directorate details subsequent experiments with John's method. John was brought to Sydney to demonstrate how it worked. In the reports, an officer betrays his incredulity at the idea, but rules out any notion that the method may be fraudulent or that John is trying to trick the Directorate for some obscure reason. 'Observers were impressed with his earnestness,' reads one note. Another says, 'He is a very highly nervous type but is perfectly sincere and would bitterly resent ridicule.'

The experiments had mixed success. Over two days, John and Directorate staff conducted 15 tests. The results of four were thrown out because test conditions were inadequate: the subject was moving, or the person's objects were deemed unsuitable. Four were deemed successful in that John could pinpoint the direction that the subject was in within a 20 per cent margin of error. John was wrong in the remaining seven tests. And while he seemed to reach some accuracy in ascertaining the direction the person was in – an officer describes his performance as 'better than chance' – his estimates of the subjects' distance away were 'all grossly incorrect'. The Directorate ultimately concluded that the method would need further development before it could be viable.

The word 'divination' in its broadest sense refers to rituals that bring what is real, but ordinarily unknowable, into focus. They find a truth-seeking path (to water, or the will of the gods, or a missing person…) by making contact with the supernatural or by picking up vibrations imperceptible to most of us.

It's an enduring mode of dealing with ambiguity. Although divination seems unscientific, the notion that solving mysteries may require investigators to draw on a set of transcendent abilities – gut instinct, intuition, even special powers – runs through popular culture. There are plenty of criminal investigators in TV dramas who are more or less the diviners of the contemporary West. When an impossibly difficult case needs to be solved, in comes Allison DuBois (played by Patricia Arquette) on NBC's *Medium*, whose psychic visions make her an effective consultant during police investigations. In comes Dr Cal Lightman (Tim Roth) in the Fox series *Lie to Me*, who has the near-magical ability to read suspects' body language so well that he meaningfully assesses their likely guilt. In come superheroes like Spiderman, who has an uncanny 'spidey-sense' to apprehend imminent danger. These characters act on visceral feelings that barely make sense, rather than rational information.

While these and television crime shows like the *CSI* franchise are exaggerations of actual policing, 'gut instinct' still plays a role in determining the police response to a missing-persons case, particularly in its early stages. There are a lot of quick decisions that must be made about the likely relevance and reliability of the information gathered at the start of the investigation. Police need to come up with a story about what might have happened by sifting through the data and attending to what seems most important in the same way you might throw out cards in a game of poker without knowing what hand you're going for.

❖

I travel by bus from Oxford to the English commuter town of Milton Keynes, 70 kilometres north-west of London, to meet Charlie Hedges, an expert on missing persons who has spent nearly 40 years working in local, national, and international policing and is now self-employed as a consultant. His current work is multifaceted: he develops prevention strategies and systems to find missing persons – particularly missing children – quickly and effectively, and he also offers training and advice for agencies across the world that work on missing-persons cases.

When I get off the bus, Charlie comes straight over to greet me. Clearly, I look like the kind of person he's imagined from our email correspondence. Maybe it's a gut feeling. And I suppose his appearance accords with my image of an older policeman. He's built solidly and stands with a straight back. His hair is grey and his eyes are watchful, taking in the surroundings. As we talk in a nearby chain café above a sporting-goods store, it becomes clear that Charlie doesn't value spidey-sense.

There is, says Charlie, 'a bit of an indefinable quantity' involved in being an investigator but 'in the world of searching, I would rather we work more on hypotheses. Which is intuition but with a bit more thought behind it … There's nothing worse than a closed-minded investigation because you're not accepting the information that's coming in.'

Good guesses are nothing compared to the minutiae of gathering evidence, cataloguing, and recording anything that might be of significance, tirelessly questioning the people left behind, and following possibilities that might not go anywhere, even if it's just to rule them out. Along the path to true knowledge, investigators deal with dead ends.

My questions about instincts remind Charlie of a case he advised on a few years ago, when a four-year-old girl went missing, who I'll call Bess (I use pseudonyms for all the cases Charlie discusses). She'd been outside playing with her five-year-old friend one afternoon in the far west of Wales when she disappeared. Her friend found Bess's mother and told her a vague story about a man in a van. The police were contacted immediately. The investigating officer called Charlie for advice. It was the early evening. He remembers picking up the phone, listening closely to the story, and the feeling of his stomach lurching.

'All they had was this uncorroborated information from a five-year-old child. Something happened, and Bess hadn't turned up at home. So, that's a bit concerning, but it was still daylight, not that long a time had elapsed.' Plenty of children are found safely at this point in an investigation. Charlie rehearsed the avenues the investigators could go down. He reiterated reassuring thoughts. As he said these words, they felt wrong. He expressed his intuitive concern too: 'This is going to be big,' he told the investigator. He points to his gut. 'I just knew.'

Charlie would be the last one to advertise psychic powers. Although I find him friendly, I can see how his icy-blue eyes could pierce a suspect. He's far more grounded than whimsical. Even when confronted with Bess's case and the sinking feeling that it was going to be serious, he turned to the rational.

'We had to go back to the basics of the investigation. What do we need to do? Are we going to attract the attention of the public?' It did end up being big. After a massive investigation, it appeared likely that Bess had been murdered, although her body was never found – she is still missing. 'I just had that feeling when we were talking on the phone,' Charlie says. 'But that didn't tell me what had happened to her.'

We talk about some of the procedures over our coffees as inoffensive café tunes play in the background.

The first important step is cultivating empathy with those left behind. This seems like a subjective process rather than a scientific one, but can help to bring about better results. Once, Charlie tells me, during a search not far from Milton Keynes, a dour gamekeeper with a shotgun over his shoulder told a group of volunteer searchers that they had to get off his land. They were searching green, rolling woodlands for an older man and, when faced with this obstacle, went back home. Unfortunately, they neglected to tell the police that their search had been aborted and so that area remained unsearched. The family of the missing man was increasingly worried the longer he hadn't been found. They decided to retrace the steps of the search party. They found the man where the search party hadn't reached – hanging from a tree.

Charlie looks down into his coffee. 'It's just a nightmare experience for them,' he says. Ideally, when the volunteers had been stopped by the gamekeeper, the police would have searched the area instead, saving the family from making that horrendous discovery. It was a big mistake. Charlie sat down with the family and apologised. He explained what had happened. The family looked at him. While they were heavy with grief, they forgave the police. The reason was empathy.

'Because I had such a strong relationship with them,' Charlie explains, 'they were completely onside with me and the police and said, "We accept that you did everything possible."' Throughout the investigation, the family was supported and continually informed about the strategies and rationales behind the police's investigations. Charlie thinks that, as a result, they were better able to cope with the devastating outcome.

At the workshops Charlie facilitates, he gets participants – usually police officers on professional-development days – to imagine a time where someone they loved wasn't where they were expected to be. Perhaps they were late home, or they never showed up to an event they'd made plans to attend with you.

'You get them to think about how they would feel in those situations. How long did it go on for? You know, was it five minutes? Was it an hour? How did those feelings escalate? And then try to visualise yourself getting to the end of the day and still not knowing where that person is. And to the end of the week. And the end of the month, and so on. To try and get people to understand just what it's like to experience that sort of loss. There's a lot of people who don't understand that.'

But families and friends of missing persons need to feel empathy from police. For them, being able to access information about how the case is proceeding and knowing that the case is a priority can mitigate some of the anxiety of ambiguous loss. At least something is happening, at least the authorities are taking it seriously. Additionally, understanding the family's concerns and listening to their insights about the missing person can help solve the case.

In contrast to the story about the gamekeeper, Charlie has a story about a time when empathy failed. About 20 years ago, Charlie fronted an investigation to find a 19-year-old man missing in the Milton Keynes area. Joseph had travelled from Wales to go to a rave with some friends. After their loud weekend, the friends arrived home, but Joseph didn't. Charlie sighs and characterises the investigation as 'a complete disaster'.

It started with a dispute between local police in Milton Keynes and police in Wales about who should be in charge of the investigation. 'It left the family in a really difficult position,' Charlie remembers. The search was not thorough. Few investigators took the case very seriously, thinking that Joseph was probably just a lad on a post-rave adventure. Perhaps he went off with a girl, they suggested, or changed his plans. Joseph's mother thought these theories sounded unlikely and out of character.

'She went to police and said, "He would not, ever, not tell me he wasn't coming home ... he would ring me and let me know because we have that sort of relationship."'

After some arguments, the case was eventually escalated. They found Joseph's body in a stretch of water that had already been searched, but so inadequately that he hadn't been discovered. As Charlie tells me this, my eye is caught by the sporting-goods store below us. There's a green tent and camping equipment, and a mannequin wearing a puffy red jacket with a walking pole leaned up against it. The countryside can get so cold and dangerous. Charlie doesn't say how Joseph ended up in the stream, but I feel a chill as I imagine his exposure to the wind and the water.

His mother, says Charlie, 'didn't get the answers she wanted from the outset, because I was running around like a headless chicken, trying to do 101 things and couldn't spend as much time with her as I wanted to – and wasn't given the resources to support her. She was having to drive up from Wales – several hours' journey – and when she got here she was so difficult and grumpy. It was really difficult.' Her stress could've been alleviated had the authorities listened to her. She revealed important information about her son's character that could have been used to escalate the case and, if not find him alive, at least find his body earlier.

The mismanagement of missing-persons cases was what attracted Charlie to this area of policing. After the discovery of Joseph's death, he wrote up a report about what had gone wrong and how improvements could be made, which was then circulated at the station. But over and over, through different cases, the same mistakes kept happening.

One day, he knocked on the door of his area commander's office and asked him, 'Why? Why did I waste my time?' Charlie's face was warm with anger. The area commander sat back in his chair, nodding in all the right places. He understood Charlie's frustration. But instead of offering sympathy, he said, 'If you want to actually make anything different, you have to get off your backside and do it yourself because no one's going to do it for you.' An effective police officer takes initiative. 'And I've been at it ever since, really,' Charlie says. The levity in his voice contrasts with his description of ranting to his boss. He even smiles. His early notes have snowballed into reports on best practice for police procedure when dealing with missing-persons cases, national policy and strategy documents advising the UK Home Office, and the fostering of international cooperation with investigations. Procedures don't erase the ambiguities involved in a case, but they are designed to give the families and friends of missing persons some answers that are grounded in reality.

The next step in investigating a missing-persons case is to decide the likelihood that the missing person is in danger, or that their disappearance may cause danger for others. It's reassuring that missing-persons cases tend to resolve quickly. In the UK, 80 per cent of missing persons are either found or return by themselves within 24 hours. According to 2016 statistics from the UK Missing Persons Unit, the vast majority of people who go missing (96 per cent) do not come to harm. For most cases, there is legitimately very little reason to worry. The trouble is trying to figure out which cases do require attention. After all, the 4 per cent of cases where someone does come to harm still amounts to over 7000 people a year in the UK alone.

The job of investigators is complicated by the fact that family members of the missing person may have their own opinions about the seriousness of a case which may not be in line with the calculations police make. There's a balance required for an effective investigation. Friends and family members need support and can offer valuable information.

'And yet,' says Charlie, 'there are cases where parents have a different feeling about what's happened; sometimes that will be good, but you have to be careful because sometimes that's wrong. Sometimes parents can be over-anxious or misinterpret things. We've had cases where parents have thought, you know, their children, their lovely little children, they're only doing right. But actually, they're well into drugs and all sorts of bad scenes. And the parents have no idea at all and that could cause a problem. And it's difficult then, trying to manage how you work with the parents.'

In one chilling case detailed in a University of Glasgow study, police assumed that a young man had taken his own life because they had found an old dictaphone with a suicide note on it, even though voice specialists confirmed that the recording had been made years earlier. The parents doubted the suicide theory and instead pointed to his recent interest in an underground bunker that was near some cliffs close to their house. He had even looked at a website about the bunker the morning of his disappearance. Frustratingly for them, police kept to their suicide hypothesis without exploring the bunker. At the time the study was conducted, the young man's parents had been asking police to excavate the bunker for three years.

Charlie recounts a case he worked on where the father of a missing 15-year-old girl, Rita, was less active in searching for her than Charlie felt was appropriate. Rita – who was living with her father at the time – had left for school one morning and instead of returning home as usual she'd got on a bus and vanished. Charlie remembers the father telling him that if Rita wasn't at home, something terrible must have happened to her. He fatalistically shrugged his shoulders when he spoke to Charlie. He resolved to move on, to get over it. But Charlie thinks that his main concern was being seen as not in control of his own family. The idea that she had chosen to leave was too shameful for him to consider. So, there would be no grand search, no media to draw attention to his failure.

Charlie disagreed with the father. He said to him, 'I'm so concerned for your daughter that I'm going to ignore your wish. And I don't really care if you don't agree because I think you're actually putting her at greater risk.' Charlie had an article about Rita put in a teen magazine. Within a week he'd received a phone call from her.

'I read this bloody awful article,' Charlie recalls Rita telling him over the phone. 'It's dreadful!' Charlie laughs. In the months she was missing, she'd been safe, living in a different city. She was near the seaside. As she'd turned 16 while she was away, she had reached the age of majority in the UK and had the right to refuse to return home. She was okay.

At the same time, Charlie's concern was sensible given what we know about the dangers faced by young people who run away or are thrown out of home. According to The Children's Society in the UK, 11 per cent of young runaways said they'd been harmed while away; 18 per cent had either slept rough or took the risk of staying with someone they had only just met; 9 per cent said that they had begged for money or food for survival. There is also the risk of sexual violence. Sometimes children run away to escape abuse; sometimes they're abused while they're away from home.

'That's what paedophiles and abusers are switched on to,'

says Charlie. 'They can recognise vulnerability in a flash and they hone in on a particular child.' Investigators don't know if the person they're looking for is at risk, but factors like age are clues they use to assess potential dangers.

It's a near-impossible task to try and come up with a story of what has happened to a person. Sometimes profiling is helpful; sometimes it sends investigators down a path of unhelpful assumptions. Sometimes listening to those left behind is useful; sometimes their suggestions are red herrings. The fact that someone is absent is inherently worrying. Yet that doesn't necessarily make it wise to prioritise the case given that police work with limited budgets and that, in all likelihood, any missing individual will be found quickly and unharmed. Additionally, prioritising some cases may even impinge on the privacy of those who are simply exerting their right to be where they like without others knowing. Important decisions about risk have to be made and revisited by police, and it's not always clear if their assessments are correct.

Another helpful step in the process is to figure out why the person went missing. To some extent, this is as impossible as knowing their intentions, their vulnerabilities, and their grievances. But it's important to try.

'People get very task-oriented thinking about, "Oh, we've got to find this person, and then we get them back, it's job done,"' says Charlie. 'Whereas actually you do need to give a significant amount of thought as to why they've gone missing. Because that "why" might tell you where they've gone.'

There are many reasons why a person might go missing. They may have chosen to leave voluntarily, or they may have been forced to do so, or perhaps the reason falls on a spectrum somewhere between these two extremes. People may intentionally go missing to create a new life for themselves, to rebel, to escape a difficult situation (such as abuse or debt), to avoid arrest, or before taking their own lives. While there may be factors that have made them feel as though they have limited choice (for example, wanting to escape an abusive or dangerous situation), their decision to go missing is made consciously. Choosing to go missing may be a right, but police will intervene if there's reason to believe that the person will come to harm.

Then there are those who 'drift' away. This includes people with dementia or mental illness who may have wandered from their usual surrounds and are either unable to find their way back or don't realise they're missing. While the prevalence of going missing is low among dementia patients, it can be very risky when it does happen – resultant deaths have been reported. This category of drifters can also include people who have simply lost contact with friends, or moved without telling anyone, but are not purposely trying to hide their whereabouts.

Unintentionally missing persons can also include people who have got lost, or been in an accident, or lost their phone (or have a dead phone battery); it can include those who've forgotten appointment times, or missed their train home. These are people who don't mean to worry others but aren't where they're expected to be and can't be contacted.

Then, there are people whose disappearances are forced. Who've been abducted, or murdered, or are victims of a crime, or injured in some way, and can't be located.

Figuring out where a missing person is on this continuum can be challenging, but it is crucial. Police have to look at the situation the person was in *before* they disappeared. Charlie talks me through the process with the fluency of someone who has gone over it many times.

'What are the likely scenarios? What might have happened to them? What is the information suggesting to us? You could start off with a list of maybe 10 or 12 things. And you think, well actually, they've decided to go to the seaside for the day. But there's nothing to support that, so we'll put that to one side. But we know that they've been in contact over the internet with an older male. That's obviously important, I wouldn't mind an inquiry to follow. It may not be pertinent in this particular case but ... You want to refine it down to maybe three of the best scenarios that you think are applicable in the case. And to do that you need to have information that supports that theory so it's a bit more than just gut instinct or an intuition.'

Police may also look at personal items such as phones, computers, and diaries – anything that may have information that's important to the case. However, just because these things can be searched, it doesn't always mean that they should be.

'That has to be proportionate to the circumstances and lawful in its purpose as well. Because you can't be intrusive just because you want to be. It has to be justified,' Charlie says. There's a balance between throwing a team into an investigation and protecting a missing person's privacy. What's known about why the person went missing should determine – although not always with certainty – where the balance lies.

What people do when they're missing is idiosyncratic but according to an analysis of hundreds of missing-persons reports made to Police Scotland, there are some correlations between the different groups and particular behaviours. Those who go missing because they need space from the stress of everyday life (often people in this group are living with mental illness) are more likely to travel alone and to walk around aimlessly. They are more likely to be under the influence of drugs and alcohol while missing, but they are also more likely to seek help from mental-health professionals or a helpline.

These tendencies contrast with those of people who go missing to escape difficult situations like abuse. They are more likely to use a method of transport like a car and deliberately evade police while missing. They're similarly more likely to spend time in quiet contemplation.

Unintentionally missing persons act as though they weren't missing. Most don't even realise they've been reported missing, but if they do, they try to go to the police as quickly as possible to correct the mistake. As you might suspect, they are also more likely to suffer a misfortune of some kind (like car trouble) while they are missing. A small number are actually on holiday and have forgotten to inform others, or others have forgotten their plans.

Once you have a picture of the missing person – some idea of who they are and some working theories on why they have gone missing – you can then proceed to consider possible locations to search. Investigators want to limit the parameters of their search to places the person is most likely to be. Locations are ruled in or out so that the search area doesn't seem frighteningly big. They colloquially call the edges of this space 'the end of the world'.

With each passing hour, the end of the world expands as the possibilities increase. For this reason, and contrary to the popular belief that you shouldn't call the police until someone has been missing for over 24 hours, it's very important that family members and friends of missing persons make a report as soon as they begin to worry about them.

A search is likely to start in the missing person's home. 'Particularly if they're young children,' says Charlie. 'They can conceal themselves in quite small places. It's embarrassing sometimes when you do all this, you get all the dogs and the helicopters and everything else and they're still hidden behind the sofa, fast asleep.' I can't help but smile at this image and Charlie laughs. 'It has happened in the past.'

If the person has been sighted – or captured on CCTV – or

if investigators can access phone records that roughly point to the person's whereabouts, or access data from a travel card or credit card, they may be able to pinpoint where to begin the search. Profiling the missing person can also bring some helpful clues as to their possible whereabouts. For instance, children aged between one and four are, on average, likely to be found within 26 minutes and 750 metres of the place where they were last sighted. So, it may be prudent for investigators to frame their search with this in mind. Your world might end up being very small if they're a child on foot. It also turns out that missing persons under the influence of alcohol likewise tend not to travel far. But of course your search area can also be very large if there's reason to believe that the missing person got on a bus, train, or plane.

An investigator also has to be aware that a small number of people will not want to be found. People have a right to leave the familiar and never come back. In these situations, the police become protectors of the secret of the person's location. They do not solve ambiguity as a diviner would; instead, they actively maintain it.

'If an adult goes missing and we have sufficient concern for their welfare then it's appropriate that all effort should be made to find them,' says Charlie. 'But if they don't want their whereabouts disclosed to their family that should not – definitely not – be done.' All they can say is the person is okay, but they don't want to talk or for any more information to be shared.

When a case is opened, investigators are compelled to understand the life, the personality, the relationships, and the thoughts of the person who is absent, while constantly acknowledging that they could be wrong, and that those closest to the person could be wrong too. They supplement evidence with experience – their best guess, their gut – to define the framework for the search. They carve up the world and hope that the person is somewhere in the section that's allotted for them.

❖

Missing-persons investigators are sometimes plunged into the middle of ongoing dramas. Cases are *in medias res*, in the middle of things. Police can go as far as their definition of the end of the world, but much exists beyond these physical parameters. Other ambiguous, ill-resolved forces always surround the case.

The first, Charlie tells me, is the disproportionately few resources – and concern – allotted to many missing-persons cases. The second is that each case stems from issues beyond what can be covered in a police investigation. Its origins may be embedded in history, in socio-economic circumstances, in despair or abuse. Police need to come to grips with this broad context when they commence their investigation in order to get anywhere. How to do that, exactly, is difficult, even in a profession accustomed to unwrapping enigmas. The third struggle is that finding people isn't always a solution; it doesn't mark the end of the problems that may have caused the person to go missing in the first place. If these issues are not addressed once the person has returned, then the biggest drivers of the case remain, albeit out of view. Going missing should be seen as a symptom of a problem, says Charlie, not the problem itself.

The top three demands on police time in Charlie's experience are road accidents, property matters (such as theft), and missing-persons cases. Realistically, he says, road accidents are over-reported because when an accident occurs everyone in close proximity seems to call emergency services. Property matters tend to be simple to deal with and rarely require urgency.

Charlie argues, therefore, that missing-persons cases take up a relatively larger degree of police time and resources. Indeed, in the UK alone, around 1000 missing-persons reports are filed each day. Missing-persons cases are also the most expensive area of UK policing in absolute terms. A medium-risk case is estimated to cost over £2000 to investigate. In total, over £700 million per year is spent on staffing costs for the hours taken to complete the tasks of searching, liaising with other agencies and the media, use of equipment and licensed software, and the services of specialised teams. It means that missing-persons cases end up requiring more time and resources than cases of either theft or assault.

Despite the number of missing-persons cases – and the expense of investigating them – they aren't always seen as priorities. 'For many, many years,' Charlie says, 'the KPIs have been looking at how many things like burglary or robbery or violent offences or violent sexual offences have been occurring in your policing area … How many are recorded and how many are you solving? How many are you preventing? And it's those things that catch the headlines and those things get government setting performance targets against them.'

With the exception of criminal abductions, missing persons aren't widely seen as a serious issue. A lot of Charlie's work has focused on missing young people in particular. A missing person is most likely to be between the ages of 13 and 17, but when a young person goes missing it rarely sparks concern. In fact, it was with derision that, in 2015, a host of news websites around the world (such as the *Courier-Mail* and the *New Daily* in Australia; the *Daily Mail*, *The Mirror*, and *Express* in the UK; and others such as *Yahoo Parenting*, *CBC News*, and more) covered a story about what the *New Daily* called the 'latest dangerous teen fad' where young people were said to dare each other to go missing for 72 hours

– 'The Game of 72'. The teen would leave home and make no contact with their family for three days before coming back without providing any explanation as to why they had left or where they had gone. Apparently, it's big in Europe. When fact-checking website Snopes examined the story, they found that there was no evidence at all behind it.

Of course, wrote Snopes content manager Kim LaCapria, 'a lack of any confirmed incidents whatsoever and a corresponding absence of any social media chatter (aside from people wondering why kids would undertake the 72-hour challenge) didn't discourage news outlets from advancing the rumour'. It was easy enough to believe, though, as it tapped into the stereotype of teenagers as irresponsible adventurers.

Even investigators sometimes lack appropriate concern for missing teens. Abduction specialist Geoff Newiss notes in a report for the UK Home Office that it's common for police to express views such as 'young people aren't really vulnerable' and that they're likely to commit crimes while missing, even though the reality is that missing young people often become victims of crime. Police officers also felt frustrated when they dealt with this demographic. 'What can we do with them if we find them?' one asked. If they were to force a teenager back home, they believed that the person would swiftly go missing again.

Charlie has worked on cases where a single young person has gone missing over 100 times. The UK Missing Persons Unit estimated in 2016 that about half the incidents of missing children are repeat cases. In such cases, many investigators just fill out the missing-persons report and wait for the young person to turn up. They think that once they've come back, they're no longer at risk. But this is not always true.

'The risk isn't [always] about being missing, it's about what's happening in their life,' says Charlie. Why are they running away so often? Additionally, 'The more you go missing

– particularly as a young person – the more extreme your behaviour is likely to become. Kids become – I hate the word "streetwise" – they think they know what's going on, they think they're grown up and brave, and they go into increasingly risky situations.' They become more inclined to sleep rough, to use illicit drugs, to beg, and to go along with people who may exploit them. According to The Children's Society, young people who go missing multiple times are more likely than one-time runaways to become homeless. The fact that leaving home is so risky says a lot about the potential risks of staying. The Children's Society also found that repeated runaways are more likely to have ongoing problems in the home, as well as at school, and within their friendship group – which may factor into their decisions to leave.

A young woman from Birmingham, Danielle McKinney, was placed into social care at age 11 in 1998, after her teacher saw belt lashes on her back while she'd been changing for PE class. After that, she was put into 39 different children's homes, was raped three times while in care before she turned 16, and ran away from care multiple times. She told the BBC, 'I don't think any of us [in care] felt safe. Half of us ran away because it was safer to run away than to be in the home sometimes.' Her story is hardly one of an adventurous, disobedient kid. It is a story of how abject fear in untenable living conditions can turn going missing into a viable option. These threats were in play well before each of her missing-persons reports were made to police.

I think back to my earlier conversation with Sarah Godwin, who, like Charlie, emphasised the fact that going missing isn't just about the act of disappearance itself. She said to me, 'It's a thing of joining up the dots in terms of policies and campaigning and everything to see where all these problems are interlinked. If you had good social workers and social-care networks, if you had good mental-health funding and care in the community, we probably wouldn't have so many missing.'

The more layers of disadvantage a person experiences, the more likely they are to go missing. In this sense, the rate of missing persons is a litmus test for how well or how poorly the most vulnerable people in society are supported. By the time a case is referred to police, the test has long been failed.

It's counter-intuitive to think of disappearances as a social issue when the story behind why an individual goes missing is so personal. A person who is abducted may just be in the wrong place at the wrong time; someone who decides to leave home may do so because their particular circumstances are making them unhappy. Yet these personal stories nonetheless fit into wider social trends that it would be remiss to ignore. According to US data, about 75 per cent of young runaways are women. There are also other groups more likely to run away from home. For instance, the US National Conference for State Legislatures estimates that up to 22 per cent of pregnant teenagers run away from home, and that somewhere between 20 and 40 per cent of young people who are homeless (many of whom are runaways) identify as being lesbian, gay, bisexual, and/or transgender. In a UK study, 19 per cent of those surveyed with a disability had run away from home for at least one night at some point in their lives. Further, 18 per cent of young people who said that they had a learning disability had also run away from home at least once.

An entrenched social issue – for instance, homophobia – has demonstrably real effects on the lives of individuals, including the probability of their going missing. Ivan Cabrera was 12 years old and living in New York City when he witnessed his boyfriend jump in front of a train. He was distraught. And when he told his conservative mother what had happened, he also came out to her as gay. Journalist Lena Masri interviewed

Ivan as a 22-year-old adult looking back on this experience. Ivan said that his mother's initial response was to tell him 'not to touch her because he would spread a virus'. Such attitudes aren't rare. As Colorado State University's Pride Resource Center states:

> … the repression of gay sexuality is enforced through the life patterns and institutions that make up our society. Family, educational system, church, government, business, media, legal, medical and psychiatric professions, all effectively combine to enforce the heterosexual model with its rigid role structures.

Even if homosexuality is not explicitly condemned, in all these arenas, heterosexuality is often assumed as the default. The stereotypical view Ivan's mother held that equated homosexuality with disease was a particularly aggressive manifestation of these systemic threads of discrimination. When discrimination entered Ivan's house, his series of exits began. Through his teens, he alternately ran away or was kicked out of home on many occasions. Ivan says he and his mother now get along, but he lived a risky adolescence.

Race is also a risk factor for going missing. In the US, black teenagers make up almost 38 per cent of people under the age of 18 who have been declared missing and whose race has been recorded (note that not all of these cases will be runaways), while, according to 2015 census data, only 13 per cent of the total US population is black. This means that black teens go missing at almost three times the rate of non-black teens. Other races in the US may be disproportionately affected too, but racial categories aren't well-defined in the FBI's data. Race can also be seen as a factor elsewhere. A study in 2011 in the UK from The Children's Society found that:

> Lifetime running away rates were lowest amongst young people of Indian, Pakistani and Bangladeshi origin (around 4 per cent) and higher amongst young people of mixed ethnic origin (13 per cent) than amongst young people of Black – African/Caribbean origin (9 per cent) and white origin (9 per cent).

In both Australia and Canada, First Nations people have also been identified as being at particular risk of running away or being reported missing. In 2019, the ABC revealed that Australian First Nations women are over-represented in open missing-persons cases.

Social responses to a person's racial and cultural background can also create impediments to even being able to search for a missing person, and may have an impact when investigations commence. In a survey conducted by the UK children's charity Barnardo's, one service provider commented that:

> I think there is more work to be done in general in relation to the workforce's assessments of risk in minority groups ... I think there's a lot of fear around getting it wrong ... about doing the wrong thing, saying the wrong thing and not understanding and not relating ... And we assess risk in a very different time span than say in comparison to a British white girl.

Authorities can also propagate bias in their investigations. In Canada in the last 30 years, as many as 4000 First Nations women have gone missing and been murdered. Racism renders them vulnerable to violence – they are up to three-and-a-half times more likely to be victims of crime than women from any other racial group in Canada. On top of that, the families of the missing and murdered women say that authorities do not address the cases in the same way they treat other deaths or disappearances. Sometimes highly suspicious cases have been ruled not to involve foul play, to the dismay of the families left behind. The Canadian Broadcasting Corporation profiles hundreds of these unresolved stories on their website. One woman, Andria Meise, went missing in 2006, when she was 32 years old. Her sister, Danielle, tried to report her missing on eight separate occasions until authorities finally registered her as missing in 2012. Danielle thinks the authorities were reticent to accept the case not just because of Andria's indigeneity, but also because she was a sex worker and she struggled with addiction. Danielle is left to wonder if vital evidence about her sister's case – now cold – could have been found if it had been taken seriously earlier. Another case is that of Chantelle Bushie, who was 16 years old when she went missing in 2007. She was a wonderful drawer, great at maths, and the mother of a young child. She was also troubled by memories of sexual abuse, and she was clearly struggling in the last few months before she disappeared, skipping school and running away from home several times in that period. Her case has been referred to a unit that specialises in cases of vulnerable missing persons but the last time Chantelle's mother heard from investigators was in 2012. A national inquiry has been launched into the enormous number of missing and murdered First Nations women in Canada, but the incidences are still accumulating. Many of the families left behind feel that the investigations have failed them.

Aside from prejudice, certain cultural beliefs and vulnerabilities may also be a barrier for young runaways in getting adequate support. In some cultures there are taboos against disclosing abuse. Beliefs that problems should be settled within the family, a mistrust of police or embarrassment about losing control of the family can all lead parents of runaway children to decide not to report them as missing. Some young people in migrant communities may also face the threat of being sent back to their country of origin or being forced into marriage by their families if they disclose abuse. This can be a barrier to getting help if a young person has run away or is considering it. Barnardo's in the UK gives an example of a young Asian man who was gay and had experienced sexual abuse perpetrated by an older man. When his family found out, they were more concerned about his sexuality than anything else. In an attempt to counter it, they began the process of arranging a marriage on his behalf. He ended up running away from home as a result. A report by Railway Children also found families applying for refugee status might decide not to report the disappearance of a child to authorities for fear that it will affect the outcome of their application.

For missing persons – young or otherwise – who are in desperate places in their lives, having better resources they can access for support is crucial. The young man Charlie worked with who had gone missing more than 100 times later went on to campaign on the issue of missing persons after he managed to gradually stabilise his life. He was asked by a parliamentarian at a governmental meeting what reforms were needed to improve the situation for missing persons. His answer had nothing to do with the process of finding them, but with the even more complicated task of helping them. Charlie recalls the young man saying, 'All I want is for you to keep on offering, consistently offering, the things that are available so that when I'm able to accept them I can take them and move forward.'

If the resources are lacking, police become the very last line of keeping people safe. They might do the bandaid work of finding the person, but there's so much more that's unaddressed. The person is still *in medias res*.

7

MORE THAN ONE AT A TIME

WARS AND NATURAL DISASTERS

I'm standing at the top of a lookout tower at the Australian National Memorial in Villers-Bretonneux, a small village just east of Amiens, in France. The tower has four windows, each facing one of the cardinal points. Most of what I see is farmland, bright yellow crops and fields that seem too green for eyes habituated still, after ten months living abroad, to the dry Australian landscape. This place was part of the old Western Front, a moving line near the borders of France, Germany and Belgium that was the main theatre of World War I. I look down and see the graves of Commonwealth soldiers. These people are buried close to where they fell on these plains around 100 years ago, far from home.

The tower looms over a wall of names; 11 000 Australians who don't have graves because nobody knows where their bodies are. I am a relative of one of the men listed here, William. This man is my great-grand-uncle, the uncle of my maternal grandfather, but that's obviously a posthumous label. There's no way he could have imagined me.

Every story I've heard about an individual going missing seems enormous. When I ask people for their stories I get autobiographies and cultural histories. The incident never stands alone, and raises important questions about how we can handle these incidents better. Everyone is implicated: governments, communities, law enforcement, social agencies. These questions become multiplied in the case of mass disappearances.

History is rife with examples: people go missing as a result of war, under repressive governments silencing dissidents, and in the wake of disasters – both natural and anthropogenic. And just as an individual missing-persons case might tell you a lot about that person's social context, mass disappearances also stand for bigger things. The missing become symbols reflecting ongoing political concerns. We project meanings into the void left by missing persons, and deal with the ambiguity of mass absences not by sitting with our collective loss, but through our imaginations.

The memorial tower in Villers-Bretonneux has many stairs, and after hiking down them my knees begin to wobble. In a chamber off a wall at the foot of the stairs, there's a plaque. It has the text of a speech about missing soldiers, made by Prime Minister Paul Keating on 11 November 1993, the anniversary of Armistice Day. In that year, the body of an unknown soldier was exhumed from a cemetery four minutes down the road and taken back to Australia. It went to Canberra, and was interred in the great, cold dome of the Hall of Memory at the Australian War Memorial. 'We do not know this Australian's name and we never will,' said Keating, making the point that if you don't know who it is, it could be anyone: 'He is all of them. And he is one of us.'

The symbolism appeals to me, too. The Australian War

Memorial is open for visitors to see the tomb and contemplate the atrocities of war every day of the year except Christmas. Not having a name doesn't mean that your life was insignificant. You may have one of the most visited graves in the country. The idea that it could be your relative must offer some comfort to the families of those missing. But I know that they didn't pick my great-grand-uncle William.

William was a member of the AIF 29th Battalion. It comprised men from rural Victoria and was formed in 1915 after news of the disastrous Gallipoli campaign – which killed or wounded almost 188 000 Allied soldiers – had hit Australian shores, so the recruits could, perhaps, anticipate the kind of horror they were voluntarily signing up for. There's no way to glean any insights into what William was thinking, but the records provide a vague story. He arrived in Europe in April of 1916 at the age of 22. His battalion fought a major battle in Fromelles that July. It was relatively quiet for the battalion for the rest of that year, although they moved in and out of the Western Front. In October, William was reprimanded for drunkenness on the field. In November, he fell ill. He was taken to hospital twice over the following months.

His first hospitalisation was for 'chilled feet'. The records don't elaborate on his condition but the winter in France that year was bitter and icy – 'chilled feet' would have been far more serious than it sounds. November in northern France is always cold, but that year was exceptionally brutal. A British soldier, Victor Fagence, recollected, 'The winter of 1916–17 was notoriously a very, very cold winter. And for my part, I think I almost in my own mind then tasted the depths of misery really.' Frostbite and trench foot were very common on the Front.

After being sent back to the field, William got mumps. Again, this was a common affliction. Vaccinations for diseases such as mumps and typhoid weren't as widespread as today and the poor sanitation and cramped living quarters of the trenches meant that microbes could be as dangerous as grenades.

William was discharged from hospital and was back in the field on 17 March 1917, just in time for German forces to attempt to delay the British advance on the Front. On 23 March, the battalion faced an aggressive counter-attack at Beaumetz, a tiny commune north-east of Amiens. It was on this day that William was declared Missing in Action. The response of his family – my family – to his disappearance can only be imagined; it's not part of the record.

Five months later, in August 1917, a fellow soldier, Private McDougal, gave an account of what had happened. William, he said:

> … appeared to lose control of himself and ran into where the shells were falling thickest. After the stunt was over, all we could find of him was his haversack with his name on it, which was covered in blood. No trace of anything further could be found of him.

His body was obliterated.

As I ponder this story and stare at William's name, the sadness of it disfigures the benign, familiar landscape around me. In the absence of very much detail about William, I imagine his experiences in the gaps. Northern Europe seems far more foreign than it did this morning. And for the first time since I've been living in Europe it hits me how far away from home I am. In my experiment with empathy I cultivate an odd fear. The fear doesn't belong to me, or to anyone in the epoch of Boeing 747s and global positioning systems. It's a fear of how large and unwieldy the world is, and how difficult it is to find your way home. I can't imagine how to navigate back across the continents. What seemed expansive and full of opportunities for adventure now feels like claustrophobia. He was frightened and so he disappeared.

His disappearance – which the Army later found likely to be a suicide – doesn't accord with what I've been told about Australian war heroes. We learned about the unique spirit of the Australian troops in school, a lesson we repeated each year in time for Anzac Day on 25 April. Those men were resourceful, strong, cheerful and a bit cheeky with their pranks in the trenches. But they were good. They came all the way over here in the first place to fight for freedom as part of the British Commonwealth. And to get a bit of travel in while they were at it. They found clever ways to eat their impermeable, mouth-cutting rations and used the time between battles to write love letters to their waiting fiancées and to play cards. They told each other 'chin up' and didn't think too much about the future. These dead and missing persons guide us on how to act: be chipper in the face of adversity, be patriotic and adventurous.

How many soldiers were really like this? I don't know. I don't know what it's like to be a person who could be so buoyant and tenacious in the mud and the ice and the decay and the blood. I think it may have been possible that William would have survived the war had he kept going somehow. But under the circumstances it's easier to imagine that *keep going somehow* is an unreasonable demand than it is to imagine how those other soldiers did keep going. Still though, the idea persists that the fallen soldiers (many of whom are still officially 'missing') represent all that's good about Australia. We project an impossible bravery, a relentless resilience upon these invisible figures.

I have another relative who went missing in France, William's brother, Charles. I'm taken west in a minibus of military tourists from the city of Lille, near the Belgian border, to the

More than one at a time 155

VC Corner Australian Cemetery and Memorial in Fromelles. There are 410 unidentified bodies and 1100 names of fallen soldiers here, Charles's among them. There are no headstones, only names. Again, I reflect on how far from home he was when he died. Charles was 18 and living in Bairnsdale in rural Victoria when he joined up in December 1915. He was recorded as missing on 19 July 1916 in the Battle of Fromelles, a disastrous attack by the Allies on the German front, designed to draw the Germans' attention away from the ongoing Somme offensive in the south. According to the Australian War Memorial, 'A seven-hour preparatory bombardment deprived the attack of any hope of surprise, and ultimately proved ineffective in subduing the well-entrenched defenders.' The Germans realised it was a trick, not a serious advance. There were 5533 Australian casualties. A further 1547 British soldiers died.

Despite the fact that someone reported 'missing' in such circumstances would more than likely have been killed, it took over a year to declare Charles dead. On the record is a letter from his father, written in curly, cursive handwriting, dated 19 September 1916, pleading with the Army for information about Charles, and for the authorities 'to search the doubt that exists in reference to my son'. He was promised very little in the typewritten reply, sent a month later and written in the passive voice favoured by bureaucrats: 'Enquiries will be instituted, and the result communicated to you in due course.' Charles has no grave because there are no remains that can be identified as his. Despite recent efforts by the Australian government to exhume corpses from the mass graves and identify the bodies using DNA testing, he – like many others – has not been found.

To me, these stories demonstrate what happens to individuals when geopolitics is treated like a snow globe. You shake soldiers around to get 44 000 square kilometres of real estate in places like Alsace-Lorraine, West Prussia, and Northern Schleswig, then it's time for the gentlemen to sign the Treaty of Versailles. William will not be found. Charles might, one day, but it hasn't happened in the last century. Those flat fields stretch out beyond the horizon, as though rolling on forever.

The bus I take heads north, gradually moving towards Belgium, stopping at other small cemeteries and memorial sites. We get to the place where the German and Allied soldiers played football during the 1914 Christmas truce. All along the front for a brief moment soldiers put down their weapons and were young men together. They played the same game, they knew the same rules, they could cooperate – the war was nothing for a soldier to take personally. We get to Ypres, a town in Belgium where several battles took place. It's home to the Menin Gate, a memorial listing the names of all the 54 395 Commonwealth soldiers who fought and died in this area before 15 August 1917 whose grave sites are unknown. The cut-off date is arbitrary, made only when the designers realised that the memorial was too small to fit the names of at least another 34 984 British soldiers, let alone the other Commonwealth soldiers who went missing in the months after. Even though the list of names is incomplete, the monument includes two archways 14.5 metres high and a hall of memory that stretches for more than 36 metres; it sits on a bridge with traffic passing through it. There's nothing personal about it at all.

❖

When someone goes missing along with many others, it may be fair to assume that they have died. My relatives who went missing most likely died in the war and at first I thought that they were not really missing persons, that there was no lingering ambiguity. But looking over that flat landscape I begin to reconsider. The uncertainty is manifest in the old letter my great-great-grandfather wrote to the Army, begging for information. Being missing in these situations does not mean being unambiguously dead. And even if you could accurately conflate the two, absent bodies are different to dead ones. Absent bodies hold within them the possibility of life, even if it looks unlikely.

There are still people missing from the 2004 Boxing Day tsunami that hit 13 nations throughout Asia, including Indonesia, Sri Lanka, India, and Thailand. Over 230 000 people, mostly from Indonesia, are confirmed dead. In the wake of the disaster, 45 752 were unaccounted for. You would think that if you survived a natural disaster as massive as this, you would make every effort to contact the people you know and reassure them that you're safe. But in this disaster, and in other cases of mass disappearances, missing does not mean dead. In the decade after the tsunami, missing people were still turning up. In 2011, for instance, as *The Guardian* reported, a girl who went missing during the tsunami in the Aceh province of Indonesia was finally reunited with her parents. The girl was eight years old when she was swept away by the waves. She survived but was soon 'adopted' by a local woman who forced her to beg in the streets long into the night. Eventually, at age 15, when the girl was too old to gain the sympathies of passers-by and failed to raise much money from begging, the woman kicked her out. She tried to find her family, though she had very little information about them to assist her search. Nevertheless, eventually they were reunited. While the chances of finding someone lost in that tsunami are remote, families may still hold out hope that they will see their loved one again.

Even people who have the power to inform those close to them that they're still alive sometimes don't. For instance, in the Soviet–Afghan war between 1979 and 1989, 300 Soviet soldiers were reported missing in action and presumed dead. Bakhredtin Khakimov was among them; he was wounded and captured by enemy forces in 1980. But Khakimov was not dead, he was in hiding. When he recovered from his injuries, he converted to Islam. He married and had children. He loved Afghanistan as his adopted home. He was eventually discovered in 2013 by an NGO searching for the missing soldiers.

Perhaps in part because of these exceptional cases, the close association between mass disappearance and death doesn't necessarily make it easier for loved ones. The stories we tell (or don't tell) about those who are missing say a lot about us, our values, our politics. The missing person is empty yet fertile space upon which to project stories and ideologies.

❖

In Argentina, those close to *los desaparecidos* – some 30 000 political dissidents who vanished and were killed or captured during the military dictatorship of the 1970s and 1980s – experienced intergenerational trauma. The state tortured and murdered dissidents. But the suffering didn't stop there. It was near-impossible for immediate family members to recover from their personal loss because their accusations against the government were so horrendous that they weren't always believed. The government claimed it was innocent. People who attempted to investigate what happened to the missing were themselves threatened by the state. Because authorities denied *los desaparecidos* and punished those who publicly acknowledged them, they restricted friends' and families' access to grieving. The absence of physical bodies disrupted traditional Argentinian funeral rites, in which the dead are buried as soon as possible after death. It also disrupted the grieving process because there was no certainty that each death had truly taken place, no sense of finality. Witnesses to kidnappings were especially affected, fearing their government and thrown into confusion by the state's denial of any involvement in the horrors they had seen. There were few avenues even to talk about these things. The families of the missing persons were alienated by mainstream society; their loss couldn't be acknowledged.

The families who took in the orphans of *los desaparecidos* had trouble explaining why the parents weren't around. The pressure to be silent and the fear of causing further pain meant that many children were lied to. Often they were told that their parents had abandoned them. Some psychologists advised families to tell the children that their parents had simply died of an ordinary cause such as a car accident – again, the need to lie was fuelled by the force of government rhetoric. Strangely, the children were aware of *los desaparecidos* as a phenomenon through banter with friends and by paying attention to pop culture. Some children of *los desaparecidos* even knew the true reason for their parents' absence, but themselves felt pressured to keep the 'family secret'.

The lingering pain carries through to people who do not remember the initial disappearance. Multiple generations deal with the aftermath of the absence of someone important; multiple generations are forced to suffer politicised distinctions between truth and fiction, real and not real; multiple generations have no safe, supportive space in which to digest their trauma; and multiple generations are raised by those whose lives and outlooks have been formed by these festering issues. Moreover, when the Argentine dictatorship removed the dissidents, they were also removing important political thinkers – the social impact of their loss is immeasurable.

In the absence of 30 000 people, the official narrative was to pretend it never happened. It wasn't until 2004, more than 30 years after the disappearances began, that the Argentine government acknowledged this 'dirty war' and announced that the children of *los desaparecidos* would be entitled to compensation. Still, there are ongoing issues. While the disappearances, torture, and murder of left-wing dissidents have been widely publicly recognised, an unknown number of right-wing dissidents also suffered the same fate, something that has not been recognised as readily. A human-rights group comprising older women whose children were among *los desaparecidos*, Asociación Civil Abuelas de Plaza de Mayo (the Grandmothers of the Plaza de Mayo) are still looking for the children of the disappeared – their grandchildren.

While many of the children of *los desaparecidos* were left behind, others were born while their parents were in captivity and many were put up for adoption illegally. These children are now in their thirties and may have no idea that they were adopted, or that their biological grandmothers are looking for them. The members of the group buy each other clothes, intended for their grandchildren to wear when they finally find them. They have not lost hope. The organisation has tracked down over 100 missing grandchildren so far.

On top of these lingering ambiguities, many of the torturers in the dirty war are still walking around Argentina. An episode of ABC radio program *Earshot* features the story of a survivor of state-sanctioned kidnapping. She saw her torturer – who did not recognise her as his victim – one day in public. He met her eyes and spoke to her – he gave her a lacklustre pick-up line. The survivor recounts, 'I started screaming because he has no right to talk to me. My daughter had to grab me by the arm because I couldn't stand up.' As well as the possibility of seeing their torturers, for many victims the fear persists that they could be kidnapped by the state again, at some point in the hazy future.

In other cases, the mass missing are exploited as a political symbol, which in turn can shape the experience of loss for immediate family members. Anthropologist Paul Sant Cassia investigated the lingering effects of the mass disappearance of people in Cyprus between 1963 and 1974 during ongoing hostilities, including the Greek military coup and the subsequent Turkish invasion. Over 2000 Cypriots – Greek and Turkish – went missing in those years. Few bodies have been recovered.

This mass disappearance – even decades after the conflicts took place – continues to be a symbol of trauma and of the political differences between the two groups. In the years since 1974, Turkish Cypriots have been encouraged by their political leaders to view their missing as dead. The situation is thought of as irreparable and unchangeable, an analogy for the broken relationship between Turkish and Greek Cypriots. For Turkish Cypriots, those missing are presumed dead, their deaths evidence that their people cannot live peacefully with Greek Cypriots and therefore need their own state. Greek Cypriots, who favour a single-state Cyprus, have been encouraged to view their missing as missing, maintaining hope that those unaccounted for may still be alive somewhere. Unlike the Turkish Cypriots, says Sant Cassia, 'the Greek Cypriots wish to maintain the issue as open in a present continuous tense, as an issue that is very much alive'. The groups grieve for their missing in different – but political – ways.

The Turkish Cypriots memorialise those missing in the same way they acknowledge the sacrifice of those they know died during the conflict; memorial statues conflate the two groups. Cassia argues that missing Turkish Cypriots were turned into 'ancestors' – the glorious dead and national heroes of long past – so swiftly that immediate family members didn't have sufficient opportunity to digest their personal loss. 'Relatives were left with very little space and few socially approved roles for private and familial mourning,' he says. This became strikingly clear to Sant Cassia during an interview he had with a Turkish Cypriot family about their missing relative, who was a young newlywed when he was abducted, his daughter conceived only days earlier. That daughter, who as an adult was in charge of translating her family's interview with Sant Cassia, learned of this history for the first time during that interview. She had never known he was missing; the topic had been off-limits. 'There had been little collective working through,' Sant Cassia writes. 'It had just been shrouded over.' It was not acceptable to discuss the personal impact of what had happened within the family because it had already been shaped as a remote event that stood for the necessity of a separate Turkish state in northern Cyprus. It was nothing personal. Yet the young woman was so affected by this news that she had to leave the room.

Because the disappearances aren't talked about, the grief has no end, and the immense level of personal loss from the missing is unacknowledged. The individuals stand instead for lofty principles: martyrdom, and the need for political self-determination among Turkish Cypriots. The individual losses are subsumed by big-picture politics.

The mourning patterns of Greek Cypriots were different, Sant Cassia observed. There were few memorials to the missing, because it is strange to memorialise people who may still be alive. In fact, Sant Cassia knows only of one memorial, and it plays on the concept of ambiguous loss, recognising the potential for return. It's the outline of a silhouette that the viewer can stand in and see through, more an emotional piece of art than an icon of sacrifice in the style of a war memorial. Sant Cassia argues that the lack of closure represented by this model of grief is politically expedient – Greek Cypriot leaders want to restore Cyprus to a time before the conflict, and likewise restore the missing to where they were before the conflict. 'Greek Cypriots thus face a more existential and hopeless trauma,' Sant Cassia says. 'They need to change their losses into a means of redemption.'

❖

In a similar vein, in 2015 social scientist Kirsten Juhl traced how the 30 000 people who went missing between 1992 and 1995 as a result of the Bosnian war were heavily politicised. The losses were personal ones as well, but Juhl explains their enormous, and ongoing, political implications. In part, the fact that locating missing persons is considered government business in present-day Bosnia and Herzegovina is a good thing. It shows a commitment by the government to the families' right to know what happened to their loved ones. Yet the issue of missing persons has also been used to promote particular political agendas and spur ethnic tensions within the region.

Immediately after the war, three different groups were formed to recover the missing persons of the three different ethnicities named in the country's constitution. One organisation was formed for Islamic Bosniaks, one for Orthodox Christian Bosnian Serbs, and one for Catholic Bosnian Croats. This was despite members of other ethnic groups in the country, for instance the Bosnian Roma, having also gone missing. Later, there was a move to merge the organisations as part of the International Commission on Missing Persons, which was established in 1996.

But despite this eventual unity, Juhl argues that one political faction of Bosnian Serbs makes use of rhetoric 'to fuel interethnic suspicion and distrust, and promote its own political agenda' (noting, of course, that this faction does not represent the views or interests of all Bosnian Serbs). This faction has undermined the work of the International Commission on Missing Persons, claiming that the Serbian missing have been neglected in search efforts and unfairly treated. The work of creating mistrust in the Commission, Juhl argues, is part of a wider campaign to establish political dominance through fear and rage. There is no evidence that any of the allegations against the Commission have merit, but the strong emotions involved in ambiguous loss and ethnic tensions make this an easy site for politicians to manipulate.

❖

The ease with which missing persons as a group are manipulated is partly due to their lack of voice. When someone is absent, those left behind may speak for them. This could be seen in the wake of the 11 September 2001 terrorist attacks on the US, particularly those attacks on New York City's World Trade Center. As at 2002, there were 105 people classified as missing as a result of these attacks and a further 1616 death certificates were issued by authorities – at the request of families – for people assumed dead but whose bodies have never been found. Political scientist Jenny Edkins writes in her book *Missing: Persons and Politics* that in the years following the attack, it became clearer that the remains of those missing would never be found. 'The missing would disappear. The cloud of dust that hung over Manhattan for some days would be all that lingered of many of the dead.'

The missing-persons posters that were stuck to walls and handed out across Manhattan acted as a way for family members to assert the existence of their loved ones – that they were real, that they were individuals who desperately needed to be found. But ultimately this quest to put faces to the missing was ill-fated. Official ceremonies read the names of those lost and killed in the attack, at once both acknowledging human suffering and, according to Edkins, glossing over 'differences of political view, religious affiliation, or role'. The diversity of the victims, and indeed of the entire nation, was erased by governments looking for an excuse for vengeance. Despite many families of the missing claiming, 'Our grief is not a cry for war', wars were waged in the names of the silent missing. The Afghanistan and Iraq wars were highly controversial but possible partially because the missing provided a strong symbol that was less about who they were as individuals and more about the harm done to the United States of America, an all-encompassing, simplified narrative of victimhood.

Other incidents illustrate the way in which politics informs a response – humanitarian or otherwise – to missing persons around the world. Until very recently, the largest cause of mass displacement of people was World War II. According to historian Ruth Balint, an estimated 20 million people were displaced by the war. And, she argues, the ways in which people were searched for were informed by the political and moral agendas of governments and tracing services.

At the time, it was unprecedented that so many of the displaced were civilians. But the civilian toll reflected the nature of the conflict – it was ordinary people who were pursued in targeted killings. The Nazis targeted Jewish people and other ethnic groups, people with disabilities, homosexuals, communists, dissidents, and anyone they considered undesirable or getting in the way of realising Hitler's deranged vision. Ordinary people were removed from their homes by force; others had to flee their country to escape persecution. Family members became lost to each other. Putting the world back together from the rubble of war was challenging. Although there are many stories of happy reunions, many others were lost forever.

Separated families posed an urgent challenge. 'To many contemporary observers of 1945,' explains Balint, 'the destruction of the family was the most visible and devastating consequence of war. Its reunion was often promoted as humanity's only possible salvation.' Consequently, in those years after the war the mantra of the Red Cross Tracing Service became 'to reunite the dispersed family'.

About 170 000 displaced persons, mainly men who had been in displaced persons camps, came to Australia between 1947 and 1952. Some of these men had families in Europe whom they intended to bring out as soon as they could. But others met someone new and deserted their wives and fiancées in Europe and committed to a new marriage. As Balint writes:

> The tracing files are littered with examples of migrant men sought by former wives and partners, often mothers of their children, who were discovered to be in new marriages without having yet annulled or broken off their former commitments.

In studying the tracing files, Balint gets the strong sense that some people came to Australia after the war specifically to disappear.

However, alongside reuniting families, Australia had another goal: assimilation. It was important to keep new families together and for them to thrive in their new country at a time when the government's catchcry was 'populate or perish'. And so, when the Red Cross Tracing Service found a remarried man that a woman in Europe was looking for, they would tell her there was no sign of him. The consequence of this decision was that those left behind lived with the ambiguity of not knowing what had happened to their loved ones. For those deserted women in Europe, information about their missing loved one was heavily mediated by political considerations. Again, while this ambiguity would be painful for individuals, the policy was nothing personal.

❖

In France, I'm confronted by some ghosts of the mass missing, but I also find some hope. I don't think you have to be close to people to care about them. In between war memorials, I visit Victoria School, a primary school in Villers-Bretonneux named after the Australian state. In 1918, Villers-Bretonneux was saved from German occupation by Australian soldiers, most of them from Victoria. But while the village was safe, it was still scarred. The school had been destroyed. And so, when school children in Victoria heard what had happened, they collected pennies to donate to the rebuilding efforts.

The school is on Rue de Melbourne. In the playground there is an enormous sign, in English: 'Never Forget Australia'. This message is replicated in every classroom and in the main hall. There are also murals, which look as though they've been painted by students, full of koalas and kangaroos.

In February 2009, 90 years after the war, one of the worst bushfires in history broke out in multiple places across Victoria. One hundred and seventy-three people were killed on Black Saturday, most of them in their own homes. Many of these people had been declared missing and remained so for a month, which was the time it took for the forensic analysis of the remains to be completed. The impact was devastating. The Victoria School hadn't forgotten 1918 or the Australians. They too sent money to help rebuild affected areas.

These two populations – one threatened by war, the other by fire – are geographically remote. We are strangers. And yet it's still possible for us to forge a connection based on the events of a previous century. It's still possible to care. We offer what we can, not because we know each person affected but because we know that they are all human beings. This is surely reason enough for tracing the mass disappeared: people matter.

I think we sometimes forget this, and forget those who are absent. The scenarios of mass missing I have described are a bare fraction of the mass disappearances that have occurred in the world. I feel some discomfort leaving it here, when there are so many more examples: the contemporary, politically charged disappearances of people in North Korea and Sri Lanka, and of the Rohingya people in Myanmar, and the mass murders in Mexico. In the 20th century, there were the thousands of missing 'undesirables' in the former Soviet Union, the forced disappearances during the Spanish Civil War under Franco, the people who went missing during the Algerian civil war in the 1990s, and the multitude of disappearances in Mao's China, and many more. There are unending natural disasters across the world, and hundreds of kidnapped schoolgirls in Nigeria. And this list is pitifully incomplete. The identities of all these many missing have, in their different ways, been subsumed by narratives about politics, justice, and ideology. We are still doing it now. Everyone is still implicated.

8

I DON'T HAVE TO LIMIT MY LOVE

LOOKING FOR MISSING REFUGEES IN EUROPE

Mina Jaf was born a refugee. I meet her in Copenhagen, a long way from where she started life. She tells me about her birth in 1988 in the middle of a chemical gas attack ordered by Saddam Hussein's government on her village in Iraqi Kurdistan.

'From then to when I was 11, we moved back and from and between cities in Iran and Iraq to settle and start our life,' she says. She was displaced. Mina and her family lived in different refugee camps before coming to Europe. Then she lived in an asylum centre for a short time in Germany, and then another asylum centre in Denmark for four years. After her time in limbo, she was finally granted refugee status. The Danish government recognised the danger and instability her family had fled and Mina was finally allowed to settle in one place.

Being displaced means being forced to leave home. It's different from being missing, but the chaotic conditions of displacement can mean that loved ones get lost or separated from each other. If you don't know a loved one's whereabouts, they are missing. For Mina – and for the refugees she has worked with – the conditions of being displaced and of being missing have been woven together.

Mina has spent her adult life working with and advocating for refugees in Europe. She previously worked in Belgium, coordinating volunteers who visit reception centres for asylum seekers – places for people who have come to a new country fleeing violence or persecution but have not yet been assessed by authorities. Asylum seekers have some rights and access to some resources through government and non-government organisations, but these rights and resources vary depending on the country, and the particular centre. It's not until an asylum seeker is recognised as a refugee that their right to live in their new country is guaranteed. This process can take years. Mina has lobbied for better conditions for asylum seekers and offered them legal support from the time they arrive. She has visited many asylum centres and camps across Europe. Now she's set up her own non-government organisation, Women Refugee Route.

The UNHCR reported that as of 2019, a total of 70.8 million people have been displaced at some point in their lives by ongoing persecution and conflict. While most displaced people stay within their country's borders, almost 30 million displaced people are refugees and asylum seekers. The rate of displacement steadily rose over the 1990s, but recent increases have been far more dramatic as a result of long-term conflicts in Somalia and Afghanistan; ongoing insecurity in Syria, South Sudan, Yemen, Burundi, Ukraine, and the Central African Republic; gang violence in Central America; and the persecution of the Rohingya people in Myanmar. And resettlement takes a long time – the newly displaced join an already large crowd of people waiting for a stable home. Between 2015 and 2019, the European Commission identified a 'migration crisis'.

In 2015 alone, over one million refugees arrived in Europe, which is over three times the number who arrived the year before. While the numbers of new arrivals appear to be trending downwards, many issues remain with migration policies in Europe.

'Part of being a refugee is you're always missing something,' Mina tells me. We meet at a café that has a balcony directly over a rectangular lake. The August day has been windy and bleak, and the sky threatens summer rain. For now though, we are insulated in glass, and as we talk we watch the swans pass by below.

'Even though the conditions of the place we were in were really bad and we needed to immediately leave that place, as a child, you don't understand why you should leave it,' Mina says. 'You have friends, neighbours, the supermarket and all those things which are nearby … It's really difficult for a nine-year-old, eight-year-old, or six-year-old girl to understand that you have to start again. You have to leave all your cousins, all your friends. And you know you'll never meet them again.'

The flux of movement over the years has meant constantly embarking on uncertainty in the pursuit of safety. It means losing track of people and sometimes eventually hearing bad news about them.

'I had this very good friend in one of the camps,' says Mina. The two of them spent long afternoons playing together, but they ultimately had to part ways. Later, Mina found out that his application for refugee status in Europe had been refused. He was sent back to Iran along with his mother. 'Later on, when I'd been researching – because I remembered their names – I found out they had been killed in Iran.' Mina pauses. 'For this reason, you grow very fast, you understand very fast that people in your life will not stay all the time. And that you will not stay here forever.'

Mina is a year older than I am, 27 when we meet. This seems young to have accepted the transience of life. I am at the limit of what I can imagine now, so I say something feeble. 'That must have been dreadful.'

'I was very shocked,' she replies. 'I didn't know what I thought about it. It was just a very emotional time … You don't know what you feel, you don't know what to think. You do not have the atlas or road map, you can't describe it even to yourself.'

But this experience that is so painful that it evades language – even the private language of thought – is not an isolated one. In her work with asylum seekers, Mina has heard lots of stories about loved ones losing each other. One story in particular, told to her by a woman in a refugee camp in Greece, has stuck with her.

'I was helping this mother with some translation and that sort of thing. And she had four kids, but she was really, really sad. Because I got close to her, I could listen to her stories. You can have a really trustful conversation.' Mina found out that the woman actually had five children. The eldest had disappeared in the chaos of crowds in a street in Istanbul. She has never seen him again. She doesn't know if he is safe, or alive.

'I carry all these stories of so many women,' says Mina. 'So many people around me don't know where their kids are, whether they're alive or not.'

A large proportion of missing children in Europe are unaccompanied minors who have fled dangerous situations across the world. They may have fled their home country without their parents, or they may have been separated from their parents, or their parents may have been killed during the dangerous journey to somewhere safe. Indeed, in a single week in May 2016, the UNHCR believes that at least 880 migrants died trying to get to Europe by crossing the Mediterranean Sea on unsafe boats. Unaccompanied minors are considered missing if they escape or are taken from the camp or centre where they've been placed until their refugee status is determined. Europol, Europe's criminal intelligence agency, reported in 2016 that there were at least 10 000 unaccompanied migrant children missing in Europe. But Missing Children Europe has said that this figure is likely an underestimation of the scope of the problem because some children go missing before they're officially registered as asylum seekers. Some of the national figures are striking. The EU agency for Fundamental Rights, in its February 2016 report, states:

> In February 2016, [unaccompanied] migrant children disappeared at an estimated rate of 90–95 per cent from Hungary, after spending one to three days in reception institutions. In Slovenia, about 80 per cent of children have gone missing. In Sweden, about 7–10 children are reported missing each week. In Austria, 100 children have gone missing from a single reception centre.

Unaccompanied children go missing for a range of reasons. A lot of these have to do with the precarious nature of seeking asylum in Europe and the additional vulnerability of children. The staggering figures from Hungary have been attributed to delays in assigning guardians to unaccompanied minors as well as inadequate care facilities. They may also be artificially inflated by the wider trend of asylum seekers choosing to move beyond Hungary to wealthier, neighbouring countries. Although Mina was not an unaccompanied minor herself – she was always with her mother and siblings – she tells me how difficult the experience was and how precarious it would be for children without guidance. When Mina's family first came to Europe they took shelter in Germany for a short time. There, her family had to share a bedroom with ten other families, including men. They felt unsafe.

Conditions for refugees vary across the world, and even throughout Europe. There are places where people live in tents and converted warehouses, while others sleep on the floor for months at a time; some places are overcrowded and basic services – water and medical care, for instance – aren't guaranteed. There are places that detain refugees, such as Greece. As an Australian, the conditions experienced by refugees directly implicates me. Successive Australian governments have indefinitely detained asylum seekers who have arrived in Australia by boat, sending them to camps in Nauru and on Papua New Guinea's Manus Island. By world standards, Europe is a relatively good place to be a refugee; far more unsafe and inhumane conditions are experienced elsewhere.

The Danish asylum centre Mina's family lived in for four years was relatively good. The family had their own space, but they were still in cramped quarters with other people. Her whole family had one room to themselves, and next door would be another single room with another family. They shared a kitchen with people from all over the world. While Mina benefitted from learning about different cultures, it could be tense.

'Sometimes it is really complicated to communicate with the others if you don't have the language skills and you all come from a war zone. Like, you don't have the patience to have a discussion or to have a dialogue. There were a lot of fights.'

Mina and her siblings could go to school, but this came with its own set of problems as they tried to integrate into Danish society. Mina had barely attended school during her years of moving backwards and forwards across camps in the Middle East.

'I had this fantasy of going to a library every day,' she says of that time. 'Just to have a library, not have a teacher to teach you things, but just to have the choice to go to the library and choose the books you'd like to read.' When she started going to school again, having missed six years of education between second and eighth grade, she felt behind. 'It's just weird ... I had this moment once, when I was like, "Why do people think that I have to do as well as the students I'm with?" It was really complicated for me to start school in such a way.'

The last time she had been in an educational setting she had been learning the alphabet and playing. 'And then I started school where you have to write, and analyse novels and dramas. Like, I really didn't understand what that meant. And there was nobody around to explain it to you.' Different integration programs have become available in the years since Mina was at school, and the UNHCR reports that many nations have managed to improve access to and the quality of education for refugee children. Even so, the experience of being confused and disengaged could contribute to unaccompanied minors wanting to run away.

Mina has made up for lost time – she now knows seven languages and has spoken as an expert on refugee issues at the United Nations in New York – but she spent years bouncing between the stress of school and the stress of the asylum centre. In the four years between applying for refugee status and actually receiving it, it was hard to cultivate a life.

'In waiting you cannot create any hopes or dreams. It's like they hold you from the society.' The conditions got 'too cosy' in the asylum centre sometimes, as Mina puts it. It was hard to get away from it outside of school hours. Her family lived an hour's walk away from central Copenhagen, and they couldn't take the bus because they didn't have much money and Copenhagen has a very high cost of living. Plus, without a father around, Mina's mother was worried about the dangers of leaving the centre. 'She was always afraid to let us go out because people could take advantage of us.'

It's difficult to ascertain the rates in which refugees suffer violence because, according to the European Union Agency for Fundamental Rights, 'victims rarely report their attacks'. Even if they always did, no member state of the EU collects data on the number of reports of violence towards women refugees. But the Agency points to the types of conditions refugees are often subjected to that make violence far more likely, like bathrooms and showers that are shared among people of all sexes, a lack of locks on doors, and poorly lit corridors. Victims of violence under these circumstances are often afraid to speak up because they fear that the perpetrator may seek revenge or that making a complaint will affect their application for asylum. Wanting to escape some of these settings seems understandable.

Mina grew up among these stories. Throughout her childhood, she knew her mother to be a trusted confidant of many of her fellow asylum seekers. Long into the night they would talk about their experiences of violence – Mina's mother herself experienced it at the hands of her ex-husband – and Mina would listen in, pretending to be asleep. 'Some of them faced violence from the smugglers, all the way to Europe. There were all kinds of violence but nobody was able to talk about it to authorities because they were afraid of what would happen to their case … I always listened in when they cried. They had really hard feelings and you could see and hear them break down as you fell to sleep.'

These stories were everywhere, but always lingering under the surface. They were saved for the cover of night and the folds of friendship. 'I have been aware of it since I remember myself,' Mina says. These stories never really stopped for Mina. Travelling to asylum centres and camps across Europe, she hears so many accounts of women being raped, of women being abused by family members or other members of their community. It's just not spoken about publicly.

'Did you think that that sort of thing was normal?' I ask. For violence to be so pervasive but unremarked upon must surely damage your expectations of other people. But Mina seems alarmed by my question. Her eyes widen.

'I think this was not normal!' she says. 'Because I also come from a family with a mum who has given me a lot of love and I think that's normal.'

Mina thinks it's unsurprising that young people in these conditions would want to escape, especially if they aren't being protected by their parents. Additionally, as with other asylum seekers, many unaccompanied migrants fear that their application to live in Europe will be rejected and they'll be sent back to the country they fled from. Some children deal with these fears by never applying for asylum through the proper channels or by evading officials.

Moreover, according to Missing Children Europe, some children who have grown up in the midst of conflict may not know *how* to act in a relatively peaceful society; they may not trust authorities because they've only seen power wielded violently; they may face ongoing psychological issues such as PTSD, depression, anxiety, and aggression. These stressors can also factor into their decision to leave official centres and camps.

It's crucial, however, not to assume that all missing unaccompanied minors left their camp or centre of their own volition. Child refugees who aren't adequately protected are vulnerable to trafficking and exploitation – that is, criminals coercing, deceiving, or forcing them into harmful situations. Forced labour, sexual exploitation, slavery, and even organ harvesting are all possibilities. Europol warns that crime syndicates that force children into slavery and sexual exploitation have been specifically targeting unaccompanied refugee minors. Mina herself has seen people lingering around camps grooming young girls and convincing them to leave.

'It is so unbelievable, you don't want to believe that. But you see it in front of you, people from outside coming, taking girls, and telling you, "I'm going to offer her a shower."' Some camps lack clean, quality, easily accessible facilities. 'But they never come back,' says Mina. 'And you see it right in front of you.'

Mina sighs and looks around her. She's sick today with a cold and says her head feels foggy. But she continues. 'I mean, you shouldn't get surprised because you have seen it. But of course, they are sensitive cases. There are so many cases like this that don't get talked about because it's taboo to talk about it.'

A child may also go missing because of financial and family pressures, which are exacerbated by naivety and a lack of education. Missing Children Europe reports on the case of a 15-year-old boy in Italy who had travelled from Eritrea. Upon arrival, he didn't want to live in a reception centre and access school and the other resources he was entitled to. Rather, he wanted to make money so that he could send it home to his family. Luckily, there were staff at the centre who were able to convince him to stay in school and learn the local language. At age 20, he was employed in linguistic mediation. He told workers at the centre that they were right, and that as a 15-year-old he didn't understand what skills he would need to thrive in his new environment, nor did he have the temperament to want to stay in school.

Missing Children Europe also details a case of an 11-year-old boy who was taken into a refugee shelter by police in Greece after being separated from his mother. Within a month he had disappeared. In the course of an investigation, it became apparent that the boy had turned to a human smuggling ring to try to reach his mother, who was bound for the UK. Unlike trafficking, smuggling is consensual – the person being smuggled wants to be taken elsewhere and they make an arrangement (such as payment) with the smuggler to that end. But being smuggled can still be very dangerous. Sometimes people face abuse, threats, violence, and torture at the hands of smugglers. Sometimes they are murdered. Because of the dangers of smuggling, a case manager for a Greek NGO, The Smile of the Child, attempted to find the boy through a publicity campaign. He was soon identified by police at a roadblock on a smuggling route, 'inside a truck headed for the UK squeezed between cargo crates'. He was provided with temporary accommodation in Greece, but days later he escaped into the hands of smugglers again. Although the boy was eventually successful in reuniting with his mother in the UK, it was an unnecessarily precarious journey.

Without guidance, the expectations of children newly arrived in Europe – and their families – may be unrealistic and lead to risky plans. In another case, a 13-year-old boy who arrived in Italy had plans to travel to Germany, where his uncle was living. Reception-centre staff were able to convince the boy to stay. But then the boy spoke to his father at home. The father told the boy he couldn't stay in Italy. The father had his own plans to come to Europe and did not want to live there. Instead, he wanted to live in the UK. The child decided to follow his father's directions to meet up with his uncle in Germany and then they would proceed together to the UK.

The Missing Children Europe report asks, 'Did the father know what the child would have to go through on his way to Germany? Was he aware of the conditions in which children live in Calais?' Although the camp at Calais – the departure point for the journey across the Channel from France to the UK – has since been bulldozed, at the time it was referred to as 'The Jungle' because of its density and makeshift living conditions. Many asylum seekers have met their deaths attempting to stow away on trucks and trains bound for England. The Missing Children report continues, 'Was the father reunited with the child that he forced into this trip?' They don't know.

Looking out over the cold, clean city of Copenhagen and the tourists out on the lake pedalling swan-shaped boats, I notice the unusual clarity of the water. It's hard to reconcile that so much hardship is being experienced at this very moment. The UNHCR says that one person is forcibly displaced in the world every two seconds, and their problems rarely end there. 'It's like you have to keep telling yourself this is real because it just doesn't seem like the sort of thing that you want to accept,' I say.

'Yes. It's true. You don't want to accept it,' says Mina. This is a problem for her, she explains. She is always surprised – even though she's been working in this sector for years – by the extent of the issues asylum seekers face in Europe. She can't get used to these realities. She keeps being surprised, even though each new, sad fact accords with everything she already knows. 'You don't want to accept any of the things going on right now because it's too hard.'

Despite the emotional difficulty, Mina does stare cruel realities in the face on a day-to-day basis. She wants to address the unsafe conditions. 'It happened to me and I cannot just be eyes [when I] see things happening ... I have to raise my voice. I have to raise my voice for the ones who can't. I have a voice and I think it's a form of violence against human beings to not use it.'

There's an urgency to Mina's words, and my heart starts beating a little faster. I think of hummingbirds and moral responsibility. Mina is relentless. In 2016, for speaking out on this issue, the Women's Refugee Commission awarded her a prestigious Voices of Courage Award. The award acknowledges refugees who are working to solve the ongoing problems that other refugees face. Other winners have included Nobel laureates Malala Yousafzai and Leymah Gbowee.

For Mina, it's necessary to provide spaces where refugees can speak and be listened to. 'I think it's really important to ask them what they need ... Just to ask them, I think, will be enough.' The idea behind Mina's NGO is to train volunteers to go to refugee camps and centres and give women in those places the information they need in their own language in a safe environment.

'It would be female-to-female because most of the time, the women feel more comfortable with having a conversation with another woman. They can get the right information about the asylum procedure, what rights they have, and how they can access services in case they've been facing sexual violence or abuse.' Mina laughs. 'It's very basic!' I smile at this, but it occurs to me that even basic things can be peculiarly difficult to put in place. Every single thing is fought for.

Mina has seen NGO staff come into refugee centres and drop information in one big, monolingual lecture. It doesn't work – partly because the information isn't tailored to the diverse needs of the audience, and partly because those most in need of help wouldn't be able to ask for it in this sort of setting.

'I don't think it's a way to give information,' says Mina, 'because then you have a lot of men who are coming to this, and the women tend to want to hide themselves.'

Ultimately though, Mina wants displaced women not to be seen as passive recipients of this support, but for them to advocate for their own rights as refugees and as women. She wants them to be included in decision-making processes, and for humanitarian workers to listen to the issues they identify from their lived experience.

It's happened throughout history: innocent people get caught up in sweeping conflicts and turmoil. As in the past, it's still a struggle to see beyond the political symbolism that has become attached to each group, and instead to see each asylum seeker as an individual. Basic things – like asking people what they need, what could make their situation better and safer, what could be done to connect them with existing services and resources, letting them know what their rights are – aren't so basic if groups of people are fundamentally seen as a set of abstract ideas. To reduce disappearances, establishing better support for asylum seekers is a good first goal.

It's impossible to generalise the various practices and attitudes across Europe when it comes to unaccompanied minors and refugees – it's a diverse continent. While there are government agencies and NGOs that support those seeking asylum across Europe, the extent of concern about unaccompanied minors varies. A social worker at an asylum-seeker reception centre in the UK told Missing Children Europe, 'The problem with a lot of cases of unaccompanied minors going missing is it's just not always prioritised as it would be if it was a child from our country, unfortunately.' Missing refugees may be neglected, invisible. At other times, the situation is less dire and unaccompanied minors are offered meaningful support.

A group of researchers at the UNHCR undertook an analysis of media reports from Spain, Italy, Germany, the UK, and Sweden about refugees during 2014. The results varied wildly. For instance, the German and Swedish press preferred to use the legitimating terms 'refugees' and 'asylum seekers', recognising that many came to Europe to protect themselves from imminent danger. Other countries tended to use the more general terms 'migrant' and 'immigrant', erasing the fact that these journeys are propelled by a need for protection. The Italian and Swedish media focused more on human rights and humanitarian obligations than media in the other countries, reminding readers that it's the duty of peaceful states to give refuge to those who need it. The UK press presented the most fearful language and anti-refugee views of all the countries by far:

> Despite the presence of newspapers such as *The Guardian* and *Daily Mirror*, both of which were sympathetic to refugees, the right-wing press in the United Kingdom expressed a hostility towards refugees and migrants which was unique. Whilst newspapers in all countries featured anti-refugee and anti-migrant perspectives, what distinguished the right-of-centre press in the UK was the degree to which they campaigned aggressively against refugees and migrants.

I noticed myself, particularly in the lead-up to the 2016 Brexit referendum – politicians and media commentators talked of their fear of refugees, of being *inundated* and *flooded* with a crisis. The water metaphors the UK press used to talk about people made me uneasy. It felt as though the mass displaced – and the mass disappeared among them – were measured volumetrically, purely by how much space they would take up rather than who they actually were. There were few discernible faces, few individual names. In such a context, it's easy to forget what the many missing refugees have to confront, and to ignore that their risk of harm is an urgent, moral reality.

'It's a really easy weapon to use on your own society,' says Mina. 'To make them afraid, to handle it the way they are handling it.'

Mina is quick to point out, though, that many politicians across Europe do want to take responsibility for the fate of refugees and do want to solve problems. She thinks many are genuinely concerned about the prevalence of missing unaccompanied minors and want to make conditions for asylum seekers better across the board. But sometimes, the problems require individual attention more than wide-reaching policies.

'Most of the action is taken on the ground,' argues Mina. 'There's a lot of fancy events and conferences going around about refugees and all these things, but they don't have any effects on the ground.'

She thinks that the people who change things are the people who are best equipped to see refugees as individuals. They are the non-profit workers, case managers, social workers, and volunteers. They are people who would notice if a child went missing. 'These are the ones you see making progress for the conditions of these people.'

Still, it's not fate or an accident that those seeking refuge face these difficulties. It's politics. It's what happens when vulnerable people are represented as threats. The circumstances they've escaped from and the dangers that linger going forward are too often set aside.

❖

Problems of insecurity, invisibility, and ambiguity are all part of the experience of seeking asylum. I wonder what kind of effect this has on someone who has been through it and then has to think about it as part of their work every day.

'When you've gone into so many new situations and you know you might not be there for very long, do you try not to get too close to new people?' I ask.

'I always get too close,' says Mina. 'You know how there are some bad people you meet in your life? They shouldn't let you doubt the other people who are out there. It's the same here. Because my experience has been losing so many people, it does not mean I have to limit my love. It's part of my personality to be close to people who I may only meet for one hour. Because maybe I can give them something that can stay with them their whole life. And what they can give me for this limited time, it'll maybe make me a different person too.'

'Yes,' I respond, 'but, you're opening yourself up to that risk that something bad will happen to that person, or you'll be sad, or you might not know what ends up happening to them. And I guess that's a very brave thing.' Perhaps Mina is naturally in tune with impermanence not having to mean pointlessness or powerlessness. Every interaction *can* have a point, and *can* be powerful. It still feels like a big, difficult concept though: to be okay with getting too close to someone who may soon be lost to you.

'I cannot be here forever, so why would the people around me be here forever? If you realise that you will not be here forever, it'll be much easier. I have this view that I should smile into the day I'm here and I should smile at the people around me right now. It's also important that we don't think, "What will happen?"' Mina adds. 'When it has happened, then you can be emotional about it. And it's good to be emotional because it helps you to stand up again.'

Mina lives with the fearlessness of a survivor. When she was young her mother told her, 'You cannot fear anything because what you fear has already happened to you.' Mina can embark on the future knowing she'll be able to keep going because she's already done it.

And so, even though it's painful, or frustratingly ambiguous, Mina continues to search for loved ones to try to find what has happened to them. 'I want to always know. I always want to know, to understand. But … you meet new people all the time and you live with the thought, "Okay, you don't find them when you did research. They may come one day in your life."'

When we end the interview, Mina offers me some suggestions for things to do in Copenhagen. She tells me to see the Royal Library, a building known as the 'Black Diamond' that lives up to its name and casts a grand shadow on the crystalline harbour. It's brimming with books. It's the kind of place Mina would have fantasised about as a child. She reaches over to hug me before we walk off in opposite directions. I feel sad and worn out talking to people about the hardships of knowing someone who is missing, or who had to go missing to escape threats, violence, and abuse. Multiply those experiences by millions and this is the world today. It is overwhelming. But having the courage to get 'too close' – learning to see each asylum seeker as an individual, listening to their stories, asking them what they need, and even embracing the threat of more ambiguous loss – is Mina's way of making things better.

9

THE BIGGER PICTURE

MISSING CHILDREN EUROPE

Mina is one of many people looking to make a difference to the rate of missing persons. There are other organisations around the world that grapple with this issue directly. The challenge for all of them – and for all of us, really – is to face the inherent ambiguity of these cases without helplessly giving up. And there are paths. They are difficult to navigate, and they have an uneven terrain, but they are being carved out.

My next stop is Missing Children Europe, an organisation headquartered in Brussels that focuses on missing children across the continent. EU member states and other European countries run their own hotlines specifically for people to ring if they need help or advice regarding missing children (some also take calls about both missing children and adults). Callers may include children who are missing or thinking of running away, or adults who are concerned for a missing child or a child at risk. These various hotlines can be reached on the same phone number throughout Europe – 116 000 – and operators are tasked with responding to urgent inquiries. They may link callers with police, undertake mediation to help bring home a missing child, or otherwise offer emotional support. Missing Children Europe (MCE) operates at a remove from the hotlines, from which it gathers data. It's through this data that we get a sense of how many children go missing (MCE estimates the figure to be around 250 000 per year, or one child every two minutes) and why. MCE also contributes to research in order to help mitigate the risks of children going missing, lobbies governments to invest in solutions, and provides a point for national organisations to share knowledge.

MCE was born from Child Focus – the Belgian organisation that Griet works for – in 2001. Child Focus had been working on the case of two young girls who had gone missing. It looked suspicious. Authorities worried that the girls had been abducted and taken to a different country. They could have been anywhere in Europe. The staff at Child Focus had to call over 300 different law enforcement agencies and non-profit organisations across Europe as part of their search effort. It was so inefficient because the national systems lacked any level of integration. Staff naturally realised that there was a need for an agency that could coordinate with missing children's organisations across the EU. After all, cross-border cases are common. They accounted for about 18 per cent of missing children cases in Europe in 2015. It is so easy for a child in a tiny country like Belgium to get to any number of other countries. From Brussels, a child could get on a train and reach Amsterdam, Paris, London, or Cologne in a few hours. Today, MCE provides a point where 31 different national non-profit organisations in 26 different countries can communicate with each other, sharing resources and information.

Brussels is a major hub for a range of international organisations, including the European Union. On the walk between my accommodation and the MCE office, each door I pass has the embossed names of a charity, lobby group, or non-government organisation. They all seem to be packed into a grid of streets adjacent to the curvy European Parliament building. I imagine the offices of all these organisations are similarly functional to MCE's, which has a floor in a shared building. The office is mostly open plan with a few smaller spaces for meetings, and slender bands of natural light make their way through the venetian blinds. At MCE I meet Gail Rego, their communications officer, and Mette Drivsholm, when we speak, a project officer whose work focuses on children who have run away from home. We talk over a round table with generous glasses of water beside us.

Gail grew up in Dubai and has an Indian background. 'I knew that I wanted to work in an NGO or a social enterprise – somewhere where I'd have a positive impact,' she tells me. 'I knew that I wanted to do something good and I knew that I wanted it to be in human rights. I'm very passionate about gender equality. It's also based on where I grew up and how I was treated and where I was born – as a woman, as an immigrant, as an Indian.' She sees social issues as fundamentally connected. Missing children can be a manifestation of things like gender issues, negative views of migrants, and racism. At the same time, she thinks that helping missing children can be a way to address broader social problems too.

'Whether it was working with women or in shelters or something else – I mean, it's all the same. It is so cyclic. If you make sure that children get the love and respect and attention they deserve, they will one day grow up to become better parents. And it's a cycle that will just get more positive.'

Mette, who is originally from Denmark, is more specifically concerned with children's rights, particularly after interning with Save the Children in Denmark as part of her studies in political science, which focused on child rights and refugee education, and then working in Save the Children's EU office in Brussels.

'I draw upon my knowledge base and my passion for working for those that are vulnerable in society and who wouldn't have as strong a voice towards decision-makers if we didn't speak up for them,' she says. She's worried about children and families who go through poverty, abuse, violence, and other conflicts. 'They often don't have the means to advocate for systemic changes which would benefit them.' She sees that as her job. And whenever children go missing, it means there's still work to be done.

The good news is that MCE is making a difference. It's very hard to measure its impact because if the number of children reported missing increases, that might just be because more people are aware that the hotlines exist or more people are taking the problem seriously. But you can look at stories too. I think of Salma getting her son back to Belgium from Portugal after his father had abducted him – it's an example of the good that can be done through international liaison (even if the process is slow). At the turn of the millennium, if a child was abducted and taken to a different EU country, cross-border assistance would have been limited. MCE included a cross-border case study in their 2015 annual report to showcase the kind of quick response that international cases can now get that would have been impossible before 2001.

There were two people in Italy, parents of a small baby, who had broken up but were cooperating so both could play an active role in their child's life. They went to the supermarket. They decided that the father and baby would wait in the car while the mother went to get groceries. When she came back, the car was gone. At first, she thought she had forgotten where the car was parked, but she soon became frantic.

The father had been having some mental-health difficulties; she was not afraid that he would hurt the baby on purpose, but he didn't have the things he would need to take care of the baby, and the baby was still being breastfed.

She called the missing-children hotline in Italy. The hotline informed local police. They were able to track the car with GPS technology and found that father and baby were already in France. So, the Italian hotline called up its French partner, which connected with local police. It then seemed the car was headed to Spain, so the Italian hotline informed the hotline in Spain. Eventually, the car was spotted by a CCTV camera at a petrol station in Valencia and the Spanish authorities were able to intervene. The baby – who was well but hungry and tired – was swiftly reunited with his mother.

One of the more exciting things about working in this sector, says Mette, is that international cooperation can work really well. There's a real advantage when you're pooling together so many agencies, and you get the opportunity to share the best parts each has to offer.

'It's really gratifying when you see that the hotlines manage to learn from each other, or sometimes they go and study each other [on secondment] and take a lot away from it. We've invited different hotlines that have good practices to share what they do. In the weeks after a meeting, I've had several hotlines contact me and say, "Wow, that was so useful."'

Through opportunities such as these, good ideas can be more easily disseminated and put into practice. But there are many challenges, too, including the stress of working in the sector. When I ask Gail what she finds the most frustrating part of her job, her immediate response is: 'Where do I start?' Each problem seems to lead to another problem which, in turn, leads to yet another problem. There's a dense network of obstacles.

For one thing, progress across different nations is uneven.

Mette points to two countries that have particularly good policies – Portugal and Belgium. 'In Portugal, the hotline does great follow-up work on missing children. They have psychologists, lawyers, and social workers. And when a child has been found and reunited with their family, they have a system where the psychologist will contact the family and follow up and ask, "Are you addressing the reasons why the child ran away?" The case is not seen as resolved just because the child has returned.' This is a huge achievement: the recognition that being found isn't the end of the journey, that the missing person may still need ongoing support.

'In Belgium,' Mette continues, 'the hotline has really good cooperation with the police and the judiciary and there's not a single missing child in Belgium that doesn't get followed up.'

Part of the frustration for MCE is seeing these good policies being put in place, knowing what works, and knowing that not every organisation or government has been able to implement them. Diplomatically, neither Mette nor Gail name the countries performing poorly.

Part of the uneven response to missing children isn't just a matter of some countries being more competent than others. Although it is a global issue, it has different textures and different problems in each country. Geography plays a huge part – unaccompanied migrants, for instance, are much more common in Cyprus, because it's more easily accessible to asylum seekers arriving from places like Syria and Iraq.

'Whereas in Croatia,' explains Mette, 'they have a lot of runaways from care institutions. And in Austria they just have a lot of runaways in general.'

This leads me to an obvious question. 'I'm just curious as to why there are more runaways in somewhere like Austria or Croatia,' I say. 'Is it a cultural thing?'

'Well, we have to be careful,' says Mette. 'Just because

they're reported in Austria or in Croatia doesn't mean that it's not also a problem in Bulgaria or Hungary. And this is one of the main problems in the field of missing children: under-reporting.'

Every figure I've mentioned so far about missing persons, children and adults, is imprecise. It's always a case of 'the figure is *around* this', '*estimates* say that', and so on. Nonetheless, it's pretty easy to skip over these caveats and feel as though you know something about the sector. It's worth pausing here to say that, in fact, we know very little.

Most of MCE's data is collected from their hotlines, yet, as Gail tells me, in many countries, 'awareness of these hotlines is very, very low'. Part of Gail's job is improving awareness and it works – the number of calls to the hotlines has increased over time. But it's impossible to tell what proportion of the total is actually being reported to them. On top of that, in MCE's 2015 report, two hotline operators didn't report their figures at all – another clear cause of underestimation. This is not a problem isolated to continental Europe, or a particularly new problem. A UK parliamentary panel once noted that there's better national data on stolen cars than on missing children.

Because the extent of the phenomenon of missing children is hidden from view, we can't really determine the scope of the problem except to say that it's probably even bigger than we think. The statistics say that about a quarter of a million children go missing in Europe each year. The reality is that probably *more* than a quarter of a million children go missing each year. And this is part of the fundamental ambiguity of advocating for missing-persons issues. How do you get adequate funding to solve a problem when you don't know how big it is? How do you know the best ways to find children if you aren't sure how many are lost in the first place? How do you prevent children going missing if you don't know who is at risk?

'There is so much more work to do before we can say that we have a complete picture,' says Mette. 'Probably we'll never be able to say that.' A first step would be to get better integration of the hotlines with other parts of the child-protection and policing systems throughout the EU.

The frustration about the poor-quality data merges with frustrations regarding the attitudes people have about missing children. Gail and Mette here echo some of Charlie Hedges' observations that law-enforcement agencies tend to neglect cases when it seems there is little risk of a child getting hurt. But the problem of neglect can seep into the process earlier: some missing children are never reported to police in the first place. Runaways are often under-reported because sometimes guardians don't realise the seriousness of the situation. Going missing is seen as an act of delinquency, or even an annoying habit, something children do to free themselves from the responsibilities of curfews and school attendance. 'There's this image of children as the problem,' says Mette, 'rather than [seeing them as] the vulnerable child.'

Sometimes under-reporting is because of the burden of paperwork, especially in situations where a young person has run away from a care facility.

'Maybe staff know that the second they report it'll just be too cumbersome,' explains Mette. 'If they know the child, they're sometimes like, "Well, we actually don't think he's in danger, so we'll just hold off reporting it."' Just as Charlie pointed out that sometimes police don't take cases seriously, sometimes cases don't get reported to police at all because caretakers don't take it seriously, or they know the police won't.

Under-reporting in these instances is a problem because even if children come back as predicted, there's a failure to understand why they keep going missing and what they're trying to escape – these problems aren't going to be reflected in the numbers. And even if there aren't any compelling reasons why a young person would run away – which Mette concedes is possible – the behaviour still needs to be addressed.

'In a case of a child allegedly running away for amusement or fun, then you need to discuss boundaries with the child,' says Mette. 'This is part of the education of the child. They have to learn to respect boundaries. It's part of growing up and becoming a full-fledged citizen who has rights and responsibilities.'

As I explored with Mina, the situation is particularly worrying when it comes to cases of unaccompanied minors. 'It's really hard to know what happens to these children,' says Gail. In part, it's because the cases aren't always prioritised by authorities. 'We'll see that police will prioritise missing children who are national citizens. And many times they will say they're a priority because of a lack of resources. But you have young children – as young as six – who are by themselves and don't speak the language and they're not given the attention they deserve because they're not a citizen.'

The problem of attitudes extends to the media – another frustration. Missing children are given inconsistent coverage.

'Very often,' says Gail, 'we see that the media will only focus on a specific type of child. Anything that can create a furore or a buzz, or something that's very dramatic. And usually they tend to focus on younger children. They tend to focus on white children. They focus on that view of that angelic child who has been taken by a stranger because that's really what's going to push headlines or sell papers.'

Most missing children don't conform to that image, says Gail. They don't always make for sympathetic victims. She points out that abuse often leads to poor school performance and drug and alcohol use. 'Of course these children are not perfect angels because they're coming from homes that obviously have issues. Their family has problems within the home.'

It's been somewhat heartening to Gail that in recent years unaccompanied minors – who are of diverse nationalities and racial backgrounds – have received more media attention. However, she has concerns that turn out to be prophetic.

'You could almost say they're giving them too much attention, because people are so saturated by the amount of stories and information they can get. But three months later – or six – when the same number of children, if not more, will be coming to these shores – and drowning, and being exploited – will they still be focusing on the issue?'

We both take a deep breath. Gail sips her glass of water.

The attitudes towards missing children may also be shaped by the fact that they're politically neglected. Gail reflects on the struggle to get politicians to take the issue of missing children seriously.

'Before I came to Europe, I didn't know what "lobbying" meant,' she says. 'It's very simple. It's just building a relationship with a politician and making them understand what you're talking about and seeing if they care.

'Usually they do care. But part of the role of the politician is to go out there and say they care. And that's it. What do they do after that? It's very frustrating as an NGO to say, "Look, we've done the research, this is the problem, these are our solutions, listen, take this to heart, do something about it." It's very upsetting for us to go time and time again to the same politicians who said the same things three years ago and still the situation is the same.'

In fact, the situation for the hotlines has recently got worse. The European Commission withdrew funding to all the hotlines across Europe in 2015. MCE is hoping that national governments will step in to cover some of the deficit, but in the age of austerity, it's not looking good. At least ten of the hotlines (which are run by grassroots organisations) have received no funding from their national governments, and they have had to rely more on volunteers who are well trained but have limits on the amount of time they can dedicate compared to paid staff. It's adding to the frustrations of the job. The hotlines have less money and resources to do more work.

'The issues that cause children to go missing – family conflicts, alcohol abuse, et cetera – haven't been fixed, so the problem is only going to increase,' says Gail. 'The number of calls we receive is never going to decrease. It's only going to increase. There's only going to be more awareness, more people calling, more people needing help.'

Mette nods, and adds, 'Everybody working for the hotlines was basically just running faster in order to keep up and still provide as good a service as they possibly could.'

The worst-case scenarios are already playing out. Some hotlines run on reduced hours, and many don't have the capacity to take every call they receive.

'One of the things we identified was that the hotline had to be accessible 24 hours a day,' says Mette. 'Because you don't just run away during the day, or you don't just get abducted during the day. And if you want your service to be used and to be effective, it's better that people know they can call no matter the time of day ... Because otherwise they might not turn to anyone else, or they might turn to someone who doesn't know how to help them.' By European law, all hotlines beginning with 116 have to operate at all times, but it's a difficult task in the wake of cuts. Sometimes, there's nobody to answer the phone. Because of a lack of staff in Hungary, in 2017 only 10 per cent of incoming calls could be answered. Everyone is doing their best to provide a vital service, but the challenges for the hotlines are ongoing. The future of managing missing children in Europe is itself ambiguous.

However, there are reasons to be optimistic here, as well as reasons to be frustrated. There is a meaningful, international exchange of information and ideas, though best practice isn't always followed. There is concern for missing children in the wider community – the hotlines are increasingly utilised and media reports about missing children proliferate. That concern, however, is delivered unevenly. Children of colour, foreign children, less-than-innocent children, poor children, and male children are given less attention. Under-reporting remains a problem. We still don't have a good grasp of who goes missing and why, and what the impact is. We know more about missing cars. Most crucially, the concern is not reflected in funding for urgent services.

Missing persons by their nature are an ambiguous reality. We don't know where they are. But the extent of unknowns surrounding the issue are not so inevitable or impenetrable. Mette and Gail have shown me that effective policies and practices are within reach. To be effective, though, we have to look at the reality of the situation, to look into ambiguity and find within ourselves – our societies, our governments – the will towards action. There are ways forward along the shadowy path.

10

THE STOLEN GENERATIONS

SUSAN'S STORY

Mina's story demonstrates how individuals can become pawns in international power plays. She had to flee her home as a result of Saddam Hussein's mission to dominate the region. His regime had received international support because of the economic importance of oil and the arms trade. It's interesting that the first European country Mina escaped to was Germany, a key provider of the chemical weapons that Hussein used to bomb Kurdish villages. Germany also didn't provide her with safe refuge when they arrived. They played a role in creating her displacement, while doing little to make up for it, and in some ways even compounding her precarity.

When it's time to leave Europe and go home, I see this dynamic mirrored in the way power-holders in Australia have perpetuated the disadvantage experienced by First Nations people, manifested in significantly lower life expectancies and worse health, employment, and education outcomes. First Nations people are over-represented in the prison population

– while they comprise only 3 per cent of the Australian population, they make up over 28 per cent of prisoners. Almost half the juvenile prison population is First Nations. According to statistics provided to the ABC in 2019, First Nations people make up 17.5 per cent of unsolved missing-persons cases in Western Australia; nationally, First Nations women are disproportionally represented among the long-term missing. These disadvantages were created, reinforced, and compounded by the decisions of colonisers and settlers. The weapons of choice are different to Hussein's, though. One of them is stealing children.

❖

I'm wandering through the Australian Botanic Gardens in Mount Annan, south-western Sydney. It's early November and while humidity hangs in the air, the ground is dry, the grass crunchy underfoot. Native desert flowers bloom happily near the information centre; they're faring far better than the rest of us. Susan Moylan-Coombs suggested we meet here as a midpoint between where she lives in Sydney's Northern Beaches and Canberra, where I'm living now. I told her I'd have a big, yellow backpack, and as soon as I walk into the café, she beams at me and laughs, 'That is really yellow!'

Susan's background is in broadcasting. She's previously been executive producer of the ABC's Indigenous Programs Unit and head of production at National Indigenous Television (NITV), a division of SBS. She's worked on iconic Australian programs, including *Play School*. Now she is the CEO of the Gaimaragal Group, which works with organisations and communities throughout Australia to provide cultural competency and immersion opportunities, and facilitating community development in projects that ensure First Nations voices and stories are heard. She meets me with her partner, Justin

Bergholcs. We have coffee and slices of citrus cake.

In 2019, in a self-described 'moment of madness', Susan ran as an independent for the federal seat of Warringah, then held by former prime minister Tony Abbott. She didn't win but the campaign for the seat was competitive, and Abbott was ousted, replaced by lawyer and former Olympic skier, independent Zali Steggall. Justin declares that they'd never put themselves through it again.

'I wanted to contribute,' Susan says. 'I have something to say. Change was needed and I put my hand up thinking I wanted to do things for the community.' She wonders aloud how she would've fared in parliament had she won.

'Look at the circus that's going on now,' she laughs. 'Could you imagine? I would have been too disruptive. I just speak the truth too much.' Susan is politically engaged yet bemused by it all, and quick to laugh. She's a mix of lightness and seriousness, earnestness and cynicism.

We're down the road from the Stolen Generations Memorial, a quiet space in the bush with a sandstone statue depicting a downcast First Nations family overlooking a river of tears. Susan is a member of the Stolen Generations, one of the many First Nations children taken from their parents by government agents. She was born Susan Calma in 1964 at a hospital in Darwin. Immediately taken from her mother, she was sent to Garden Point Mission on Melville Island – one of the Tiwi Islands off the coast of the Northern Territory, about 100 kilometres from Darwin. Once Susan was born, her parents were sent away from this same mission, her mother to become a domestic – basically a maid – her father to work as a labourer. I can only use the passive voice here because we don't know who made these individual decisions in carrying out government policy, who did the taking and the sending; we only know that people were taken, people were sent.

Her parents had been stolen and taken to Garden Point Mission when they were kids too. 'That's why it's not the Stolen Generation, but the Stolen Generations,' says Susan. 'Sometimes it happens for two or more generations within a family.'

That plural is important – generations. There are different estimates of how many children were taken: records weren't well kept in the first place, and some have been lost or destroyed over time. A 1994 survey by the Australian Bureau of Statistics estimated that 10 per cent of First Nations people over the age of 25 had been taken from their families. Extrapolating from the ABS data gives an estimate of between 20 000 and 25 000 removals between 1910 and 1970. Separating children from their families – the state-sanctioned creation of mass missing persons – is inexorably stitched into the history of European settlement of Australia. It's linked with the history of political thought in this country, and thoughts about race, and the evolving ways governments justified such a harmful practice.

As early as 1814, when New South Wales Governor Lachlan Macquarie and his wife Elizabeth set up the 'Black Native Institution' in Parramatta (later moved to Blacktown), First Nations children were separated from their families under the pretext of education. As Rosemary Norman-Hill, CEO of the Kirrawe Indigenous Corporation and a descendant of one of the Institution's first students, told the *Sydney Morning Herald*, 'It is clear from [Macquarie's] General Orders that the intention was for these children to lose their language, their culture, their heritage and their Aboriginal way of life.' While children were taught reading, writing, arithmetic, domestic duties, farming, and the Bible, Macquarie stipulated that they weren't to leave until they were teenagers – even if their parents or other relatives came for them. Parents were allowed to see their kids through an open-slat fence and at annual public conferences. Enrolments were never very high – 20 was the most at any one time. In 1821, several students died and others consequently fled. The Institution was largely boycotted by First Nations families, but its remit was a precursor to later Stolen Generations policies.

As well, says Susan, 'There weren't a lot of women that came out on the First Fleet, or the subsequent fleets that came. So there was rape of Aboriginal women.' Young women, according to historian Henry Reynolds, 'were forced in concubinage'. Reports from the Northern Territory in 1899 show that white men would regularly kidnap young First Nations women, pursuing them on horses before taking them away, locking them up for weeks at a time, even tying them up at night to prevent their escape. It's not clear how widespread kidnap and slavery was, but it was officially noted throughout the country as a regular practice, and officially condemned by governments (although they failed to prevent it).

'You had these so-called "half-caste" children being born,' Susan explains. Most of them had an Aboriginal mother and a white father, and in many cases the mother had been raped by the man. Often he had little to do with raising the child. 'So they had the problem of, "Who are these kids?" They're not white and they're not black.'

The authorities theorised that mixed-race children would display the worst traits of each parent. As academics Quentin Beresford and Paul Omaji describe in *Our State of Mind*, they were alleged to be 'disinclined to work', 'loafers', and 'beggars'. Their high birth rate was a looming social menace.

At this time, Australian states enabled First Nations children to be taken from their communities in the belief that they should be 'absorbed' into white society, to 'breed out the colour'. The office of Chief Protector of Aborigines was created in all states except Tasmania and was designated the legal guardian of all First Nations children in their jurisdiction. (The Tasmanian government didn't believe the state had any First Nations people, just some 'half-castes' on Cape Barren Island.) An English-born civil servant, Auber Octavius (AO) Neville, the Protector in Western Australia, asked a conference of administrators in 1937, 'Are we going to have a population of one million blacks in the Commonwealth, or are we going to merge them into our white community and eventually forget that there were any Aborigines in Australia?' The practice of removing children from their parents and communities was the practical expression of this attempt to merge, to forget.

In those decades, the theory of eugenics was adopted by many scientists and policymakers. Eugenicists believed in making humanity more powerful, civilised, and modern by propagating 'good' genes and eliminating 'bad' ones. These were the theories used by the Nazis to justify the Holocaust from 1941 until the end of World War II. Eugenics was not fringe thinking at the time; it was considered 'science', supported by research grants and included in university-level textbooks.

In Australia in the 1920s and 1930s, federal parliament was presented with three different Mental Deficiency Bills, which would enable the state to forcibly sterilise or institutionalise 'inefficient' people. According to historian Ross L Jones, such people would include:

> ... slum dwellers, homosexuals, prostitutes, alcoholics, as well as those with small heads and with low IQs. The Aboriginal population was also seen to fall within this group.

In 1939, one of these Bills passed unanimously. By that stage though, World War II had broken out and parliament had other things to worry about. By the end of the war, they no longer had a taste for legislation that seemed so easily comparable to Nazism.

Coincidentally, on the day I meet her, Susan has just come from the Sydney Jewish Museum in Darlinghurst. She was there as part of their 'Be a Mensch' campaign. *Mensch* is a Yiddish word meaning a person of integrity and honour, and the campaign reflects on how people do good in times of atrocity. Violence is enacted in different ways, with differing social and political dynamics, but, reflects Susan, 'There's a similar experience, really, of Jewish people in the Holocaust and Indigenous people's removal and dispossession. Groups of people share these critical moments in their personal stories – the Stolen Generations, the Holocaust, children abused within churches. They all need to be addressed and recognised for the unique experiences they are, and we need to understand how people see themselves in the world today as a result of that experience.' When groups of people have come so close to annihilation, there's going to be a deep, collective trauma. But they're also likely to be wise to the opportunities for integrity and compassion.

People spoke out against the treatment they'd suffered or witnessed under the Nazis. They debunked eugenics. The Stolen Generations continued, but under different rhetoric. As Robert Manne traces in *In Denial*, the policy of 'breeding out the colour' was replaced by 'assimilation'. Policymakers asserted that First Nations children were better off in white families or white-run institutions so they could be educated for participation in a white-dominant society. Laws focused on the child's welfare as justification for removal, but it was very easy under these laws to establish that First Nations children were 'neglected', 'destitute', or 'uncontrollable'. Families were closely watched by authorities for any missteps.

Poverty itself was used as evidence that a child was being neglected, and poverty was easy to find in First Nations families because it had been forced upon them. Settlements were neglected by governments and it was also hard to get a job. Employers were required to get a permit to hire First Nations workers, which was a discouraging hassle. Where permits were procured, it created a system of bondage because employees couldn't miss a day of work or quit without government approval. Negotiating wages and conditions is impossible if you can't threaten to find a new job. The jobs available to First Nations people were mostly odd jobs and seasonal work, tasks such as picking 'dead wool', which involved searching paddocks for dead sheep and plucking wool from them by hand. First Nations people were not entitled to social security payments until 1966, or to statutory minimum wages until 1967. First Nations poverty was created by settlers and then used as an excuse to remove children from their families.

When children were removed, some – like Susan – were taken at birth from the hospital. Authorities also regularly rounded up children in raids on First Nations communities. Some were dragged from the arms of their parents. The 1997 *Bringing Them Home* report, which summarises the findings of the National Inquiry into the Separation of Aboriginal and Torres Strait Islander Children from Their Families, tells stories of parents crying and running after their children, attempting to rescue them. Sometimes the scenes of separation weren't so visibly harrowing. For example, a parent could send their child to care pre-emptively, to prevent them from being taken away under more traumatic circumstances; or authorities could tell a young mother that she'd have to give up a baby or else be charged with 'carnal knowledge', thereby making it seem as though she chose to give the baby away. Children were sent to church missions, government training institutions, and private families. Once a child was stolen, conditions in 'care' were often rough.

In the post-war years, children throughout the Northern Territory – including Susan's parents, and Susan herself for her first three years of life – were sent to Garden Point, a Catholic-run mission. The accounts of children who were sent there show that it was a scary transition. Some had lived in the desert and never seen the sea, so the journey on the boat from the mainland was terrifying. The children could enjoy nature there, and they received a basic education, but there was abuse and grief. Sexual and physical abuse by priests and nuns, as well as older children, was reported. One man, Nicholas Flowers, told *The Guardian*, 'They'd strip us and flog us with a sewing machine belt ... The priest had one of them and used to flog us naked.' They were deprived of their families and knowledge of their own culture, knowledge that had accrued over millennia. Instead, missionaries imposed Christianity, often conflating First Nations' beliefs and cultural practices with barbarism and sin. Once they grew up, there was hardly any paid work for First Nations people on the island, so many were sent back to the mainland to work as labourers or domestics.

These memories aren't unusual among members of the Stolen Generations. In care, brutal physical abuse took place. Children often went cold and hungry. In some states, girls were taken into care until they turned a certain age (sometimes as young as ten), when they'd be sent out to work, apprenticed as domestics in white homes. Many of these girls became pregnant, usually as a result of rape. Often their babies were then taken into care, continuing the cycle of Stolen Generations.

In 2016, researchers at the University of New South Wales published a report called *No Child Should Grow Up Like This*, a study of the experiences of those placed or forced into care between 1930 and 1989, including child migrants and

Forgotten Australians (children taken into institutional care for a variety of reasons) as well as Stolen Generations. Almost every participant in the study had experienced some form of abuse. Over half experienced sexual abuse perpetrated by an adult, and 41.8 per cent experienced sexual abuse by a peer. Most (81.5 per cent) reported that they commenced work before the age of 13, and their labour tended to be physically demanding. Pay was poor, amounting to mere pocket money, and some children didn't receive any.

Stolen children were prepared for menial work and life on the lower rungs of white society. Teachers on missions aimed to educate their students to the level of a ten-year-old in the mainstream state school system. Members of the Stolen Generations, according to *Bringing Them Home*, didn't significantly differ in their educational achievement from First Nations children who had stayed with their families.

In official eyes, First Nations people were held in open contempt. One witness spoke of hearing a welfare officer talking to their foster parents 'about how they were hoping our race would die out'. Some members of the Stolen Generations report that while in care they were told that their families didn't want them or were dead. Letters their families wrote them and letters they wrote to their families were not always passed on. Some were forbidden to talk to their families at all, and their names were forcibly changed. Some were encouraged not to think of themselves as belonging to First Nations communities, and to abandon their spiritual practices. Some were never told of their heritage.

Things began to change by the end of the 1960s. In 1967 a referendum was held to amend the Constitution to include First Nations people in the census and allow the Commonwealth government to make laws for them, including reforms that would allow them greater rights. Almost 91 per cent of voters agreed to these changes. At that time, the rights of First Nations people varied between states: they could vote in federal elections, but they couldn't vote in state elections in Western Australia and Queensland, nor could they marry freely in every state. In most states, they had no rights to their own children, nor the rights to move freely or own property or to be paid award wages. Things didn't change overnight, and these reforms didn't immediately stop child removals, but the referendum paved the way for greater legal equality into the 1970s.

By 1969 the government had taken control of Garden Point Mission, and all the children there had been returned to the mainland. In 1967–68, almost 18 per cent of First Nations children in the Northern Territory were in institutional care, but after the referendum, many institutions began to close (although not all – some continued to operate in the Northern Territory into the 1980s). The children, however, were not returned to their parents.

'There was a need for families to take Aboriginal kids,' says Susan. 'So I was flown to Sydney and adopted into the Coombs family.'

The referendum had a significant impact on Susan's quality of life, and it had come about as a result of tireless campaigning by First Nations people, prime minister Harold Holt's interest in the issue, and Australian voters' wish to see changes in the way First Nations people were treated.

Yet as Susan and I talk about the Stolen Generations as a historical policy, she points out that First Nations children are still being taken from their parents and their communities across the country today.

'We're just doing the same things,' she says. 'They dress it up differently, but it's the same stuff.'

More than one-third of removed children in Australia

today are First Nations children. They're removed under welfare legislation, but the removals can be suspicious. In the Northern Territory, it's possible to remove children from their parents with only hearsay evidence of abuse or neglect. Officials fly to remote towns early in the morning and take children thousands of kilometres away with no explanations and no guarantee that they'll ever return. How concerned can child protection workers be for the child's welfare when they literally airlift them from their home, from everything they know, their culture, and from relatives who are able to take care of the child if their parents can't?

And how concerned can policymakers be for children's welfare when only limited programs exist to support families? It can be difficult for adults and communities to navigate through the entrenched trauma of being stolen, or knowing your family tree is dotted with missing persons. It's hard to learn how to be a parent if you were stolen from your own at a young age and subjected to institutional abuse; and it's hard to ask for help if you've seen children taken away at the slightest hint of parental struggle. Yet, in the Northern Territory in 2012, more money was spent on surveillance of First Nations children and removing them (some $80 million), than on supporting families experiencing poverty (a measly $500 000). Instead of providing support to parents such as counselling, education, and resources, instead of trying to build trust, government practice is to watch for failure and intervene at the first sign.

'They're stealing kids up instead of giving parents skills and acknowledging the trauma,' says Susan.

The 2019 *Family Is Culture* review independently examined the cases of 1144 First Nations children taken by authorities between mid-2015 and mid-2016 in New South Wales. The review team found that child protection workers gave misleading evidence to the Children's Court; and that against the department's own guidelines, they omitted details about the parents' strengths or evidence of their positive approaches to parenting. A quarter of the cases they examined were of babies who had been taken at birth or soon after. There were also cases where not only did families not know where their removed children were, but the Minister in charge of their protection did not know either. There were reports of removed children being abused in care.

Removal practices persist despite the rhetoric of the New South Wales Department of Communities and Justice, which notes that removal isn't the only option child protection workers can choose in cases of abuse or suspected abuse. The Department says that 'the best place for a child is in their family home. Most families can get help to cope with difficulties while the children remain at home.' And yet, First Nations children continue to be removed at staggering rates. In the cases examined by the report, workers consistently chose removal over alternatives like early intervention programs, or parental responsibility contracts. There were cases of children being removed from families despite there being no evidence that they were at risk of harm. Workers also ignored other family members who were willing and able to take care of the kids, routinely separating families unnecessarily. They also routinely separated siblings – even twins – unnecessarily, placing them into different care settings.

The report found that less than 2 per cent of cases conformed to the Department's own policies to plan how the child's cultural needs would be met after their removal. These plans should be made in consultation with the child's family and community. Contact time should be scheduled with parents, other family members identified that the child can connect with, and the child's connection with their culture promoted.

The state is still creating missing children, still separating children from their communities.

❖

Susan had a middle-class upbringing on the Northern Beaches of Sydney. She thought she was the only First Nations person around (she wasn't, she just didn't know many others), and was always aware of her heritage.

'I was black and my sisters weren't,' she laughs. 'It was really obvious.' She was only three months younger than her older sister, so when people asked them their ages, they'd give the same answer. 'They'd kind of look at us, and we'd let them ponder that for a bit, and then my sister would go, "Oh yeah, she got left in the oven a bit longer, that's why she's brown."' Susan would pause before explaining she was adopted. 'People were really stupid about it.'

While nobody ever hid Susan's background, she didn't have a lot of information to go on to understand where she was from or what it meant to be a First Nations person. Her adopted grandfather was the first governor of the Reserve Bank of Australia, economist HC 'Nugget' Coombs, who, she says, 'was fairly influential in Indigenous Affairs'. He'd travel to communities around Australia and bring back objects, 'boomerangs and bark paintings. There were artefacts in the house, and he would talk to me about things'. Her adopted mother, Jan, also told her as much as she could, although Susan was confused, 'trying to understand what it all meant'.

When she shared her story with the Sydney Jewish Museum, Susan was trolled online by someone who argued that her fortunate upbringing meant that she wasn't really a survivor of the Stolen Generations.

'Someone made the comment, basically saying, how dare I say that I'm a survivor. I was horrified.' She frowns. 'And this was a non-Indigenous person saying this to me too.' They were a former social worker, someone who'd held senior positions in their profession. 'I was like, how dare you suggest to me that my story, my experience of being removed and part of the Stolen Generations, isn't a survivor story?' The hurt registers in her voice. 'I was taken at birth, I was sent to a mission, I was adopted into a non-Indigenous family at the age of three. I have continued trauma.'

Silver linings exist alongside trauma for members of the Stolen Generations. Some children were placed with loving families, and material circumstances likely improved for some. But being stolen always has a cost. Accounts from members of the Stolen Generations share a sense of loss, even of feeling *lost*. The University of New South Wales report observes that the feelings of grief and loss experienced by many who have entered care are lifelong. They found that 70.2 per cent of participants experienced mental illness at some point in their lives, and most attribute their distress to the trauma of being placed in care. It's easy enough for non–First Nations people to connect with this loss in imagining the pain of being separated from your birth family, of spending your life wondering who they are, and who you are. But there are other types of loss that may be difficult to grasp for those of us who don't come from cultures with a strong sense of place. Being stolen, explains Susan, 'causes huge issues around culture, and Country, and language, and spirit, and belief, and the western mindset doesn't see this'.

When Susan was about 12 or 13 years old, she didn't talk much; her words seemed to dry up. 'I just stopped talking because I didn't understand where I was. I was trying to work the world out, and I needed time for silence.' Her parents brought her to a children's mental health clinic. The clinician she saw asked her parents to imagine how one of their birth children would cope if they were sent to a foreign country. He explained Susan's silence as a natural response to 'culture shock'.

She reflects, 'I was trying to integrate and make sense of the world.' And so, she was allowed to be silent when she needed to be. 'And that's okay,' says Susan. 'That's just the way I deal with things.'

The world was giving her signs, but her ability to read them had been taken away from her. When someone is taken away from their culture, they're spiritually injured – they lose a context to make sense of what they perceive around them. It results in a kind of void.

'In my brain,' says Susan, 'there's a level of disconnect with Aboriginality because of being removed. But there is bloodline, there's DNA, there is a knowing. There's a whole way of thinking I have.' Susan sees it as inhabiting two different worlds: what she's been taught growing up in a predominantly white society, as well as what she seems to have been born *knowing*. Susan's adopted father was a barrister, so she grew up with an understanding of the law, of right and wrong. But she's also inherited a sense of Lore, a body of knowledge accumulated through cycles of teaching and learning. Lore is story, history, and wisdom. It's also about right and wrong, but in a different way to the western legal system. It's closer to the sense of natural justice, or cause and effect, where the consequences of an action are inherent in the action itself – the way bulldozing a forest can cause soil erosion, ecosystem imbalances, and impacts on human health – rather than imposed by someone else as punishment. 'I grew up just knowing things, and I didn't know why I knew them, and I thought everybody knew them. Things around energy, feeling Country.'

These concepts are difficult to articulate in English, but

they revolve around intuition, and a connection with the environment and living things.

'Like, I didn't understand it – I just had a sense I was being protected.' Susan was one of the first female lifesavers in Australia and swam at the notoriously rough South Curl Curl beach. 'Just before going in, it's almost like I would talk to the ocean, just to watch and see what she was doing.' She swam in events, often beating the men ('Some of them didn't like that,' she laughs), and even when the tides were so rough the organisers were contemplating cancelling races, she still felt confident. 'I just knew how to navigate it. I just saw it. I knew what to do, and to trust it.'

Although Susan's ancestors are from the Northern Territory, she's been raised on Gamaraigal land, and this is the landscape she knows.

'When I'm walking, I know when I'm meant to be there or not to be there; I kind of get pulled in certain directions. There's totems there. One of them is a black crow or raven; it's always around when I'm driving, so I know everything's fine. I see it and go, "Thanks," just in my head.' During a meeting with NITV, she remembers the boardroom having enormous, floor-to-ceiling windows, and for the entire time there was a huge raven sitting outside, looking in. After the meeting, the non-Indigenous CEO asked Susan what she made of the bird. Susan told him, 'I think he was just there to witness what we were doing. He was just making sure we were doing the right thing.'

This connection to Country has enriched Susan's life. She credits it with keeping her safe from accidents and injuries and it's helped her avoid people and situations that didn't quite feel right.

'But for me,' she says, 'I didn't have words around Lore until I was in my twenties.' She had to search for the context, find an Elder and Lore-woman to teach her what it all meant. Throughout First Nations cultures, men, women, and children have specific roles which require them to draw on Lore. The continuation of culture, and of life itself, requires this Lore to be passed on and practised. Learning women's business allowed Susan to make sense of what she knew. It gave her a way to talk and think about the cycles of nature, honouring the environment, fostering connection and synergy with the earth. It gave her words.

'Cultural wounds require cultural medicines,' Susan says, quoting a Canadian research paper from the University of British Columbia about the trauma experienced by First Nations people. One of the ways of dealing with this sense of loss, and of being lost, is trying to find some of those experiences that were stolen from her when she was taken from her mother.

❖

Place is important in First Nations culture. The idea of songlines – that the journeys of creator-beings and ancestors are imprinted on the land itself and contain important Lore and cultural memory – isn't easy to grasp for people with backgrounds like mine. I've lived in four different cities in two different countries; I'm the descendant of British and Northern European people who were either transported to Australia for petty crimes or who came opportunistically to search for gold, or sun, or to get out of post-war Europe.

As Claire G Coleman pointed out in *Meanjin* in 2017, the ancestors of settler Australians were basically nomadic; they travelled vast distances with only a vague understanding of what life would be like once they got where they were going. They're particularly nomadic compared to First Nations people, who had been living on the same land for at least 60 000 years, perhaps moving through the bounded tract that constitutes their Country in accordance with seasonal shifts, but with the same kind of stability with which one might move between a summer home and a winter home over countless generations. As Coleman observes, 'Many of the average Anglo-Australians I knew would not hesitate to move countries, mostly for economic reasons but sometimes just for the hell of it.' Many of us dream of travelling, of living out of vans and backpacks, unencumbered by borders, free of all responsibilities to be anywhere in particular. Obviously First Nations people travel too, but Coleman argues that by comparison:

> To many Aboriginal people the Country of their ancestors, the place where they were born, the places where their parents were born, are beloved members of the family who are missed when they are not present.

Abducting a child from their family doesn't just take them from their relatives, but from their culture, their spirituality, and their place, all of which are woven together.

Reclaiming place in the wake of the Stolen Generations and mass dispossession is not easy. Native titles legally recognise the ongoing rights of First Nations people to their traditional lands and waters, and their right to use those spaces for traditional practices, as well as to earn royalties and rent from other users of the land. But native title rights are contingent on you and your descendants having an unbroken connection to the area in question since before colonisation, and those rights can't have already been sold off to someone else by the government. These connections become legally severed where First Nations people have been dispossessed of their land. They're severed when a person is stolen, too: as the *Bringing Them Home* report says, 'In all jurisdictions the ability to bring a native title claim will generally be extinguished by forced removal.' That said, where members of the Stolen Generations are accepted back into the fold of their ancestral community, they can become part of a collective native title claim or enjoy their community's existing native title.

However, it gets even more complicated when the mix of child removal, frontier massacres, and disease means that some nations become so small they're near-forgotten, or they get absorbed by neighbouring nations. Over time, Susan has gained a better understanding of where her parents are from.

'That's been really exciting, looking at what that means,' she says brightly. On her mother's side, Susan is Woolwonga, from part of the Northern Territory near Katherine. It was thought that no Woolwonga people had survived a massacre in 1884, but descendants are still living today. The problem is that because the whereabouts and history of those descendants are so fragmented, seeking land rights and cultural information is fraught. The Woolwonga Research Committee undertakes archival research, and writes to museums to request information. One of the most important documents they've found details their totems, drawings, and language, and had been housed at the Royal Anthropological Institute of Great Britain and Ireland. It's ongoing work.

The Woolwonga haven't made any native title claims, but some are seeking the right to hunt and fish on their ancestral lands, to be able to enjoy it.

'It can cause huge conflict,' says Susan. 'The destruction of culture and identity and connection by the government has caused contemporary issues around Stolen Generations people being able to reclaim their identity.' As the Jawoyn Association told the National Inquiry into the Separation of Aboriginal and Torres Strait Islander Children from Their Families, 'Significantly, very few people in this situation have said they want to receive a share in rentals or royalties (except perhaps as a symbol of recognition).' The intent is to understand themselves better, to no longer be quite so lost.

❖

When Susan says that her grandfather was 'fairly influential in Indigenous Affairs', this is an understatement. He was one of the leaders of the Council of Aboriginal Affairs, established by Prime Minister Holt after the referendum. The Council was ill-fated – once Holt disappeared in December 1967, government interest in rights for First Nations people waned. But Nugget Coombs continued to work with both major political parties to promote these rights, and in 1979 launched the Aboriginal Treaty Committee, calling for a formal treaty between the Australian government and First Nations people, affirming that sovereignty was never ceded during colonisation.

'He was a huge advocate for Indigenous people, before it was fashionable,' says Susan. 'He just couldn't understand why a race of people who originally came from this land were being treated so poorly.'

His interest in improving rights shaped his and Susan's connection. 'It was a really lovely relationship, that was special to me.' When she was in her mid-teens, he asked her if she wanted his help to find her biological parents. She didn't feel ready at the time, but in her early twenties she took him up on his offer. They wrote a letter to a government department in Darwin, who then passed it on to Maxine, Susan's biological mother. She wanted to make contact too, so the Department forwarded Susan her phone number.

'So, I rang her,' remembers Susan. 'It was lovely.' Maxine had been looking for Susan with the help of her husband. They'd assumed that Susan would still be in the Northern

Territory, and they searched in secret. Maxine never told her other kids they had an older half-sister until she spoke on the phone that day.

'It was a beautiful experience,' says Susan, smiling. When they met, Susan took Jan with her too. 'So, my Sydney mum came and met my Darwin mum. One woman had given birth to me, but the other woman had raised me. So, I had two mums. For me, emotionally, I just need to be able to see both women at the same time.' Susan says Jan had been the most influential person in her life in defining who she became. She thought of her as a friend. 'I could talk to her about anything. We had a really strong relationship.' And Maxine was the person Susan had been wondering about.

'It was the beginning of a renewed relationship. When we'd been split up, it caused her huge trauma, and it caused me huge trauma.' Seeing both women together was like being able to see all the pieces of her life for the first time, getting a sense of how they might all fit together.

Maxine was born in Darwin, and having been stolen herself she's had to research her family line as an adult. That's how she found out that she was Woolwonga. Because her nation has been absorbed by neighbouring ones, it's been hard for her – and for Susan – to explore their identity. 'She just wants to be able to say "This is Country,"' says Susan. 'She wants her and her family to be able to go to Country and just be on Country.' But simply finding Country hasn't solved everything.

Susan returned to Sydney, but the relationship with Maxine remains. As well as rebuilding a relationship with her mum, she also made contact with her siblings and other family members. She visits often, navigating that contradiction of being born of the desert but living life by the sea: the two-world mix of law and Lore.

At first, Susan had been focused on meeting her mother,

but in the lead-up to turning 40, she decided that she'd like to meet her father too.

'The life expectancy for men is a lot younger,' says Susan – the average lifespan of a First Nations man in the Northern Territory is just under 67 years. She worried that time was running out. The children of Garden Point Mission stayed in touch with regular gatherings for Wednesday lunches and, sadly, for the funerals of their fellow survivors. All this time, Maxine had kept in touch with Susan's biological father. Maxine gave him Susan's phone number and they chatted. Susan flew to meet him on her 40th birthday. Maxine came with her so that she'd be able to spot him – Susan didn't know what he looked like.

'It was really special,' she says. 'I have this hilarious photo of the three of us together which I call "The Three Garden Gnomes" because we're all so short.' She laughs. But learning about her father's life was also sobering. 'You can see the trauma in him, you could see the impacts that removal had on him and how he was living his life.' He is Gurindji; he was taken from Wave Hill, more than 700 kilometres south of Darwin. His housemate told Susan that he could walk Country, and that he'd walked over 900 kilometres from Borroloola to Darwin with just a knife. For thousands of years, walking was the main means of getting around the continent of Australia, over intersecting trails that have been walked generation after generation. He is part of that enormous legacy. And so, says Susan, 'There was a lot of trauma for him in the disconnection.' Susan's grateful that she got to meet him, but they've fallen out of touch and Maxine hasn't seen him for a while either. She's not sure if he's alive.

❖

The impact of being stolen, of being missing from your family, your culture, your spirituality, and your Country, never ends. These traumas are the result of the laws, policies, and ideologies imposed upon First Nations people by colonisers and settlers. As I sit with these facts in the Campbelltown café, eating my cake in tiny forkfuls and drinking my coffee, it's hard to know what to do with them. The idea of separating children from their families and communities because of bizarre assumptions about First Nations people is hard to grasp. But my capacity to imagine it isn't relevant – it happened, thousands of times. And as this discomfort unfolds in my body, there's an additional discomfort: this isn't about me, or my feelings. Listening to these stories is necessary to understand what happened and why it was so traumatic. But it's not enough just to know and to feel bad.

Susan shared her story for the inquiry that culminated in the *Bringing Them Home* report, and she was invited to various events to speak about her experiences.

'I did that for a couple of years with some other ladies from the community,' she says. It was difficult, but possible 'for me to tell my story and not completely lose my bundle'. This isn't true for many members of the Stolen Generations, for whom telling the story is often re-traumatising and extremely distressing. 'But after a couple of years of telling my story, I decided I needed to stop,' Susan says. 'It was so voyeuristic. You're not doing anything ... People just love to hear the trauma – that's my perception of it. And I kept saying, "So what are we going to do about this? How can we support healing and wellbeing?"'

One of the problems of settler guilt – and white guilt in particular – is that it doesn't do anything or help anyone. It can fuel denial – the belief that what happened is so absurdly horrible people conclude it didn't occur, the nation they love couldn't do something like that, or maybe it's not as bad as everyone thinks, for one reason or another. Denial is thinking there's a way to justify the Stolen Generations, but it requires you to ignore the historical evidence and those who, at great personal cost, offer their stories. After the *Bringing Them Home* report was released, this kind of denial rang through the right-wing press. Some white people seemed to think that they were being manipulated into feeling guilty, as though the guilt itself was a grenade to shelter from. This isn't the goal of truth-telling, but some people are so resistant they can't listen any more. A few months before Susan and I meet, a member of the Senate unsuccessfully moved a motion that 'It's okay to be white', as though anyone had claimed otherwise.

Guilt can also be a self-congratulatory stance, as if to immunise yourself from the racist movements of history because at least you understand it was wrong. This might be the appeal of voyeuristically sponging up survivor stories: the knowledge sets you apart, grants you immunity.

'I started getting annoyed,' remembers Susan. 'That's me being polite – I used to get pissed off.' The groups of people she spoke to seemed interested in learning about the history of the Stolen Generations. 'They educated themselves. But they've done nothing with it, other than using it as a dinner table conversation, something they could share among their friends.' Listening doesn't mean you're doing anything constructive to transform a racist past into a better future. 'I have issues with the reconciliation movement because nothing practical has really come out of it.'

Susan notes there have been some successes – Kevin Rudd's 2008 apology, for example, and the thousands of people who walked across the Sydney Harbour Bridge in 2000 as an expression of reconciliation – but to her they feel more symbolic than concrete, especially when it comes to the Stolen Generations.

Cognitive dissonance limits our gains in racial justice. From 1971, Australians were heavily involved in protesting apartheid in South Africa. The South African Springboks, a then all-white, racially selected rugby union team, toured Australia and were met with vehement protests. The government then banned racially selected sporting teams from competing in Australia, a boycott that lasted over 20 years. Australia also enacted trade and investment sanctions against South Africa as part of our opposition to apartheid. Yet it was Queensland's Aboriginal Protection Act of 1897, limiting the rights of First Nations people, that inspired apartheid. South African lawmakers studied the Act as a template for their own laws. Clearly Australians know what injustice looks like, but it's not so easily perceived when it's your own society that's enacting it. In Australia, child snatchers could see the tears of First Nations parents and took their babies anyway.

It's important to learn from the Stolen Generations. 'Maybe Australia needs to have a mental health plan,' says Susan. Justin rejoins the conversation and agrees that, as settlers, 'We need to look at ourselves and say, "There's trauma on my side of the fence as well that I need to look at, and own that shame for things we've have done, for the countries we've invaded, taken, raped, pillaged, and plundered." Because if you don't take responsibility, you keep doing the same stuff.'

Australians who are not First Nations people might do well to reframe the Stolen Generations not as a set of sad stories from the past but as a vast series of injustices to be redressed today. Whether or not we're personally responsible for the past, we are responsible for addressing these injustices in the present. This will take time. As the Lowitja Institute reports, where First Nations people maintain 'a driving role and [have] legitimate decision-making power', where the expertise and cultures of First Nations people, and connection to Country are embedded into programs and organisations, the benefits are striking. The most effective strategy for redressing injustice is to provide First Nations-led groups with resources and support rather than imposing rules from outside. Settlers have done enough imposing. Aside from creating the conditions to allow self-driven development, political actions such as providing compensation to survivors of the Stolen Generations and working towards a Treaty are also among the opportunities for healing.

Susan believes people also need opportunities to heal from their personal and intergenerational trauma. 'It's still living trauma, the after-effects still ripple and reverberate through our community.' As with the other stories of missing persons I've encountered through this project, the impacts are never-ending. 'We've not actually healed people, or allowed families to start to look at the trauma and put in programs that really address it.'

How to address it is a complicated question, but Susan has sources she draws on for hope. She mentions the work of Michael Yellow Bird, and his concept of 'neurodecolonisation'. Trauma can impact both the mind and brain function, and the trauma of colonisation – along with dispossession, poor health, a lack of rights, and forced separation from your community – is no different. Trauma seems to affect regions of the brain such as the ventromedial prefrontal cortex and the amygdala, both of which are involved in regulating emotions like fear and anxiety. This keeps people trapped in the feeling that they're under threat, even in safe environments. It's hard not to panic all the time, to think clearly, to make decisions. The stress hormones that flood the body can increase the risk of illness, to the point where trauma (especially adverse childhood experiences) has been identified as a public health issue. In addition to these health issues, colonisation has suppressed spiritual practices – like rituals and ceremonies – that help people cope mindfully with difficult circumstances and make sense of things in relation to their enduring beliefs. Brains, however, are changeable. People can come to teach themselves to feel calmer and safer, even after extreme trauma. Neurodecolonisation involves using traditional and other practices to help bring about positive neurological changes and healing.

Susan's also interested in investigations of epigenetic shifts caused by colonisation, and how this might also hold a key to healing. Epigenetics describes changes in the way genes are expressed as a result of one's environment – even when there are no changes in DNA, the way someone's genetic make-up manifests is variable. New research may show that exposure to the stress of colonisation has an epigenetic effect, and may – alongside continuing social disadvantages – account for the increased health risks we see among First Nations populations around the world. Trauma survivors pass their trauma down to the next generation – so if you're constantly stressed, fearful, and anxious, that's likely to affect the way you treat your children. There's also an increasing body of evidence to suggest that intergenerational trauma could be propagated through genetic codes: changes in the ways genes are expressed as a result of stress may be inherited, and future generations may be born with the imprints of the trauma of their ancestors. If this is true, it's evidence that the human body is malleable, that supportive environments could allow for healthier gene expressions. And, as a way forward, it's possible to create those environments.

Susan's current work fosters wellbeing among First Nations people on an organisational level. One of the projects she's worked on was to create resources for the Northern Sydney Primary Health Network in collaboration with Relationships Australia NSW as part of a program called Caber-ra Nanga –

a Gai-mariagal term that means 'resting the mind', gifted by Dennis Foley, a Gai-mariagal knowledge holder. It involves, says Susan, 'changing the dialogue around mental health to be more inclusive of our way'. Services were broadened to include men and women's healing circles, cultural ceremonies, and other more cultural and social forms of fostering wellbeing than individual therapy (which is also available to people who want it). They talk about health holistically, as per cultural traditions where connection to Country is key, and where mind is integrated with body and both are intertwined with spirituality. One of the paths forward is diversifying what treatment looks like, making it more culturally appropriate, and turning to 'cultural medicines'.

For every year that passes, healing becomes more urgently needed – for everyone. Susan has the canny ability to see connections between issues, and talking to her is how I come to realise that the phenomenon of mass missing First Nations persons also relates to climate change. Separating people from their culture kills the millennia-old cycles of teaching and learning, of passing along Lore. It kills that accumulated knowledge. Right now, we need this knowledge. UNESCO has stated that First Nations knowledge will be key to mitigating and adapting to climate change on a global scale. In Australia, First Nations knowledge could likewise be better used to mitigate environmental issues such as drought and bushfires. First Nations people have always undertaken practices like farming and land clearing and food production throughout the continent, and were able to do these things sustainably because they understood land and water management, ecology, seasons and weather patterns, and cultural burning. First Nations communities across the country continue to implement these sustainability techniques, or have extended them to include things like carbon sequestering (which mitigates climate change by limiting the release of carbon into the atmosphere). But government policy has been reluctant to embrace these models.

'We are the oldest living culture on the planet,' says Susan. 'There's disregard for who we are, and then the knowledge we hold. Gracious Elders who aren't too traumatised to teach just want to share this knowledge. Because it's about their grandchildren and great-grandchildren, trying to create a better place for people to live.'

The problem, says Susan, is that there's a lot at stake for the government if they were to recognise the value of First Nations people and knowledge. 'If we truly recognise the knowledge that the oldest living culture has to share, it will potentially undo Australia. Because if we start to truly honour and respect and listen, to embrace Indigenous models, what does that say about how we got here? What does it say about the crimes against humanity?' To embrace these models, you have to admit that your knowledge is limited, you have to defer to the authority of First Nations people. You cast yourself into the intolerable unknown.

After all, Australia's political institutions were created on the artifice that their control over the lives of First Nations people was legitimate – that it was okay to raise British flags on Australian shores based on the doctrine of 'terra nullius'; that it was okay to dispossess people of their land because the settlers knew how to cultivate it better; that it was okay to take children from their families because the settlers knew how to bring them up better. To acknowledge the flaws in colonial thinking would be to admit a level of ignorance ill-befitting those in power, and it would be an admission of liability.

This is where we are right now. The story of the Stolen Generations hasn't ended. There is ongoing harm, and even existential risk exacerbated by the policy of mass abductions. But everyone on the continent has the opportunity to create a new inheritance, to make some luck. Walking out of the café with Susan and Justin, I see again the desert flowers thriving as the world around them wilts under the midday sun.

11

DRINKING THE KOOL-AID

THE ATTRACTION OF CULTS

Some people choose to go missing. Others are compelled to by forces outside of their control. At times the reason for their disappearance is somewhere in the blurry space between choosing to go and being taken. Brandy, for instance, wasn't abducted from her home, but not leaving would have posed a threat to her physical safety. Among those whose decisions are on this line, somewhere between free and forced, some would be just as safe staying where they are. But they are persuaded to cut off contact with their friends and family, and while they can say no, it can be difficult to refuse. They may want to leave, although 'wanting' in this situation can be ambiguous as well. Under the undue influence of others, or of a group – a cult, for example – desires could be imposed.

I talk to Nick Lee over Facebook Messenger, my phone and recording equipment propped on a friend's kitchen table. Nick is in New Zealand and I'm calling from Canberra. He's a serious young man with a business-like expression. He's just started his legal career in Auckland.

Nick thinks that his friend Gideon (not his real name) went missing because he started to question his beliefs. 'He was a very committed Christian,' he says. 'But he was also a very conservative Christian. He wasn't used to having doubts and questions about the church's teachings.' By Gideon's early twenties, his once-solid faith had become murky. He didn't know how what to do with his increasing religious uncertainty.

'It's a paradox,' I reflect. 'He started to have questions, and maybe dissatisfaction around religion, and then he ended up joining a group where you can't really have questions at all.'

Nick agrees that it seems paradoxical on the surface, but the sequence of events still has a logic to it. When someone joins an organisation like this one, 'a cult', he calls it, 'They start teaching them the problems with existing churches.' They validate the concerns of Christians who are searching for new interpretations of what makes a good life, and a greater understanding of the Bible, and Christians who are concerned with the top-down structure of churches like the Catholic Church, where huge amounts of money are collected and put into wealth and assets for the few at the top, and where child sexual abuse is endemic.

'And then they try to teach that their church is different. They interpret Bible verses in their own way, in a very convincing way.' At this stage, they tell members that they're a non-denominational Christian group; they don't tell them their name. 'That,' says Nick, 'is how they try to brainwash people.'

Both Nick and Gideon were born in South Korea and grew up in New Zealand. They were in Seoul at the same time, Gideon for a visit, Nick to undertake the two-year military service that's compulsory for male Korean citizens. While in Korea, Gideon searched for a church he could frequent away from home, and when he found this group – still an unnamed Bible study group at this point – he brought Nick along.

Nick looked around the tiny room the group met in, situated in a small, nondescript building. It seemed cosy, friendly. 'They introduced themselves as just a Bible study group, with people from different churches,' he shrugs. He estimates that there were around 30 to 40 people, mostly in their twenties. 'It was just ordinary church services in the beginning. But then someone who proclaimed she was a professor delivered a speech. It wasn't the same as ordinary church speeches. Something was wrong.'

Nick doesn't remember the contents of the speech all that well – it was a few years ago, after all – but he remembers the creepy feeling he experienced, his suspicion.

'They mix up numbers and words in the Bible to reach whatever conclusions they want to reach. The one I heard when I went there was about what happens to a person's soul when they die. Their use of Bible verses to support what they were saying didn't seem right.' At first he put the inconsistencies down to this simply being a different branch of Christianity to what he was used to. But the creepy feeling lingered.

'After I went there a couple times, they asked me to join a one-on-one Bible study program that would go on for weeks. I attended that once and I found something fishy about that as well. I did a bit of research and found that their ideas were similar to a cult in Korea, but I wasn't sure which one it was.'

Armed with his Google results, Nick told Gideon that he didn't feel comfortable with the group. Gideon agreed and as far as Nick knew, he quit going. 'He lied,' Nick says. Gideon secretly took an intense Bible study course with the group. 'He never told me it was Shincheonji. I found out later.'

A few months later, Gideon cut ties with his family and friends. 'The cult made him do that, so he could focus on their teachings and activities,' says Nick. When they didn't hear from their son, Gideon's parents – who were still in New Zealand – were worried. They asked Nick and some of Gideon's other friends to try and find him. 'That's when we found out that it wasn't a small group, it was actually Shincheonji – they're quite influential in Korea.'

To get their son back to Auckland, Gideon's parents stopped giving him money for rent and food, forcing his return home. Shincheonji got their recruit back though. Group members in New Zealand gave Gideon tickets for new flights to Korea. Alongside flights, Shincheonji also provided him with free accommodation, food, and a small stipend so that he could stay, becoming completely dependent on the group. He once again cut contact with his friends and family. Shincheonji even took his phone away during the week, Nick says, purportedly so that Gideon could focus on his religious education. He was not allowed out of the small area of Seoul where he lived and attended his intense Bible study.

'They tried to control him by making him cut ties with people, with his previous church, with his university. They were basically making him cut ties with his past and reform him to be a completely cult-committed person,' Nick says. In the longer term, 'his plan was to become a Shincheonji missionary and go to Europe'. Nick thinks that part of Shincheonji's goal for expansion is to recruit Europeans and other westerners into their fold. The worry for those Gideon left behind was that they wouldn't even know what country he was in.

Nick was still in Korea at this time and tried to keep in regular touch with Gideon. For his efforts, he became the only person in Gideon's pre-Shincheonji life who received any communication. Every few weeks Gideon would send Nick a text telling him he was fine.

'I had to pretend that I was okay with him being in the cult because if I told him to quit then he would have just cut ties with me as well, and that would've caused bigger problems.' Aside from a text now and then confirming his basic safety, 'I never got to see him again,' Nick says.

'We were hoping that he'd at least keep letting someone know he was safe. That was the only thing we ever hoped for at the time.'

Nick eventually returned to New Zealand. Nobody knew if Gideon would ever join him there.

❖

Cults are groups of people who share an intense common mission. Some are religious, while others have political, monetary, self-development, or mixed purposes. They tend to promote unusual beliefs and have a charismatic leader. But what a cult believes is less important than the methods they use to recruit and maintain membership. Cults require extreme commitment from followers, high levels of discipline, and a willingness to divest lifelong relationships and interests. They may require followers to pay money, to provide free labour, or to relinquish their possessions to the cult. A cult may be deceptive about its nature and beliefs to outsiders and new recruits, preferring to slowly introduce core elements of their beliefs over time, after a person has already connected with the group and is primed to accept teachings. They may be abusive and manipulative towards the membership, making it difficult for members to think critically about the group, to leave, or, in time, to entertain the idea of leaving.

The former members of Shincheonji I speak to call it a 'cult', though the term itself is subjective. It's not a term the organisation uses to describe itself, nor is it likely a term that existing members use to describe it.

Shincheonji is a Christian organisation, established in Korea in 1984 by its leader, Lee Man-hee. Followers read the Bible closely, but idiosyncratically. Quoting Psalm 78:2 in the Old Testament – 'I will open my mouth with a parable; I will utter hidden things, things from of old' – Lee teaches that the Bible is in code. Only he has the power to decode its true meaning. Some words and numbers, Nick explains, stand in for other, secret meanings. Textual references to 'heaven' really refer to Shincheonji's church leaders, 'Earth' really means 'congregations', 'sea' refers to 'the world', and so on. To be 'saved', a person must know these secret readings. The beliefs get more complicated still. They don't believe in the Holy Trinity, and Lee is both the Holy Spirit and the second coming of Jesus. They also have a novel take on the Book of Revelations: they believe its apocalyptic prophecy was made in Korea in the 20th century and is already almost fulfilled. It's the end of days.

Gideon's story sounds harrowing to me, but I don't understand how such a group could be so captivating that you'd leave everyone and everything you know to be with them. Why would you drop your whole life, your ambitions, your relationships, to get on a flight to Korea with the long-term goal of becoming a Europe-based missionary to spread the idea that the Bible is all written in code and the apocalypse is imminent? In my own googling about Shincheonji, I find an anti-cult Facebook page, 'Shincheonji Sydney', full of links and information about the group and decide to message the admin. They won't agree to meet with me until I message them my phone number and we have a chat.

And so I rush in the rain to take a call from Nicole (for reasons that will become clear, the people I speak to about Shincheonji prefer me not to use their real names) – I don't want to miss it because I'm nervous she won't call again. I tell her how I first heard of Shincheonji and why I want to talk to the group. It seems I've passed some kind of test. We arrange to meet in Sydney the following week. I later learn that Nicole got in touch with me this first time using a burner number – a phone number that wasn't her regular, personal one.

❖

Nicole meets me at Central Station, and has asked two other former Shincheonji members to join us. As we wait for them, she asks me more questions about my project. She's in her early twenties and strikes me as the opposite of naïve. I don't know if she's always been shrewd, or if her Shincheonji involvement has made her so. She keeps looking around the station, I assume to spot the people we're expecting to meet, but she later tells me it's because she's afraid she's going to see Shincheonji recruiters. When the other former members, Luke and Pedro, arrive, they smile at each other. They've never met each other before; they're all here just to talk to me. There's a palpable sense of relief that floods through our little circle of four. Another intuitive test, and we all pass. They exchange their worries that this meeting would be filled with infiltrators, current Shincheonji members investigating who these troublemaking ex-members are, who this writer is.

Nicole explains to me that she has had messages through the Facebook page from current Shincheonji members wanting to find out who she is, to threaten her into silence. The suspicion swimming around us, now slowly dissipating, is not paranoia.

We walk together from Central, past Railway Square and the Devonshire Street tunnel that opens into the back of the ABC Ultimo building and the University of Technology Sydney. We find a round booth in a café in the university, one side of it open to the world, the other three sides squished into faux leather. Nobody wants coffee or food or anything, even though it's verging on lunchtime. I get us a bottle of water to share.

Sitting across from me, Luke says to the table, 'I've seen at least 15 people today.' He's referring to active Shincheonji members. 'We met here at 12.30, I was here from 11, and I saw at least 15 people.' He pauses and looks around. 'I can guarantee there's at least a few people here. They target universities.'

Pedro agrees. 'Evening classes start at 6.30, so before those start they go out to fish. That's what their term is: fishing, getting new fish.' 'Fish' is another one of Shincheonji's secret Bible words, which, according to them, really means 'people'. 'Fishing' is their word for recruiting.

There seems to be a strategy when it comes to fishing. They like new members to already identify as Christians, but not necessarily to have much knowledge of the Bible. These people might, like Gideon, be at a point of dissatisfaction, or they might simply have time on their hands and be interested in learning more. They seem to target people of particular ethnic backgrounds: people from China and South-East Asia. International students in particular are targeted, perhaps because they're young, far from home, and searching for friends with common interests. These groups already include people who look like them, people who speak their language, friendly folks.

I ask the three former members how they got 'fished' and they share similar stories. All of them were already Christians and interested in learning more about the Bible. One joined through an online Bible study meet-up group; the others were accosted at train stations – Central and Town Hall. Recruits are invited to do a month or two of free Bible study. It's intense: a one-on-one course, held twice a week.

They start off with uncontroversial teachings, Luke says. 'They told us what the Bible is, they gave us verses to look up, and we looked them up.' It was held in a study room on a university campus, and the teacher would seem bubbly and interested.

Pedro joins in. 'Mmm, yeah. They start off by introducing the covenants.'

Confusion must wash over my face. My knowledge of the Bible is superficial. 'Keeping your word, being a good person,' Luke explains. It also deals with ideas like humankind's domination over the Earth and over animals, and God's promise to protect those who are loyal and observe the Ten Commandments.

Sometimes other people would come in and out of these lessons. The teacher would introduce them as 'a friend' who would join in and leave at odd intervals. The visitors said they were new students too, but they were actually long-time Shincheonji members posing as new students.

Each new recruit is paired with a fake new recruit, called a 'leaf' or 'maintainer'. At this point, new recruits are instructed not to talk to anyone else about the group but their leaf. On the surface, the new recruit and their leaf are meant to be buddied up, to support each other, 'To lead you to the right way, the correct way,' says Luke. Pedro suspects that the leaf's real job is 'to make you stay'.

Once the recruit has finished their one-on-one lessons, they join a beginners' class. There might be 60 or so people in the class, but about half are existing members pretending to be new, artificially inflating the numbers.

At around three to four months in, recruits begin intermediate-level study. 'That part gets really interesting and really creepy,' says Pedro. Lessons stop being held on campus and are instead held at the group's Surry Hills or Parramatta premises. It also starts costing money. The group charges students $50 a month, citing high rent as the reason. 'They introduce more about the prophecies, and the leader. They're encouraging you to believe and join the 144 000.'

I ask what the 144 000 is. The number is mentioned several times in the Book of Revelations, and for Shincheonji it represents the literal group of people who will go on to live eternally while the rest of the world is condemned. I note that Shincheonji boasts a membership of 200 000 people in 24 different countries and wonder how they pick people for this exalted group from their international membership.

During their studies, recruits are told that other churches are corrupt, that they don't teach 'the Truth'. At around the four-month mark, recruits are told to go to a church – perhaps their regular local church, perhaps somewhere new – and ask the leaders there about their beliefs, and about the Bible's secret keywords.

Nicole offers examples of what recruits are told to ask: 'What does a tree mean? What does a seed mean?' The point the teachers make is that mainstream Christian denominations lie by teaching their followers that a tree is just a tree, a seed just a seed. They're keeping the key to the Bible – the key to salvation – hidden. Their reasoning is clearly circular, but the aim is to make students feel they have an opportunity to validate what they've been learning for themselves and make the organisation look open.

The Shincheonji studies are demanding. Bible study ends up being a regular commitment on three or more days of the week and there are exams to study for.

'They're very good at making you feel bad if you aren't taking it seriously,' says Pedro.

In preparation for this interview I listened to a recording uploaded online labelled 'Shincheonji class'. The teacher's language is colloquial but bombastic, as though he's delivering a motivational speech or TED talk, employing filler phrases like 'you know' and asking 'right?' at the end of half his sentences. It's as though he carefully planned how to make himself sound approachable. The class laughs at his low-key sexist jokes about humans and beasts (mothers of daughters think that all men are beasts). Throughout, he directs the class to different Bible verses, which the class chants without prompting. There's a sternness just under the friendly surface. He makes fun of people who check Facebook, who 'hang out' on Friday nights, who get preoccupied with girlfriends and boyfriends, who party. He tells the class the Bible says you shouldn't be like that, or envy such people. They are 'wicked', they're not going to heaven, they may enjoy their lives but their 'final destiny' is sealed in hell. We should 'despise' them as 'fantasists'. He describes people who don't feel shame as 'animals in God's eyes'. Implicitly, students are belittled for their ignorance, their weekend plans, anything they do that isn't geared towards knowing God better; those outside the organisation, those not trying hard enough, are doomed, beastly, and 'evil'.

Even four or five months in, recruits still haven't been told the name of the organisation or all of their main beliefs. New recruits aren't deemed 'ready' for the details just yet. It's key that students don't artificially accelerate their studies through internet research. 'They told us not to go on the internet,' says Nicole, 'because it's the world's vomit.'

Luke agrees. 'They told us not to tell anyone: "Don't look it up." There's this verse in the Bible about a dog that'll eat its own vomit, or something like that.'

'They're very good at connecting Bible verses and explaining how what you're doing is poison,' echoes Pedro.

Recruits are advised to stay away from the poison of Google while simultaneously being led to think that they're still simply doing non-denominational Bible study. 'They're not going to say in the beginning who they are,' explains Nicole. 'Because no one would want to join them.'

'A few would,' counters Luke, glancing towards the ceiling. 'They told me who they were, but they brainwashed me so much I stayed there.'

Although misleading, the group seems very informative, and very friendly, at least on the face of it. They enjoy regular picnics at Victoria Park, adjacent to the University of Sydney; you have a 'leaf' assigned to your spiritual welfare; everyone seems interested in getting to know you. Studies are intense but the tone stays light. Nicole, Luke, and Pedro all made friends in Shincheonji – some of them they're still in contact with, others stopped talking to them after they left. They all, at some point, considered Shincheonji to be family.

As they got closer to other Shincheonji members though, they also grew more distant to friends and family outside the group.

'They told me to stay away from family, stay away from friends,' remembers Luke. 'You're there three times a week, if not more. And if family and friends notice you aren't there, they're going to ask why.'

'What are you meant to say?' I ask.

'Lie to them,' says Nicole.

'Lie,' agrees Pedro.

'Lie through your teeth,' says Luke.

Pedro explains: 'They tell students that the devil will find new people to stop you from learning.'

'The devil is everyone besides this organisation,' says Luke.

'Yeah,' continues Pedro. 'The devil will use situations and people –'

'Like your friends and family,' says Luke.

'A new job,' says Nicole.

'New girlfriends, boyfriends,' continues Luke.

Pedro finishes the sentence: '– to trick you.'

It's both surprising and endearing that these former Shincheonji members are finishing each other's sentences when they've only just met. It points to how they all shared this experience with so many others but have rarely been able to talk about it frankly with people who know what it's like.

Students are instructed not to tell anyone about the group and what they're learning. Pedro contravened this once. 'I was surprised by this one teaching that a prophet of Jesus, John the Baptist, will go to hell,' he explains. He asked his sister about it. 'And then my sister was surprised too and said, "Don't you think that sounds different to what the Bible says?"'

Pedro's sister asked him to leave the group, but when he tried to do so, they convinced him to change the times he came to Bible study so she'd be less suspicious of his involvement.

Nicole likewise hid her involvement with the group, isolating herself from family and friends. Nicole's family is part of the Hillsong church, so she told her parents she was doing one of their Bible study groups whenever she went to Shincheonji. The problem was that the Hillsong groups only ran every week or two. 'But with this,' Nicole explains, 'it was three times a week, and on Saturdays too, so they were really surprised.' Nicole liked to sleep in on Saturday mornings, so her parents became suspicious when she wasn't in the house. 'I would be like, "I'm just meeting a friend," or I would say I had something to do with uni.'

Her friends were also asking where she was. 'I was in a close-knit group. We would still hang out but we were getting more distant.' Nicole wanted to tell one of her friends about Shincheonji, but when she asked her leaf about it, they told her to stay quiet, that her friend wouldn't be 'ready' to hear about what she'd learned so far.

The groups thrive on isolating individuals. Nicole was only

in the early stages of drifting away from her friends, nothing as extreme as disappearing like Gideon. A missing person is an ideal cult member – a person who is lost, who has abandoned their former life and ready to embark on something new.

When students begin the intermediate classes, Shincheonji requests their details: their phone number, address, place of work, and so on. Nicole refused to write hers down. 'I asked my leaf, "Why do I need to give my address?"' Her leaf told her just to put down whatever information she wanted.

'It sounds like you were suspicious then?' I say.

'I was,' says Nicole. 'Throughout the whole thing. I guess that's why it was easier for me to leave.' As soon as Nicole was told about Lee Man-hee – six months after starting her studies – she left. She explains that even though the group never felt right to her, the reason she stayed a member so long was because she was interested in the Bible. Nicole describes this as an in-between feeling, not fully committed yet still studying hard for the exams; partially extracting herself from her social group, but never fully immersed in this new one; taking in the teachings, but not absorbing them as 'the Truth' either.

'Because I didn't know much about the Bible, they were able to teach me things that weren't true,' reflects Nicole. 'I guess I started to believe it, but deep down, I didn't.'

Both Pedro and Luke felt suspicious well before they left the group. In fact Pedro convinced a new recruit to leave before he did himself.

'I started having doubts when I got annoyed by this teacher who was asking me too many questions.' He felt he was being shamed for not knowing all the answers. Pedro was in the group classes at this time, but what he didn't realise was that the class was stacked with older members posing as students. This was why the teacher's attention was disproportionately focused on him. 'I was so annoyed I started asking some of my own questions,' Pedro continues. 'I started asking, "How come you guys don't believe in the Trinity?" I got so annoyed, I didn't follow the teacher's reminders not to Google their issues. So, I searched some of their lessons on the internet and Shincheonji came up. Everything came.'

Pedro sighs. 'I shared what I found with another new student, and then he left.' Group members blamed Pedro for the departure and ordered him to get him back. 'I didn't, though,' he says. 'It was becoming stressful for me. At that time, they were telling me to study more, attend more classes. They tried to encourage me to do more one-on-one classes because they felt like I wasn't absorbing the lessons well.'

Pedro thinks it's likely that he wasn't picking up the teachings because he came from a conservative Christian family and he already knew the Bible well. He eventually left after five months, but it took another member on their way out to help him do so. 'It's hard to escape. I was trying to find ways to peacefully tell them I wanted to leave.'

Luke laughs. 'You can't peacefully tell them you want to leave.'

The fact that the group had his details on file also played on Pedro's mind. 'If you leave, they'll show up to your workplace,' he explained.

I gasp. 'Did that happen?'

'I've heard of cases,' Luke says darkly, 'of teachers coming to people's workplace.'

Luke first started having doubts after around four months, when he was instructed to go to a local church and ask the leaders about their teachings. 'I just felt so guilty because I was asking all these questions and trying to destroy their beliefs. I just felt guilt in my heart, like, how can these people expect us to do this?' He tried leaving a number of times after that, over another four months, but he felt close to the other Shincheonji members and knew if he left, they might not speak to him again. 'They were like family to me. And they put guilt on me, they kept asking me to come back, so I did.'

When students finish the classes they 'graduate' and become fully-fledged members of Shincheonji. Nicole, Pedro, and Luke all left before graduation. They think that this time in between advanced classes and graduation is pivotal for determining someone's long-term Shincheonji membership. It's as if an intangible force takes some people over, and not others. They call this process 'brainwashing' (which is also the term Nick had used to describe what happened to Gideon). 'At the end, someone I knew was saying that they're going to leave,' says Luke, 'but then – ' He snaps his fingers. 'Suddenly they're staying. I have so many friends in there, but I have a broken heart because they're so brainwashed.'

'I have a friend,' adds Nicole. 'I tried to get her out, but she's too brainwashed that she wouldn't listen. It's really sad. I challenged her a lot when we had conversations about it, and then she told her teacher about what I'd said. She told me that we shouldn't talk about Shincheonji any more.' Nicole still talks with this friend, but she's not sure what to do, whether to try to convince her to leave but risk alienating her, or whether to pretend she's okay with her friend's Shincheonji membership so she can keep an eye on her.

Thanking the three of them for their time, I feel like I have a better sense of why a fringe religious group might become so appealing to somebody that they embark on a new life and try to sever ties with their old one. Nothing so dramatic happened to these three, but when I tell them Gideon's story, they understand it immediately. There's a series of mechanisms at play with these groups that are both subtle and far more effective than most of us would expect. It's a mixture of deception – not telling new members about their belief system until they've forged strong ties with the group – and pressure, getting information about people, manipulating them, and isolating them from everyone they knew before, all of whom are characterised as 'the devil'. They specifically target people who are most likely to take on their teachings and to be looking for a place they belong. They're looking for people who are questioning the mysteries and uncertainties of faith, life after death, and what we're meant to do while we're here on Earth.

❖

As I go about the rest of my day in Sydney, I keep turning over the question of whether 'brainwashing' is the right term to use for people who join Shincheonji and groups like it. I keep thinking of Gideon as a victim of 'abduction', but is he really? Cults ensnare their members, that's clear, but do they capture them? Isn't the fact that Nicole, Pedro, and Luke all got out evidence that you can escape when the desire to leave is strong enough? Gideon was enthusiastic about going back to Korea, studying the Bible, and spreading his beliefs in Europe. Adults have the right to their religion, and to go missing. How do the friends and family members of someone who joins a group know when to step in or when to let someone be?

The anti-cult movement answers these questions in very clear terms: cult members are forced into believing strange things, into leaving their families, even into killing themselves. Cult membership is a pathology, and members are victims of brainwashing or mind control.

The term brainwashing was first used by journalist Edward Hunter to describe how Mao Zedong's Red Army turned Chinese people into communists. Hunter claimed brainwashing could 'change a mind radically so that its owner becomes a living puppet – a human robot – without the atrocity being visible from the outside'. The fear that communists had somehow developed technologies or techniques that could dissolve individual will galvanised in 1953 when US prisoners of the Korean War falsely confessed to a series of crimes – germ warfare, unleashing anthrax, even dropping the bubonic plague on civilians – and helped produce radio broadcasts of communist propaganda. Most POWs – 5000 of 7200 – either signed false confessions or petitioned the US government to end the war. Twelve refused to go back home immediately when the war ended. The only way officials could make sense of these treasonous confessions and refusals to repatriate was this concept of brainwashing.

Albert Biderman, a social scientist in the US Air Force who studied the POWs, concluded that they were simply responding to their torturous conditions – to extortion, continual shaming, intense isolation, and the threat of death. Just because you strategically agree to cooperate with the people who've imprisoned you, it doesn't mean you are brainwashed. Those POWs who defected into China held realistic fears that if they were to return to the US, they'd be punished for their pro-communist statements, even though they had made them under duress.

Nonetheless, brainwashing continued to be a compelling idea and was used by the anti-cult movement when it first came into prominence in the 1970s. The '70s was the decade of the Jonestown massacre, when a farming settlement of hundreds of American members was established in Guyana by political leader Jim Jones and his group, the People's Temple. In 1978, Congressman Leo Ryan arranged a delegation of politicians, journalists, and left-behind relatives to visit the settlement to check on the welfare of members. Fourteen members expressed a desire to leave and did so with the delegation, but the vast majority ostensibly wanted to stay. Ryan wasn't concerned, and thought that a handful of defectors signified a pretty good satisfaction rate. The group might've been strange, but their settlement was picturesque, and people were entitled to odd beliefs and he wasn't going to interfere. Despite this positive report, Jones was convinced that his settlement was doomed. Members of the cult assassinated five delegation members and defectors before they could fly back home, including Ryan, who was shot 20 times. Jones had some members prepare a metal vat of grape Flavor Aid (not Kool Aid, as is commonly believed) laced with cyanide and other drugs. The members gathered around and drank it. Over 900 people – including children – died.

How do you make sense of the Jonestown massacre? Or that the People's Temple is not the only group to have had mass suicide? In 1997, 39 members of Heaven's Gate – a US group formed in 1974 whose members often went missing from their families over the years – killed themselves in the hope of reaching Comet Hale–Bopp (a real comet) where they believed aliens would grant them eternal bliss. Why would someone rationally choose such a fate for themselves?

The anti-cult movement argues they wouldn't. In the early days of the anti-cult movement, families would hire specialist 'deprogrammers' to abduct cult members, where they'd be forcibly taught about mind control and listen to ex-members reveal damning information about the cult. Today, deprogramming has fallen out of favour and been replaced by voluntary forms of counselling. On the outside, a cult member is encouraged to reclaim their right mind.

They explain that cults use techniques including inducing hypnotic states, drug use, meditation, staging spiritual experiences (for example, using 'psychic powers' to reveal information about a recruit which they've secretly already collected from their recruiter), inculcating values like discipline and obedience, food and nutrient deprivation, 'love bombing' (where cult members are incredibly nice to another member, particularly a new recruit) interspersed with shaming, blaming an individual's problems with teachings on their moral ineptitude, limiting people's access to information and to people they knew before joining the group, limiting people's privacy, provoking fear of the outside world, and making leaving seem impossible. It's like being in an abusive relationship with dozens, or hundreds, or thousands of other people.

These tactics can make someone vulnerable to influence and too exhausted or confused to question teachings, but they can't literally transplant thoughts into people's minds. Clear thinking may be more difficult, agency might be harder to find, but there's no magic through which anyone can get anyone else to do anything. Glynn Washington, a journalist who recounts the story of Heaven's Gate in a 2017 podcast, muses that from his own research and interviews 'we use the word brainwashing not because there's evidence that it's real, but because it protects us from the alternative: how could we think that our brilliant daughter or our beloved father would make a choice to destroy themselves, or to abandon us?'

We have to consider this question. After all, if brainwashing were effective, cult recruitment and retention would be much higher than it is. But since the 1970s, cult membership has diminished in western countries. Generally, people aren't drawn to cults, nor do they tend to stay for long if they are recruited. Sociologist James Richardson offers some theories about why people join in *The Handbook of Cults and Sects in America*. It may represent a rejection of the dominant society (Jim Jones gained followers as an outspoken proponent of radical social justice). Some personality traits and life experiences can draw individuals to such groups (such as being young and finding yourself alone in a new country). A group may serve the needs of its recruits (such as fulfilling a desire to learn more about the Bible), and sometimes people just get involved in regrettable things or don't heed the warning signs as quickly as they'd have liked.

Social psychologist Alexandra Stein offers another theory in her work *Terror, Love and Brainwashing*, suggesting that cult involvement is an example of 'disorganised attachment'. A cult member isn't immediately under the spell of their group, rather they oscillate between a sense of unease and love. This ambivalence was part of the stories of the ex-Shincheonji members I spoke to; they were in turns suspicious of the group and committed to it until they finally left. Group members feel fear and frustration when they're shamed by teachers, or guilt-tripped, or when they find out information that's been hidden from them. Yet they also find friendship, belonging, and spiritual devotion. Stein explains that when people are caught in oscillating dynamics like these, they can experience dissociation, a kind of surrender to their situation, where it feels less exhausting to deal with the doubts and fear by letting them dissipate. They might:

> ... giv[e] up the struggle to fight against the group and the fear it has generated ... This moment of submission, of giving up the struggle, can be experienced as a moment of great relief, and even happiness, or a spiritual awakening.

It might lead to the proud day of Shincheonji graduation, being accepted as a fully-fledged member of the group after toiling through the demanding study. The mind is 'washed' only in the sense that it's clear of too many intolerable conflicting thoughts. It's erased of ambiguity.

None of this makes the question of whether a person chooses to flee to a cult or is coerced into it any easier. Manipulation is still part of a group's apparatus, even though personal responsibility and critical thought is always part of an individual's apparatus. Maybe cult membership is a clash of these forces – sometimes they oppose each other, and sometimes they don't. And the result is somewhere in between choice and force, a belief formed and a belief imposed.

Many sociologists and religious studies scholars prefer the term 'new religious movement' over 'cult' to avoid stigmatising people and their beliefs. People in such groups don't identify as 'cult members' until after they leave, and the label can be used to dismiss people and groups that are merely different but harmless. Mainstream religions can and do take on cult dynamics where worship is intense and regulated. Likewise, relatively new and less mainstream spiritualities such as Wicca are clearly not 'cults'.

Seeing emerging religious groups as 'movements' also allows us to contextualise them. While a cult centres on a messianic leader who's charismatic enough to gain some followers, movements are all informed by political and social changes beyond the group. And indeed, new religious movements seem to take off during times of social ambiguity. In a 2019 article, David W Kim and Won-il Bang observe that during times of upheaval in 20th-century Korea, such as the period of Japanese colonisation (1910s–1930s), and during democratisation (1960s–1980s), there was a growth of new religious movements with a range of Korean religious figures proclaiming themselves to be the messiah. We see this elsewhere: in many western countries, the increased ability to travel, urbanisation, emphasis on civil rights, the sexual revolution, demographic shifts, and other key changes in the 1960s and '70s coincided with a peak in religious revitalisation, change, and entirely new religious movements (although statistically few people actually join them). The birth of these groups corresponds with mass uncertainty, and either a sense of great possibility or an enveloping sense of helplessness. Whether or not they provide meaningful direction and comfort in these times, new religious movements are as much about managing widespread anxieties as they are about erasing individual ones about the purpose of life, what happens when we die, or how to be a good person.

International human rights law doesn't distinguish between mainstream organised religion and smaller fringe groups in its provisions for religious freedom. In 2019, Shincheonji was so sure of its legitimacy that it made a statement to the UN Commission on Human Rights stating that two members had died during their forcible abduction and deprogramming. One woman was killed by her husband in 2007, and another died in 2018 after being admitted to hospital as a result of her 'second attempted deprogramming'. They called on the Korean government to curb religious 'hate speech' against their organisation.

At the same time, 'cult' is a word that the people I speak to – the survivors – use. It's important to recognise that they feel deceived, manipulated, pressured, and shamed by Shincheonji. This remains so, even if Shincheonji considers its teachings genuine, and their dubious organisational methods justified as a means of spreading 'the Truth'.

I come to think that Gideon was almost abducted, and almost a runaway. He was a missing person who had a right to be missing, a right to religious freedom; and at the same time those left behind had legitimate concerns for his safety.

❖

Cult membership isn't widespread in Australia. In a report almost 20 years ago, the Australian Human Rights Commission looked briefly at the influence of cults in Australia and found that only 2 or 3 per cent of Australians have had anything to do with them as members or as someone close to a cult member. Yet, while the raw numbers of cults and their recruits in Australia isn't high, these groups can be influential and can feel omnipresent to ex-members. Some boast great wealth, and some even influence geopolitics. They cause people to go missing.

Talking to Nicole, Pedro, and Luke, I'm reminded of when my partner and I were in Seoul one sweaty summer, on the train to Hongdae, the city's overstimulating student district. We were accosted by a man who spoke to us in English and asked us where we were from.

'Australia,' we responded. His face brightened. He explained he had been to Sydney and he'd seen the Opera House. He had travelled there for his missionary work.

'Are you Christian?' he asked. I responded no, we're not religious. He scolded us and walked away.

'Why would he do Christian missionary work in Australia?' I wondered after we got off the train and walked through the busy streets where small groups of young people were dancing to Korean pop music and attracting onlookers. 'There's already tons of Christians.' It's a question I put to the former members of Shincheonji as well. They said that this man was from a cult. It was not Christianity he wanted to spread, but his group's unique take on it.

Public transport, university campuses, shopping centres, tourist locations throughout the world, even YouTube are all common places for recruitment. Sometimes these groups will create front activities – a board game club, free Korean lessons – in order to surreptitiously recruit those who turn up. They go to mainstream churches and try to recruit from the congregations. Nicole has seen Shincheonji members 'fishing' at her Hillsong church; 'fishing' from other churches is such a common practice in Korea that churches often put signs on their doors saying 'Shincheonji, Keep Out'. Nicole, Pedro, and

Luke told me that being a former cult member means that you see their operatives everywhere. You suspect they might be tracking you, getting information on you, trying to pull you back in. I try on this mindset as I walk through to the underground train station at Sydney's Town Hall. I scan my surroundings for fishers. They look so ordinary that I can only speculate whether I actually spot any. This mundanity is part of what makes it scary – not all who believe in the imminent apocalypse are out there wearing sandwich boards and shouting at you. Group members look like students, like potential friends.

❖

Shincheonji is only one of an estimated 400 Korean cults or sects, with around a quarter of those claiming links to Christianity. Similar groups are also operating in Australia. Providence – which has around 100 000 members worldwide – was founded in 1982 by convicted rapist Jeong Myeong-seok, and imported to Australia in 1997. SBS's *The Feed* spoke to ex-members in Canberra who were recruited at the shopping centre in Civic and on university campuses. They said that the group recruited young women to worship images of the leader alongside images of Jesus. During worship, they're told Jeong was falsely imprisoned because of religious persecution.

'They said we are in the position of brides towards God and we are also in the position of brides towards Jeong, the leader, because he represents God,' says Liz, an ex-member. She was encouraged to write intimate letters to him while he was in prison, as though he were her husband. He'd respond in kind. 'He would say things like "women are much more beautiful when they are naked" and he said my white skin arouses him.' Liz travelled to Korea to visit Jeong in prison. There, she saw him caressing pictures stuck to his cell wall of women from around the world. 'He wants to have as many beautiful women believing that they are in love with him and believing they would give every part of themselves to him.'

Other Australian members have allegedly gone missing as a result of their involvement in Providence. In 2017 the ABC's *7.30* reported the case of Camilla Wagemans, who was recruited by Providence at the Australian National University and is now living in Korea. Her father, Gerry, said that he didn't realise his daughter was involved with Providence until he saw *The Feed*'s piece about it and found she'd appeared in a promotional video for the group. Although he was allowed limited phone and email contact with Camilla, it was sporadic, and the topic of Providence was off limits. Gerry experienced 'a general feeling of disbelief and also great mourning that ... I really lost my daughter'. Providence has denied the allegations made by the ABC and SBS.

❖

One of Australia's most notorious cults, The Family, led by Anne Hamilton-Byrne, was homegrown and based on the outskirts of Melbourne. It instigated many child abductions. Hamilton-Byrne preached a mix of Hinduism, Christianity, and black magic, and claimed to be the reincarnation of Jesus. By the 1970s, some followers handed their children over to Hamilton-Byrne, while other children were stolen from hospitals in adoption scams carried out by members who were nurses, doctors, and lawyers. In their 2016 book, *The Family*, Chris Johnston and Rosie Jones describe how Hamilton-Byrne amassed a following of around 500 people, and had 28 children living in a secluded compound on Lake Eildon. The children were meant to be a master race that would survive the imminent nuclear apocalypse and become the world's leaders. Members gave Hamilton-Byrne money and property, which allowed her to isolate the children. Her net worth in property, land, and cash was around $150 million in the late 1980s.

The children were overseen by Hamilton-Byrne and other adult members of The Family, dubbed 'the Aunties'. Their names had been changed, birth certificates falsified, their hair dyed peroxide blond to make them appear related. Survivors say they were regularly drugged with LSD and other psychoactive substances, and subjected to strange rituals, abuse, neglect, and starvation. They rarely saw the world outside.

The Family collapsed in 1987 when one of the children, Sarah, was kicked out for disobedience (she was the second child to have been kicked out) and alerted authorities to the compound. Some of the children were reunited with their biological parents, and then it was then Hamilton-Byrne's turn to disappear. She fled the country and evaded police until 1993, when she was found and brought to trial. Bizarrely, she served no prison time, and she and adult members of The Family were only prosecuted for fraud – for making false statements, submitting false social security claims and falsifying birth certificates. Hamilton-Byrne was later sued by some survivors and ordered to compensate them for abuse.

How did Hamilton-Byrne manage to gain so much influence over members? This is a question Johnston and Jones ask in *The Family*:

> Cult narratives are full of it: the charismatic leader offering salvation made me do it ... made me steal [children], made me abuse [children]. Made me ignore right from wrong.

Victims and perpetrators blur; the wide-eyed people who hand over their assets are also child abusers. There's an alchemical circularity to it: the same people who gave Hamilton-Byrne power through their money, their property, their labour, their skills, were the ones who felt they were under its control. Hundreds of lives were disrupted. Some children grew up never knowing their parents.

❖

Money is an important component of influence. The Church of Scientology, formed in 1952, is based on the writings of L Ron Hubbard. His heart stopped momentarily during a dental procedure and in the ensuing near-death experience, Hubbard believed that he was given a glimpse of the secrets of existence. His insights eventually became the basis of his bestselling book, *Dianetics*. The HBO documentary *Going Clear: Scientology and the Prison of Belief* – which interviewed former members who labelled Scientology a 'cult' – points out that membership numbers are diminishing over time while the group's material value increases. Ex-members say that they were under huge pressure to donate money to the church, and using membership labour keeps the organisation's costs low. Globally, the Church of Scientology enjoys religious tax exemptions in multiple jurisdictions, and owns more than a million square metres of property and a cruise ship. It is estimated to have over US$1 billion in liquid assets, more than most major world religions.

Disappearances have also been associated with Scientology. As is common in groups labelled 'cults', members are reportedly forced to cease contact with concerned or sceptical loved ones. One ex-member reports that she was cut off from her daughter and granddaughter after trying to talk to her daughter about Scientology's problems.

'She hugged me, she told me she loved me, she said, "I have to disconnect from you"… I was concentrating on smelling her hair, seeing the way she felt, touching her skin with my face. It was the last time I saw them.'

A missing-persons report was filed in 2013 in Los Angeles for Shelly Miscavige, the wife of current Scientology leader David Miscavige. She hasn't been seen in public since 2007. The LA Police Department has closed the case and Scientologists say that Shelly is simply a private, dedicated person who was never missing. However, a *Vanity Fair* investigation suggests that she may have been exiled (perhaps voluntarily) to a secret, highly guarded remote Scientology base.

In the 2016 Australian census, only 1684 people identified themselves as Scientologists (down from 2163 in 2011), yet Scientology headquarters can be found in metropolitan areas of Sydney, Melbourne, Brisbane, Perth, Canberra, Adelaide, and Launceston. Aaron Saxton, who was born in New Zealand and involved with Sydney's Scientology branch, has a disquieting account of Scientology in Australia. In 2009 he gave a statement to Senator Nick Xenophon to enter into Australian parliamentary record. He says that his mother – a Scientology member – had signed over guardianship of him to the church when he was 16 years old. He became a senior member of Scientology's elite branch, Sea Org, in Sydney and in the US. He alleges that church practices included isolating members, forced abortions, confinement, malnourishment, medical neglect, hard labour, and torture. He wrote of kidnapping dissident members and described an incident where he was involved in abducting, imprisoning, and torturing a former member on a farm in western New South Wales. The church denies these allegations.

❖

These kinds of groups can have a terrifying impact on geo-politics, waging wars and bringing missing people into their dangerous fold. In the *Journal of Terrorism Research*, Bruce Barron and Diane Maye identify ISIS as an Islamic cult:

> ISIS is trying to resurrect a medieval Islamic society under the rule of a caliph (Abu Bakr al-Baghdadi) whose word is unquestioned and final. Similar to other cults, ISIS has little tolerance for outsiders and believe they should be conquered, forced to convert, or killed.

Consistent with cults, ISIS holds views that are at odds with both mainstream Islam and society, and they maintain an impossible goal of 'world domination'.

They also cause disappearances. Abdullah Elmir was a 17-year-old from Sydney who was reported missing at the end of June 2014. He told his parents he was going fishing, but unbeknown to them, he took a flight to Syria to fight with ISIS. They didn't know where he was until October that year, when he appeared in ISIS propaganda videos.

Greg Barton from Monash University's Global Terrorism Research Centre told the *Sydney Morning Herald* that Abdullah was groomed through a western Sydney street-preaching group.

'It's like sexual predation,' he explains. 'Somebody might strike up a friendship in an online chat forum and present themselves in a different fashion – to try to get them into their web. By the time they actually meet the people they're speaking with, they may be in too deep to know better.' Of the propaganda video, he comments, 'He thinks he's the star ... but the reality is his new friends have got him a one-way ticket. He's not in charge of his own destiny at all; he's being used.'

According to *The Australian*, Australian counter-terrorism

agencies believe that Abdullah Elmir was killed in a bombing raid in Syria in 2015, but the death has not been verified. He is still missing.

❖

After a year of being away in Korea and barely talking to his family or any of his old friends, Gideon's parents sent him an email offering a deal. Luckily, he read it and took the deal. They'd found an organisation offering anti-cult education and told him if he went and listened to what they had to say and still wanted to remain in Shincheonji, they'd support him.

'Fortunately,' says Nick, 'the anti-cult group helped him realise the cult was wrong.'

Gideon left Shincheonji and flew back to New Zealand. His life is similar to the one he left behind. Gideon's case has a fortunate ending, Nick says. 'He came back, but a lot of people don't come back.'

Superficially, Gideon's story of running away is similar to Brandy's – he also escaped family members and friends who held beliefs counter to his own. Yet unlike Brandy, Gideon entered a place of dependence, where his access to food and shelter, where he was allowed to go and who he was allowed to talk to, were controlled by Shincheonji.

It's not easy to evaluate the trajectory of others' lives from the outside; it can be hard to tell the difference between freedom and control, self-preservation and self-destruction. We can't always tell how wise a decision is until the person who made it speaks for themselves upon their return – a return that's never guaranteed. But an important distinction is that when Brandy left, she carried her doubts with her too. She experienced homelessness, and took with her questions about trust and suffering, and her own feelings of guilt. This honest openness is a harder road – the ambiguity is near intolerable – but a false sense of fate is a warning sign. States of uncertainty are uncomfortable, yet danger lies in certainty, too.

12

A POINT OF CONNECTION

THE MISSING PERSONS ADVOCACY NETWORK

Both my visit to Missing Children Europe and my conversation with Susan focused, in their different ways, on the big-picture policy measures. The issue of missing persons needs to be taken more seriously by both the media and law enforcement, and resources need to be doled out more equally among cases. Critical services need greater investment, and there needs to be funding for research so we can understand the scope of the issue. Although my conversation with Gail and Mette from MCE made me feel like I understood the possibilities of constructively dealing with the ambiguous situation of disappearance, it didn't make me feel that I personally had much of a role to play. It felt like it was up to policy-makers, politicians, and institutions to do better.

When I talk to Loren O'Keeffe, who founded the Missing Persons Advocacy Network (MPAN), I still have the view that structural change is vital. But then she details how we can all interact with those searching for missing persons in helpful ways. That individuals, companies, and local communities all have a role to play. In the face of ambiguity, we are not helpless.

I call Loren on Skype. I first met her in 2015, a few weeks before I left Australia to live in Europe, and we talked in a café near her office in Melbourne's Little Collins Street in an arcade with a high, translucent ceiling, a tiled floor, and little shops selling gifts and cakes and useless pretty things. Trams hummed and rang outside and the smell of coffee wafted in the air. It was early September, the first days of spring. I think of that day and realise that both of our lives are quite different now to what they were then.

Loren founded MPAN in 2013. Her motivation was personal: her brother Dan had gone missing in July 2011. Loren's family didn't have any idea what to do. They were shocked that police weren't going to help them search. The police thought the case was low risk – even though Dan had a history of depression – and so prioritised his privacy over the family's questions. The family had to run the investigation themselves. They made some false starts and they happened on some helpful tricks. Loren's idea for MPAN was based on the belief that no person who has lost a loved one in such a stressful, ambiguous way should have to reinvent the wheel. There should be practical help for them, some guidance about what's possible and what works.

Central to MPAN's mission is the Missing Persons Guide, which essentially provides a checklist of what families can do from the moment they're worried that someone is missing, to what to do after a week, or a month, or longer has gone by. It talks about making a missing-persons report, making posters, finding people to help search, informing the media, building a social media campaign, hiring a private investigator, and managing the missing person's affairs. Loren encourages people whose loved one has been missing for over a week to contact her and see what additional support MPAN can add beyond the Guide. The organisation has partnerships with a law firm, a strategic communications firm, an advertising agency and the advertising teams of national publications, a billboard advertising company, a poster-printing company, even a bumper-sticker company. These organisations can provide professional advice and services – like answering legal questions and writing up press releases – pro bono or at low cost.

When Loren and I spoke that day in 2015, her brother had been missing for over four years. She talked about the case, the leads her family had been following, and the difficulties of trying to stay in the public eye over time when there was little new information. Similar to the PR strategy the McCanns designed after their daughter Madeleine went missing, Loren notes you need to be clever about bringing attention to cases. There's a lot to say. Whenever I asked Loren a question, she had reams of insights. Any issue within the broader topic of missing persons merged into others. There aren't really concise answers you can give. It's not easy when your goal is to keep the short attention spans of the public on your case when a page-long press release is too long, where more than a short sentence on a billboard will go unread, when you're competing with videos of puppies for likes on Facebook feeds, and so on. Despite the hurdles she'd been facing, she was hopeful that Dan would turn up again one day.

Sadly, a few months later, in March 2016, Dan's body was found in an obscure recess between a wall and solid-rock earth in his parents' backyard. He died by suicide. Loren's grief when I speak to her in 2017 is still present. She apologises to me.

'As a consequence of all the stress and intensity, I've become quite forgetful,' she says. 'My brain is all over the place nowadays.'

MPAN was always bigger than Dan's case. Having this

constructive work to do was a way for Loren to cope with his disappearance, and then, his death; but MPAN has taken on its own momentum.

In Australia, Loren tells me, those left behind can access counselling services and support groups by way of morning teas and forums. But these resources are only offered in the state of New South Wales by the Families and Friends of Missing Persons Unit, which is run by the state government. People from other states, like Loren, have to travel to access these services.

'It's good,' says Loren. 'But it's different. It's a very different type of service to what I feel like people like me – people who want to be proactive and productive – need. I went to a forum and to a morning tea. I found it quite depressing, to be honest. Understandably. It's a terrible reason why we've all come together, but to dwell on that never sat well with me. I always wanted to work on the next problem and to fix it. To try and find the person. And to keep the public engaged in the meantime.

'Sitting in a room with 20 people lamenting over their devastating predicament, and the poor treatment they've had from police or whatever it is – that's not empowering.'

Loren notes that it can be incredibly beneficial for those left behind to talk about their experiences and to be listened to – in fact, MPAN published a book, *Too Short Stories*, which conveys some of the difficulties of ambiguous loss. Some of us need to express ourselves when faced with despair. But some of us also like to problem-solve, and that pragmatic inclination should also be facilitated.

'I really want MPAN to empower people who find themselves in what is a really, overwhelmingly hopeless and helpless situation,' says Loren. 'I want to help them find something they can do.' In the face of ambiguity, there are opportunities to forge forward anyway. MPAN exists on this premise.

Loren thinks that the central problem that families and friends of missing persons face is a lack of understanding. 'It's a weird space, it's quite awkward to talk about. I mean most people – everyday people – have an opinion on things in general, but not this. This is an area where people just don't really know how to respond. One of our challenges is trying to normalise it. To make it known that it is such a prevalent issue, [that] it does impact so many thousands of Australian families every year.'

When so many people are affected, Loren believes that we all have a collective responsibility to understand the issues and to address them. From the outside, it looks like missing-persons cases are completely within the remit of police to resolve. It wasn't until Dan went missing that Loren learned just how limited police resources are when it comes to finding missing persons. It's common for family members and friends to conduct their own searches in conjunction with police, but as Loren's family found out, sometimes no police assistance is offered.

'You think the police are there to get out the heat-seeking cameras and get out the dog squad but that very rarely happens,' she says. Loren's family searched wide areas and did their own door-knocking to ask neighbours if they had information. 'And so, I think it's important for us not to have that expectation.'

It's not possible that police even *could* address the needs of those left behind on their own. The media plays a central role in publicising cases and could, argues Loren, provide greater free advertising space for this purpose alongside their news coverage. Likewise, local governments can also play a part. Loren can recall numerous times when families of missing persons have attempted to poster walls around their city only for the posters to be taken down by council workers strictly applying the council's 'Post No Bills' policies; they could be more flexible with the policy when it comes to finding loved ones. Loren's family has also suffered from the impact of inflexible bureaucracy of local government.

'Mum and Dad have been getting letters from the Sheriff's Office about Dan's parking fine for the last five years,' says Loren. Despite attempts to inform the Office that Dan was missing, and later, that he had died, they have not stopped issuing these letters. 'The Sheriff's Office said that the letters will keep coming but just ignore them. Like, really? There's no way that you can just stop them coming altogether?'

It's needlessly difficult for those left behind to do some basic, practical things to manage a missing person's affairs after they've disappeared. This is a space where utility companies and the corporate sector could make a few small improvements which would, in turn, massively help family members and friends of missing persons. Loren once helped a woman in Perth whose brother had been missing for around a year to deal with his mobile phone bills. His provider had been sending debt-collection notices because his account was overdue. The woman had called the company to explain the situation, but they didn't stop sending the threatening letters. So, Loren called the company herself.

'I said, "Look, this is ridiculous. Can you please just suspend the account?" And they did. And I said, "Okay, that was easy, wasn't it?"' She's since worked with the phone provider to put a policy in place so that if customers go missing for an extended period of time, there'll be a way for their loved ones to cancel accounts, or put them on hold. She hopes that other companies will follow in kind. 'It doesn't really affect them at all. It would probably save them money because they're not paying debt collectors to chase a missing person.'

Everyone can help. It's simple to join a Facebook group that disseminates information about missing persons and increase your awareness of ongoing cases. A Facebook group called 'The Australian Missing Persons Register' is run entirely by a woman from Queensland who posts information about missing persons in Australia every day. Followers – of which there are over 130 000 – may have leads themselves, or can share them to spread the information further. It has untold reach.

'I don't know how she stays on top of it all,' says Loren, 'but she's been doing it for years.' Anyone can join groups such as these and thus join the effort to locate missing individuals. That said, when looking online for information, it's important only to join legitimate groups and pages. Some Facebook groups post hoax reports in order to gain shares, likes, and follows; this in turn allows them to sell the page to companies wanting to use the page's existing popularity for their brand.

Privacy can also be an issue when we share the details of missing persons, or alleged missing persons. In 2017, according to Missing Children Europe, some formerly missing children found that information shared about their cases was still online. They worried how this information would shape the way they were perceived when they met new people, or applied for jobs. The lingering digital footprint of campaigns needs to be balanced with fears for the missing person's safety.

Sometimes sharing information about a child can directly compromise their safety, too, as Swedish publication *Metro.se* reported in 2013. It's possible for parents who have had a restraining order taken out against them to pretend that their child is missing on social media. Disclosing the whereabouts of a child to an abusive parent can be dangerous, leading to further violence, abuse, and even death. Nonetheless, with sensible caution such as verifying information before sharing or otherwise acting on it, helping out can be as simple as checking your news feed – something you'd probably do anyway.

'We want this to be seen as a community issue,' says Loren. It's better if multiple sectors feel responsible, because on their own, the support police can provide is not enough.

Loren has designed a number of strategies to get people to think about their personal responsibilities when it comes to missing persons. One major aspect of it is to make the topic more relatable by distinguishing it from notions that it's associated with crime. 'We try to challenge that stereotype,' she says. Just because police may get involved with missing-persons investigations doesn't mean that they're capable of preventing people from going missing, or always find people without the help of the broader public. MPAN has access to free advertising space for missing-persons posters, and MPAN's creations look different to typical police notices, which include a picture of the missing person and a rundown of their vital information.

'The artwork uses soft colours and softer tones,' Loren explains. 'There's friendlier language. So it's not "Daniel James O'Keeffe", it's "Dan". And it's his hobbies and the different roles that he played in the community. It's not just "He's 180 centimetres tall", it's "He's a brother, he's a grandson". It's all about humanising missing people – trying to get people to engage with them and their stories. Trying to make the public interested in the people behind the posters.

'And it's key, little details – like reminding the public that this is a real person who plays basketball, or speaks French, or whatever – that will make someone go, "That could be my sister" or "That could be my best friend". We want to help them realise that this could happen to anyone. Not just baddies or victims of crime like in the movies – this is much broader than that … And it's also part of straying from that association with criminality. I don't want the public thinking that missing persons is a scary, dark, criminal topic. It's not. People go missing for a number of reasons. I really want it to be seen more as a social issue rather than a police task.'

The power of social media and of helpful individuals became clear to Loren after she uploaded the last poster she ever made for her missing brother to Facebook. It was a Wednesday afternoon and her parents were flying to Darwin that day to look for possible leads on Dan's whereabouts. They planned to visit different food vans around the city because of the correlation between those who have gone missing and those who are homeless. At five o'clock that night, Loren's parents arrived at the first food van.

'And at the back,' says Loren, 'the volunteers had taken it upon themselves to print out the latest poster that had only just become available so that – in the event that someone from their community had seen Dan – they'd be aware that he was missing.

'To know people that far away from us had just taken it upon themselves to print out the A3 [size] colour poster and put it up on the back of their food van was really touching. That helps, you know? Other people sharing the load.'

Loren explains how often practical support for families of missing persons is also an emotional form of support. 'Putting up posters is one of the most exhausting tasks associated with this process – physically, mentally, emotionally. To have strangers do that for you is really, really incredible. And social media enables that, which is wonderful.'

As important as it is to assist in the search, it's not just about that. 'It's that feeling that you're not alone in this. You've got thousands of people who care about your brother and want the same end result as you do. Even if it doesn't directly lead to finding that person,' says Loren, 'it's about the hope and the sharing of that burden.' In the months after Dan first went missing, the Facebook page Loren created to help find him, 'Dan Come Home', had over 5000 followers. When the family decided to conduct a search for him through parkland near their home they mentioned it to their followers. One hundred of them – most of them strangers – came from across the state to help out with the search early on a Saturday morning.

The night before, Loren's sister realised that it would be useful to have a metal detector for the search because Dan had gone missing with his mobile phone. It was a bit late to put out a call on Facebook – it was midnight on the day before the search. But Loren did anyway, just in case. 'And a man rocked up the next morning with his metal detector,' she says. 'He didn't know why he was there, his wife just told him to be there. He just spent the whole day with his metal detector.' Nothing was found in the search, but the experience was profound for Loren and her family. 'We had the support of the community thanks to social media. We were able to reach those people who we didn't know but who cared enough to come down on a Saturday from across the state. It's invaluable to a family.'

Like Sarah, Loren has also had to deal with negative responses to her brother's case. The hoaxes over the years – people pretending to be Dan on the phone and telling her to stop searching, scammers from Ghana sending emails to those close to Dan saying they've kidnapped him and demanding ransom money, people using Dan's image for online dating profiles – have been particularly disturbing.

More quotidian and less mystifying responses can hurt too. Loren remembers the reaction her work colleagues initially had when they learned that her brother had gone missing. It had been on the news; everyone knew about it. Loren was quickly going into the office to collect some things before taking leave. From the time she walked in to the time she walked out, nobody in that office talked to her.

'Even people I considered friends at work didn't even look at me because it was too awkward. When it comes to talking about it, or having information about it, people are – I don't know – paralysed? They don't know how to broach it.'

But Loren has hope that even if the ambiguity posed by missing persons makes us uncomfortable, we're ultimately interested in their plight, and those left behind.

'It is deeply intriguing. People cannot help but to be intrigued by it. There's so much mystery and drama. And there's so much emotion around this topic.' This contradiction provides a path into people's consciousness. As much as they want to turn away, they are also attracted. 'They don't know what to do or to say but they want to learn about it. Because it is interesting. We try and manage that because in regard to media attention and everything, that's the one thing we've always got.'

The role of social media in aiding families of missing persons is a fledgling area of research. A 2016 study looked at social media as a way to crowdsource the search for missing persons. The paper is optimistic about the usefulness of social media in supporting family members and friends of missing persons, but not necessarily about its potential to actually find people.

Loren agrees this is largely true. 'Finding missing persons is the ultimate goal,' she says, 'but it's certainly not the objective of MPAN. We try and help the likelihood of that increase but actually finding missing persons is not something we could ever claim to be able to do.'

However, there are cases where people have been found or where key information about missing-persons cases has become available through social media. 'Everything seems to happen in America,' laughs Loren. 'You know how you see things on the news and you're like, "Only in America!" but there are quite a few cases of children in particular who go missing and thanks to widespread social media coverage, they're recovered in a short amount of time – like hours.'

Indeed, US television network NBC reported on a case in Richmond, Virginia, from May 2016 where a nine-year-old girl was abducted. Local law enforcement put a huge emphasis on regularly using Twitter and Facebook to update members of the local community about the case. They had pictures of the child and, when they managed to get CCTV footage of the abductor's car, they uploaded it to social media straightaway. And it worked. A member of the community was able to identify the car, and the abductor. The girl was brought home safely. Dana Schrad of the Virginia Association of Chiefs of Police told NBC, 'I don't think we could be nearly as successful without the advent of social media.' She attributed the rising recovery rate of missing children (from around 60 per cent in the 1980s to above 97 per cent in 2016) to social media because of the way it broadened the search effort. 'It really becomes a matter of everyone being involved now when a child is missing,' she said.

As part of her work with MPAN, Loren helped out with the high-profile missing-persons case of Dane Kowalski, a 27-year-old man from Diamond Creek in Melbourne. His friends and family became concerned on Boxing Day 2014. They hadn't heard from him for a few weeks. They'd expected little contact from him because he was travelling, but it was out of character for him not to get in touch at Christmas. They tried to call him but couldn't get through. 'They were the ones really getting this campaign off the ground,' says Loren. Along with approaching traditional media, they were going through MPAN's guide, spray painting bedsheets with the message '#FindDane' and hanging them across footbridges above multi-lane highways. They also set up a social media campaign with a huge following. After months of raising awareness, a woman in South Australia got in touch with them.

'Thanks to their Facebook page,' says Loren, 'she knew that a car she had seen abandoned on the side of the road out in the middle of nowhere was Dane's car. And so, she got in touch with them and said, "I think I found Dane's car" and she called local police.' The police found Dane's body 340 metres from his car. He had written a note, found on a tree nearby, saying he had been bitten by a snake. He had been dead for over three months by the time his body was found.

'Had she not followed his page on Facebook, that car may have been found but it wouldn't have surprised me if police didn't check the plates and figure out that it belonged to the missing man in Victoria. And then Dane could've remained missing for years. Or forever.'

While the idea that all of us can play a role in finding missing persons and offering support to those left behind is a hopeful one, I also wonder if we really have the skills to take on this responsibility. Of central importance to a missing-persons case is a public appeal. There are missing-persons posters that display a picture of the missing person and include identifying details and instructions on what to do should you see them. There are also Amber Alerts, a strategy first developed in the US in 1996 following the disappearance of Amber Hagerman and since adapted around the world. Amber Alerts disseminate information about missing children as quickly as possible to law enforcement agencies and communities in the event of extremely concerning disappearances. I've seen many public appeals for information as I've researched this book, yet I don't seem to have a clear picture of any of the individuals in my memory. It's disturbing, really, the idea that I could be walking by a missing person on any given day and not realise.

There hasn't been much research into the effectiveness of

public appeals for information, which is paradoxical given how much searching relies on them. Psychological research reveals that we aren't generally good at what's called 'prospective person memory', that is, remembering details of a person for a future where we might see or interact with them. Both under experimental conditions and out and about, people on average are able to identify a person they've learned about earlier only 10 per cent of the time. Other studies have found that missing persons appeals are most successful where they're relatively short, viewed recently, and contain memorable information about the person – as Loren advocates, not simply a list of facts, but a story about who the person is, and the concerns those left behind have for them. It's also important to be strategic in placing Amber Alerts, as research reveals that the more the alerts go off, the less likely people are to pay attention to them. It's possible to oversaturate people's minds with messages, especially given that the goal is to have people on the lookout for a missing person while they're otherwise occupied going about their daily lives.

NBC's *Today* program in the US filmed a little experiment in 2016. They put hidden cameras in a store, put up fake missing-children posters with a picture of a child actor, and had the actor walk right in front of the posters. Some people responded to the matching poster and child, but most did not. Even when people noticed the apparent similarities between the two-dimensional child on the sign and the child standing in front of it, they reported having been too afraid to say anything in case they were wrong. They were afraid they would embarrass themselves and scare the kid. *Today* talked to the mother of the child actor.

'That's my child, and if she was really missing … nobody wants to help,' she said worriedly.

During the 1980s in the US, the faces of missing children

were printed on around five billion milk cartons. But as podcast *99% Invisible* reports, this strategy to publicise the faces of missing children was not generally successful. For one thing, it was disturbing for families – especially children – to stare at the face of a child who had been abducted (most likely by a stranger) over breakfast. More disturbingly, very few of the 'milk carton kids' were ever found. The podcast features the story of one girl, Bonnie Lohman, who was found as a result of the campaign but under unusual circumstances. She had been abducted by her mother and stepfather. After many years of living away from her father, she was at a supermarket with her stepfather and saw herself on a milk carton. She thought it was cool. She didn't know how to read so she didn't realise she was on it because she was 'missing'. Her stepfather, in an act of hubris, bought the milk carton. When the milk was finished he offered it to Bonnie to keep, telling her not to show anyone. She was eventually 'found' because she had left the carton in a toy box at her neighbour's house and they called the authorities. Most people wouldn't have such close contact with a missing child, nor would they ever be likely to find the face of the neighbours' kid on a missing-persons milk carton left at their house by that very kid. Most of us would have to work much harder to recognise a missing person.

Facial recognition – and our general ineptitude for it – is a persistent problem for police. As the *New Yorker* reports, the London Metropolitan Police has access to CCTV footage of many crimes but 'unless somebody recognises a suspect, CCTV footage is effectively useless'. There are about six police officers in the force (out of 32 000) who have been identified as having the canny ability to recognise faces, a team known as the 'super-recognisers'. Super-recognisers can take a grainy, pixelated picture – or the merest sliver of a face that has been obscured by a disguise, or a picture of a face taken many years ago – and identify the person out in the world. The half-dozen super-recognisers are responsible for about one-quarter of the force's CCTV identifications. Facial-recognition abilities fall on a spectrum. You have people with 'face blindness' (technically called prosopagnosia) who couldn't recognise the faces of their closest relatives, and you have super-recognisers. Most of us are somewhere in the middle.

And perhaps this is enough. Even if most people aren't very good at recognising people, those who are might be enough. We may need to reassure ourselves that it's better to say something about a sighting of a potentially missing person and be mistaken than to not alert the authorities at all. Among the thousands of people who see the image, only one needs to make the brave leap between the face they saw on-screen the night before and the face right in front of them and say something.

Another hope is that the missing person themselves will see these public appeals, and realise that people are concerned and would love to have them home.

❖

Since her brother was found to have died, Loren has occupied a strange space. She's still as dedicated to MPAN as ever, but she is also conscious of the fact that she is no longer a family member of a missing person. She remembers the jealousy she felt towards families whose cases were resolved.

'We're at least fortunate that we get to bury Dan.' Loren sighs. 'Many families go on living their entire lives not knowing. It's weird. There's lots to consider. Every day is different.' The best thing for her seems to be to keep the momentum going. Keep applying for grants to allow research and service provision. Keep exploring the power of technology (aside from social media, Loren is interested in the role drones could play in future search efforts). Keep working.

'It's a really challenging environment,' she says. 'But it's a really exciting environment.' There's so much for her to do, even though her brother's story had a sad ending. There is still more to find out, more searching, more opportunities to persuade all of us to consider the ambiguous realities of missing persons. There's a lot the rest of us can do too.

13

OPEN ENDING

LIVING WITH AMBIGUITY

On the face of it, missing persons might seem like a tangible problem: *I don't know where somebody is.* This problem neatly prescribes its own solution: *find them.* Obviously, it's not that easy. Searching for people is an effortful process. There can be many hypotheses about what has happened to a person and where they are that need to be both followed up and ruled out. While the immediate concern is that you don't know someone's whereabouts, to have lost someone in such a way brings about less tangible problems. Grief. Someone you care about is no longer *there*, but they are on your mind.

In the introduction I wrote about how being missing is relational: to be missing, you have to be missed. A missing person hasn't simply disappeared from their physical world – their home, their workplace, their school, their favourite café or pub – they've also disappeared from the folds of their relationships: their friendships, their family, and their community. Talking to people involved in missing-persons cases, it's also become clear that problems in their environment can make someone disappear. Missing-persons cases are so entwined with other issues that they are hardly solvable in isolation. For this reason, it's strange that in most places the police are the ones tasked with the brunt of managing disappearances.

Psychological problems can cause people to go missing. Relationship problems can cause people to go missing. Social problems – such as poverty, discrimination, and disenfranchisement – can increase people's risk of going missing. Political problems like war and terrorism can cause displacement, which can render people missing. Political failures like inadequate funding for support services, confusing processes for people such as unaccompanied child migrants, and lack of coordination between agencies can increase the likelihood of people going missing. They can make people harder to find, too. All these problems can intersect to the point where we lose people and don't find them; and what's more, we lose people without really looking into why they were lost. The physical act of finding someone doesn't fix these underlying causes. While these issues persist, our social system is set up for people to go missing, and to keep going missing. The world is reflected in the lives of missing persons. And, given the enormous number of missing persons and the rate of displacement within populations, it's worth contemplating if things could be done better. We should be more compassionate, pay attention to abuse, and invest in agencies and programs that support people through tough experiences.

What I'm proposing, however – easier said than done as it is – is not itself a 'solution'. There is no answer to the problem. As much as it is possible to prevent some disappearances, missing persons will also always exist alongside accidents, confusion, and mistakes. Perhaps it's inevitable that people will go missing from time to time. People get held up or forget their way or wander around forests as the weather turns and the landscape becomes impossible to navigate. Going missing is an ordinary risk of being out in nature and the world at large. It might also be a common (though not an advisable) way to cope. People might sometimes need a few hours to walk away from their life, breathe, and then – having worried those close to them – come back. Anyone could go missing at any time. It's scary to fathom, but such ambiguity is woven into the world.

Moreover, because disappearances are common, it's important not to lose touch with the reality of them. Absence is an experience that is likely to affect you or someone you know over the course of your life; the stories of those who are missing and those who are looking for them are not always the stuff of true crime or murder mystery novels. Stories of disappearance are often also the stories of people living their daily lives. It is helpful to remember this, lest we continue the tendency to alienate those who are involved with missing-persons cases, when what we need to do is pay attention to their stories and work out ways we can all mitigate the risks, and the prevalence, of disappearances.

I began with two questions: How do we live with and talk about not knowing? And what can we do in this place of doubt? I have some insights now. Though, by the very nature of my project, I don't have answers.

I have met several people who live with and talk about not knowing as a regular part of their personal lives. When you look at an unsolved missing-persons case, you look at what is essentially a void. You can't ask the person why they've gone. So the best way to understand the cases is to look at the person's life at the periphery of their absence – what were things like for them before? When Sarah talks about Q's disappearance, she adds in the culture of Auckland in the 1990s, the nature of bipolar disorder, and the stigma of mental illness.

When Salma tells me about the abduction of her son, she tells me about the years of a difficult marriage and cultural differences. When Brandy tells me about her own disappearance, what she did while she was missing is the shortest part of the narrative – and almost beside the point. She explained her abusive home life, the toxic power dynamics, the culture of silence. Gideon, who went missing in Korea, did so because he was involved in a group that directly benefitted from cutting him off from those who loved him back home. The people Mina searches for have lived under dangerous regimes. Members of the Stolen Generations, and their family members, continue to search for the people – and the culture – that were lost to them as a result of government policy.

The context of what happens before a person goes missing is key to understanding why they do. There can't be clear answers because everyone is different. There are no answers to questions like 'Why do people go missing?', 'What are the lives and personalities of missing persons like?', or 'How can we get them back?' That would be like asking 'Why do people do anything?' or 'How can we solve everyone's problems?' Yet, by accepting the ambiguity of not knowing where someone is, a valuable conversation about the contexts that compel people to go missing gets opened up. We could work towards mitigating some of the causal factors. We can analyse and learn within ambiguous spaces, even if no clear facts emerge.

Investigators such as Charlie productively reflect on uncertain scenarios. An investigator has to make an educated guess about how serious a case is, how likely it is a missing person has come to harm. If they decide it is low risk, they do a minimal investigation and hope that their assessment is right. If it's higher risk they have to piece together possibilities of what may have happened using limited information, with limited time, on a limited budget. The possible scope ranges between a few metres and the whole world. And yet, even with those limitations, most investigations are still fruitful. Most people are found, and quickly.

The missing person is also in an ambiguous situation. Have they broken away from the past? Will they ever be reunited with, or will they ever have to face, those left behind? What might happen if they decide to go back? How a missing person deals with these ambiguities varies, depending on why they went missing. In Brandy's case, by running away, deliberately plunging herself into an ambiguous space, she could escape torment. And later, she could cultivate respect for herself in choosing a scary but safer path. She lived.

Researchers and advocates face the limitations of poor data, unstable funding, and the perennially challenging question of how to get people to take notice and to take action. Their response is not to ignore ambiguity – all the advocates I met explained to me very clearly how much they don't know, and how much more funding and awareness is needed. Rather, their response is to tenaciously keep trying to get answers where they can, and to keep supporting those in need.

Naming the ambiguity around missing persons and exploring how it feels has itself come with barriers. The available data have a lot of shortcomings: there aren't a lot of stories out there that reflect on the long-term ramifications of being missing or knowing someone who has gone missing; and as I noticed very early on as I struggled with the appropriateness of simple terms like 'missing persons' and 'family members and friends of missing persons', 'disappearance', 'gone missing', and so on, it's hard to find any fluency, to find the right words and phrases to talk about it. But in talking to people anyway and seeing what information is out there, I've come to see that working through these barriers is necessary. It's in the stories that the devastating statistics are attached to individuals with complex interiorities. We can't let missing persons disappear twice – once in their physical absence, and a second time by ignoring the issue. It affects too many people. As hard as it is to fathom, the ambiguity posed by absence has its own huge, if invisible, force.

When we hear the stories surrounding absence, we come to understand more about it. We also come to explore more general themes such as the human capacity for endurance. We all have impossible, unanswerable questions, and we collectively face a future that is unlikely to closely mimic the status quo. Challenges like climate change and ageing populations force us to fathom uncertainty. But I know we can face these problems because I now know people who have faced the unknown in more personally devastating ways. Often alone. And it's their stories that I take with me into the murky future.

We need more stories about missing persons. We need to know what those affected by disappearances experience, and we need their insights into how to mitigate the harms missing persons face – including the harms they encounter before they go missing. Raising awareness is crucial to support those left behind and those who are missing or have been missing.

My interviewees have each taken a lead in talking about their experiences because of their commitment to properly addressing the issue of missing persons. Several of them specifically told me that they only wanted to talk to me because it might help someone else who has been in a similar situation. They want others to know they aren't alone. They want someone else to benefit from their difficult experience. The idea of having a conversation with me – a complete stranger – for an hour or two wasn't exactly how they'd choose to spend their time otherwise. Mina told me that, as she had a voice, it was important for her to use it, that 'I think it's a violence against human beings not to use it', which struck me as emblematic of the way my interviewees have become advocates. Sarah said something similar about her charity work for Missing People in the UK: 'It's been incredibly important to be doing this work with Missing People, meeting other families, trying to make the situation better – and when I say better, it's never going to be better-better – but to try to make the situation less chaotic and painful for anybody whose child's walked out the door, whose husband, mother, father, walks out the door. Because I've been there, and I've done that, and we can help other people so that they don't feel quite so alone and don't feel quite so unsupported.' While experiences of absence are common, conversations about it are not. Finding others to relate to or some guidance to help cope with it is not easy. We need more space to articulate these stories.

We also need to know that it's okay for our lives not to fit traditional story forms. It's okay if your life doesn't have a clear structure of beginning, middle, end. It's okay if your life is full of murky middles, or features 'and then … and then … and then' as a messy refrain, or if you have no idea where the story is going or what your audience is meant to take out of it. The ambiguities that many of us face are still true of our experiences, and still important. I'm grateful that the interviewees I spoke to allowed their stories to remain unfinished, peppered with 'I don't know's, or even directly spoke against the possibility of 'closure' – as Sarah said, 'For me the word "closure" when it comes to the whole missing scenario is very overused and anybody that gets what you might call "real closure" is pretty lucky, and pretty rare.'

I'm grateful because the interviewees have given me permission to allow my own uncertainties (over my health, for instance), to remain so, not constantly locked in a struggle for answers but to accept the nature of my experience for what it is. A story does not need to be forced into arbitrary, affirmative tropes – a narrative with a happy ending, or even just an ending – in order for the telling of it to be important.

There are signs that we're culturally ready to incorporate more ambiguity in our stories. I took heart from Hannah Gadsby's show *Nanette*, which disrupts the expectations of stand-up comedy, leaving audiences without a neat resolution to her narratives on topics like sexuality, abuse, and mental health. She leaves us with question marks, for things to think about. Her truth is prioritised over the audience's cathartic laughter. It has been a huge hit internationally. We're up to the challenge of listening to difficult, ambiguous, honest stories.

After we've engaged with ambiguous stories, what can we do in this place of doubt? The physicality of the immediate problem gives ordinary people a lot of scope to help in significant ways. Your senses are tools to assist those left behind. Your awareness matters. As Loren said to me, 'The biggest thing that separates our charity [MPAN] from most others is that awareness – like, literally keeping your eyes open and letting families know that you're keeping your eyes open – is an enormous help. It doesn't cost you money. It's free to be aware. If you see something on social media you can follow it or you can share it.' And in turn, simply talking about missing persons as an issue – normalising it, making others conscious of it – is also helpful. 'Again, it's free, it's easy, and it encourages more people to say, "Oh yeah, this is something that doesn't just happen in a movie, it happens every day, all around us. And it can happen to anyone." And it's something that we all should share responsibility for, all members of the community.'

The bigger mission for all of us is to make the world a safer, more stable, and more supportive place – at least to the extent we can. People will continue to go missing for as long as there are reasons for them to do so. For as long as there are people who are unsupported, depressed, and scared; for as long as there are people who feel entitled to take another person; for as long as shifts in geopolitics cause insurmountable rifts and separations – there will be missing persons. Missing persons will exist alongside abuse, alongside war, alongside crime, alongside debt.

While ambiguity is part of our shared condition, there is no one way of coping with it. Multiple, idiosyncratic, and even changing paths seem to work.

For all of us, every tomorrow is a leap into the unknown. I've felt the panic of uncertainty in myself and now I've seen it through the eyes of others. We do our best to uncover what's there. We reserve the right to re-interpret our findings so far. And we know there's probably more that we don't see. There remain things that are both there and not there, shadows of people and experiences that are only memories yet are cast over our lives forever as things that are solid and real. And it is possible to live like this, in the dynamism of uncovering new things, changing our minds, and apprehending the future with the new clues each day unveils. Never knowing. But always trying to get closer.

FURTHER READING

Please note: links were correct at time of publication.

Ruth Balint, '"To reunite the dispersed family": War, displacement and migration in the tracing files of the Australian Red Cross', *History Australia*, vol. 12, no. 1, 2015, pp. 124–142.
Quentin Beresford & Paul Omaji, *Our State of Mind: Racial planning and the Stolen Generations*, Perth: Fremantle Arts Centre Press, 1998.
Susan Billig & Greg Aunapu, *Without a Trace: The disappearance of Amy Billig*, New York: Avon, 2001.
Pauline Boss, *Ambiguous Loss: Learning to live with unresolved grief*, Cambridge, MA: Harvard University Press, 1999.
Annie Brown (reporter), 'Milk carton kids', *99% Invisible* (podcast), 15 September 2015, <99percentinvisible.org/episode/milk-carton-kids/>.
Canadian Broadcasting Corporation, 'Missing & Murdered: The unsolved cases of Indigenous women and girls', *CBC News*, n.d., <www.cbc.ca/missingandmurdered>.
Claire G Coleman, 'When we encountered the nomads', *Meanjin*, Summer 2017, <meanjin.com.au/essays/when-we-encountered-the-nomads-2/>.
Mette Drivsholm, Delphine Moralis, Karen Shalev Greene & Penny Woolnough, *Once Missing, Never Forgotten? Results of scoping research on the impact of publicity appeals in missing children cases*, Brussels: Missing Children Europe, 2017.
Jenny Edkins, *Missing: Persons and politics*, Ithaca, NY: Cornell University Press, 2011.
Families and Friends of Missing Persons Unit, Attorney General's Department & Mental Health Association NSW Inc, *Someone is Missing: An emotional resource for the families and friends of missing persons*, Sydney: Mental Health Association NSW Inc, 2003.

Elizabeth Fernandez, Jung-Sook Lee, Hazel Blunden, Patricia McNamara, Szilvia Kovacs & Paul-Auguste Cornefert, *No Child Should Grow Up Like This: Identifying long term outcomes of Forgotten Australians, child migrants and the Stolen Generations*, Sydney: University of New South Wales, 2016, <www.forgottenaustralians.unsw.edu.au/research-findings>.

Nicholas Fyfe, Hester Parr, Olivia Stevenson & Penny Woolnough,'"To the end of the world": Space, place, and missing persons investigations', *Policing*, vol. 9, no. 3, 2015, pp. 275–283.

Geoffrey T Glassock, 'Australian families of missing people: Narrating their lived experience', PhD thesis, University of New England, 2012.

Susan Hogben, 'Life's on hold: Missing people, private calendars and waiting', *Time & Society*, vol. 15, no. 2/3, 2006, pp. 327–342.

Eric H Holder Jr, Laurie O Robinson & Jeff Slowikowski, *The Crime of Family Abduction: A child's and parent's perspective*, Washington, DC: US Department of Justice, 2012.

Independent Review of Aboriginal Children in OOHC, *Family Is Culture: Review report*, Sydney: Family Is Culture, 2019, <www.familyisculture.nsw.gov.au/?a=726329>.

Chris Johnston & Rosie Jones, *The Family*, Melbourne: Scribe, 2016.

Journalism Center on Children & Families, 'When a child dies: Dori Maynard on "Missing White Girl Syndrome"' (video), 9 December 2012, <www.youtube.com/watch?v=mc1nJgcvAQA>.

Kirsten Juhl, 'The politicisation of the missing persons issue in Bosnia and Herzegovina', *International Journal of Human Rights* vol. 20, no. 1, 2015, pp. 1–32.

Patrick Radden Keefe, 'The detectives who never forget a face', *New Yorker*, 15 August 2016, <www.newyorker.com/magazine/2016/08/22/londons-super-recognizer-police-force>.

Laura Kiepal, Peter J Carrington & Myrna Dawson, 'Missing persons and social exclusion', *Canadian Journal of Sociology*, vol. 7, no. 2, 2012, pp. 137–168.

Robert Manne, *In Denial: The Stolen Generations and the right*, Quarterly Essay, no. 1, 2001.

Miki Meek (producer), 'Really long distance', *This American Life* (radio program), 23 September 2016, <www.thisamericanlife.org/597/one-last-thing-before-i-go>.

Georgia Moodie, 'What happened to Rachel Funari?', ABC Radio National, 4 October 2016, <www.abc.net.au/news/2016-10-04/what-happened-to-missing-person-rachelfunari/7898300?sf37999360=1>.

Missing Persons Advocacy Network (MPAN), *Missing Persons Guide*, <www.missingpersonsguide.com>.

—— *Too Short Stories: The unfinished stories of missing Australians*, Melbourne: MPAN, 2016.

National Crime Agency, Statistical Tables for the Missing Persons Data Report 2018/2019, <https://www.missingpersons.police.uk/en-gb/resources/downloads/download/91>. See Table B2: England & Wales = 320 715, Northern Ireland = 10 761, Scotland = 21 338.

National Inquiry into the Separation of Aboriginal and Torres Strait Islander Children from their Families, *Bringing Them Home: Report of the National*

Inquiry into the Separation of Aboriginal and Torres Strait Islander Children from their Families, Sydney: Human Rights and Equal Opportunity Commission, 1997.

Geoff Newiss, *Missing Presumed … ? The police response to missing persons*, Police Research Series, no. 14, London: UK Home Office, 1999.

Hester Parr, Olivia Stevenson & Penny Woolnough, 'Search/ing for missing people: Families living with ambiguous absence', *Emotion, Space and Society*, vol. 19, 2015, pp. 66–75.

Hester Parr & Olivia Stevenson, *Families Living with Absence: Searching for missing people* (project report), University of Glasgow, 2013.

Hester Parr, Olivia Stevenson, Nick Fyfe & Penny Woolnough, 'Living absence: The strange geographies of missing people', *Environment and Planning D: Society and Space*, vol. 33, no. 2, 2015, pp. 191–208.

Hester Parr & Olivia Stevenson, '"No news today": Talk of witnessing with families of missing people', *Cultural Geographies*, vol. 22, no. 2, 2014, pp. 297–315.

Peter Pierce, *The Country of Lost Children: An Australian anxiety*, Melbourne: Cambridge University Press, 1999.

Doris Pilkington (Nugi Garimara), *Follow the Rabbit-Proof Fence*, Brisbane: University of Queensland Press, 1996.

Paul Sant Cassia, 'Guarding each other's dead, mourning one's own: The problem of missing persons and missing pasts in Cyprus', *South European Society and Politics*, vol. 11, no. 1, 2006, pp. 111–128.

Emilie Smeaton, *Running From Hate to What You Think is Love: The relationship between running away and child sexual exploitation*, Ilford, UK: Barnardo's, 2013.

Alexandra Stein, *Terror, Love and Brainwashing: Attachment in cults and totalitarian systems*, Abingdon, UK: Routledge, 2016.

Sarah Stillman, '"The missing white girl syndrome": Disappeared women and media activism', *Gender and Development*, vol. 15, no. 3, 2007, pp. 491–502.

Jill Stockwell (writer/producer), 'Argentina – haunted by memories', *Earshot* (radio program), ABC Radio, 9 March 2015, <www.abc.net.au/radionational/programs/earshot/argentina-haunted-by-memories/6268778>.

Chimene Suleyman, 'There's an epidemic of missing people of colour who aren't photogenic enough for us to find', *The Independent*, 18 April 2016, <www.independent.co.uk/voices/theres-an-epidemic-of-missing-children-of-colour-who-arentphotogenic-enough-to-find-a6989666.html>.

Jane Thompson, *Reaching Safe Places: Exploring the journeys of young people who run away from home or care*, Sandbach, UK: Railway Children, 2014.

Sarah Wayland, '"I still hope, but what I hope for now has changed": A narrative inquiry study exploring hope and ambiguous loss', PhD thesis, University of New England, 2015.

ACKNOWLEDGMENTS

I would like to thank those who agreed to be interviewed for this project – Cindy Bohan, Trevor Salvado, Hardy Clemens, Sarah Godwin, Griet Ivens, 'Salma', Brandy Bonner, Charlie Hedges, Mina Jaf, Gail Rego, Mette Drivsholm, Susan Moylan-Coombs, Justin Bergholcs, Nick Lee, 'Luke', 'Nicole', 'Pedro', and Loren O'Keeffe. Their knowledge, openness, and generosity has made this book possible.

This book started out as a PhD thesis. My research was supported by an Australian Government Research Training Program (RTP) scholarship. I'd like to thank the University of Wollongong, and my supervisory team, Siobhán McHugh, Marcus O'Donnell, and Cathy Cole. Being granted money and time to write while having access to resources and others' expertise has been a tremendous opportunity. The research and the manuscript also benefitted from the feedback of Sarah Wayland and Derek Neale.

Max Porter and those involved with the Portobello Prize offered much-needed advice and encouragement, as did Lauren Finger.

I'd also like to thank Harriet McInerney, Sophia Oravecz, and the other folks at NewSouth, who've been wonderful to work with. Linda Funnell has been an excellent editor. Cathy Craigie gave important advice on the Stolen Generations chapter of this book and Janette Stewart helped me discover and fact-check our family history.

Lindon Roberts has been a tireless early reader, and re-reader. I thank him for his support.

I'd finally like to thank all my family members, friends, and teachers who encouraged this project, and encouraged me to write.

CPSIA information can be obtained
at www.ICGtesting.com
Printed in the USA
BVHW031931140621
609546BV00006B/86

9 781742 236797